W9-BXP-602

DiMaggio

DiMaggio

AN ILLUSTRATED LIFE

EDITED BY

Dick Johnson

TEXT BY

Glenn Stout

WALKER AND COMPANY
NEW YORK

To my wife, Mary Hamilton Johnson, and my parents, Minna and Robert, with much love and respect

—Dick Johnson

To Siobhan . . . and Phil Rizzuto

—Glenn Stout

First published in the United States of America in 1995 by Walker Publishing Company, Inc.

Published simultaneously in Canada by Thomas Allen & Son Canada, Limited, Markham, Ontario

Library of Congress Cataloging-in-Publication Data
Stout, Glenn, 1958–
DiMaggio: an illustrated life / edited by Dick Johnson ; text by Glenn Stout.
p.   cm.
Includes bibliographical references and index.
ISBN 0-8027-1311-4 (hardcover)
1. DiMaggio, Joe, 1914– . 2. Baseball players—United States—Biography. I. Johnson, Dick, 1955– . II. Title.
GV865.D5S86   1995
796.357′092—dc20
[B]   95-31775
CIP

Permission to reprint the essays on pages 129, 220, and 246 has been granted by the publishers as follows: "The Streak of Streaks," Stephen J. Gould. Reprinted with permission from The New York Review of Books. *Copyright © 1988, Nyrev, Inc. "The Legend of Joe DiMaggio" from* All My Octobers *by Mickey Mantle. Copyright © 1994 by Mickey Mantle and Mickey Herskowitz. Reprinted by permission of HarperCollins Publishers, Inc. "The Clipper: Safe Haven at Last," Thomas Boswell. Copyright © 1983* The Washington Post. *Reprinted with permission.*

Frontispiece photograph from Transcendental Graphics, Mark Rucker; title page and chapter opener photograph by Dick Thompson, from the collection of The Sports Museum of New England.

Endpaper art by Michael Schacht

Book design by Ron Monteleone

Printed in the United States of America

2   4   6   8   10   9   7   5   3   1

Contents

Foreword

Ted Williams

My first encounter with the DiMaggio family was in 1936 when Vince DiMaggio and I were teammates on the San Diego Padres. He was a good friend as was his brother Dom with whom I share many memories from our years together on the Red Sox. Even before I saw Joe I knew of his reputation from his years in the Pacific Coast League and respected him greatly. While I was still in the Coast League he was knocking down the fences in New York. He was one player I couldn't wait to see in person.

I finally had my chance to see him when I played in my first major league game at Yankee Stadium in April 1939. I remember that Lefty Grove pitched for us that day against Red Ruffing. I also remember how impressed I was with DiMaggio and the entire Yankee team. In all the years I saw him play I never saw Joe look bad on a ball field. He even looked good when making a rare swing at a bad ball. Joe was simply the greatest player I ever saw, as well as the most graceful. Everything he did on a ball field, from cocking his arm after catching a fly ball to legging out a ground ball, was done with style.

Not only was Joe my greatest rival but he has also been a good friend for over half a century. I've always appreciated the many compliments he has paid to me over the years. I'll never forget the day he came over to me when I was managing the Senators and he was coaching for the Athletics and he told me he thought I was doing a hell of a job. That's the kind of guy Joe is, quick with a kind word at the right time. No one admires him more than myself, and I always look forward to seeing him and having the opportunity to talk a little baseball.

In this book Glenn Stout and Dick Johnson have captured the essence of Joe's career in words and pictures as they pay homage to one of the greatest figures in American sports. I hope you enjoy this book and gain insight into the life of a great ballplayer and man.

Ted Williams and Joe Di-Maggio were rivals and friends. They usually finished in the top two places in American League MVP balloting and were the subject of many a street corner argument over who was the better player. (Photograph courtesy of the Brearley Collection)

Acknowledgments

It has been my privilege once again to join forces with the gifted and amiable Glenn Stout. His skills as a researcher and writer are supreme and are matched only by his enthusiasm. Glenn and I have attempted to assemble the definitive biography of Joe DiMaggio, who was simply the best player on the best succession of teams in baseball history. DiMaggio possessed an athleticism and grace seen only in a select few; Ted Williams probably summed it up best when he said that DiMaggio was so graceful he even looked good striking out. It is our sincerest hope that our work helps illuminate and amplify the achievements of a very special ballplayer and American hero.

Both Glenn and I were fortunate to work with George Gibson of Walker and Company. It is our sincere hope that our effort with this book begins to match the magnitude of his faith in the authors. Our good friend, Luke Salisbury, once again offered his incisive comments on the manuscript and saved his best prose for the superb essay contained within this volume.

There are many other individuals who helped me edit, research, and assemble the photographs for this volume. Dick Dobbins, Mike Anderson, and Mark Rucker were most generous with their time, expertise, and the wealth of their personal collections. *Boston Herald* librarian John Cronin is the DiMaggio of his profession and a fountain of friendly advice and support. *Boston Globe* sports editor Don Skwar also lent his generous support, as did Debbie Matson of the Boston Red Sox and writer/pundit Paul Dickson. Veteran New York photographer Bob Olen came through in the clutch, as did researcher Mark Shreve and Jeff Idelson of the Baseball Hall of Fame. Old friends such as Pat Kelly of the Baseball Hall of Fame, Steve Gietschier of *The Sporting News*, Butch McCarthy of the Maxwell Collection, Mark Rucker of Transcendental Graphics, Michael Schacht, and Dennis Brearley also came through with flying colors. Kevin Grace supplied one of the best images in this book.

Special thanks go to my friend Steve Laski of London, England, who spent much of his only trip to Cooperstown researching photos for this book. My former intern Saul Wisnia left no stone unturned in the nation's capital as he also performed yeoman research duties. My good friends Michael LaVigne and Harvey McKenney were always quick with a pat on the back, as were my colleagues at the Sports Museum, who also deserve my heartfelt thanks for their support of my work. And finally, I am most grateful to my wife, Mary, who along with Bobby and Elizabeth are my inspiration and comfort.

—Dick Johnson

My batterymate, Dick Johnson, shared his extensive library and magnanimous spirit throughout the course of this project, as did his family. George Gibson of Walker and Company believed in this project when no one else did. His faith in the authors has resulted in the book we wanted to do, the goal of every writer. The staff of the Microtext Department of the Boston Public Library and of the Government Documents and Microtext Department of the Lamont Library at Harvard University were of critical help in the research of this book, as was the Thayer Memorial Library in Uxbridge, Massachusetts. Luke Salisbury again demonstrated considerable editorial talent in late-inning relief, as did Jacqueline Johnson of Walker. Dick Dobbins, Bill Weiss, Dick Beverage, Billy Raimondi, Charley Wallgren, and several sources who chose to remain anonymous provided critical information. Anthony Bedard of San Francisco interrupted his busy schedule at Past It Records to make several trips to the San Francisco Public Library on my behalf. John Dorsey agreed once again to listen to me talk about a book months before it was finished. The authors of other books and articles about Joe DiMaggio and the Yankees provided a starting point. My teammates on the Hyde Park Athletics of the Boston Men's Senior Baseball League did their best to distract me from this project and remind me that baseball is a game played. Siobhan kept me from going crazy and provided the daily support and faith every writer needs. I'd also like to thank my family—Gary, Lisa, Pop, and Joanie—the Hourihans, Al Lizotte, Sean Heaney, Joe Sarro, Charles Longley, Henry Scannell and Gunars Rutkovskis for their role in this project.

—Glenn Stout

Introduction

In the summer of 1986, I attended an "Old-Timers' Day," at Fenway Park in Boston. Most of the participants were former Red Sox players, like Ted Williams and Jim Lonborg, a few ex–Boston Braves like Warren Spahn and Tommy Holmes, and others with a New England connection, like Massachusetts natives Vic Raschi and Mark "The Bird" Fidrych.

The players were introduced to the crowd in inverse order of their contribution to the game. As expected, the cheers grew in proportion as each man stepped from the dugout and nodded to the crowd: Johnny Pesky, Luis Tiant ("Looie!"), Warren Spahn. The crowd seemingly reserved its greatest cheer for Ted Williams, standing and applauding, roaring for close to a minute as Williams alternately mugged with his old friends or looked faintly defiant.

Then Joe DiMaggio emerged from the dugout, the only player not in uniform and the last to be announced to the crowd.

A different sound took over. The lingering roars and cheers that greeted Williams were immediately silenced, replaced by a growing surge of steady applause. No one in the crowd whistled or bleated a horn or hurrahed above the simple, strong ovation from 33,000 pairs of hands. The capacity crowd stood in reverence and applauded for nearly three minutes as DiMaggio, in suit and tie, stood dignified and somehow alone at the end of a long line of former players, who also stood and applauded, recognizing that in his presence, they, too, were simply a part of the crowd.

I have since attended other games and seen other "heroes" introduced to similar crowds—the survivors of local tragedies, movie stars, military veterans, former players, presidents, and heads of state. I have yet to hear a crowd respond to anyone as they did to Joe DiMaggio.

In 1969, as professional base-ball celebrated its centennial, a poll of sportswriters selected Joe DiMaggio as both the "greatest living player" and "greatest player ever." (Photograph courtesy of The Sports Museum of New England)

In the PBS series "The Power of Myth," Bill Moyers asked Joseph Campbell, "Why are there so many stories of the hero in mythology?" Campbell responded, "Because that's what's worth writing about . . . a hero [is someone] who has found or done something beyond the normal range of experience or achievement. A hero is someone who has given his or her life to something bigger than oneself."

Perhaps no other American athlete, in any sport, in any time, fulfills Campbell's notion of the hero more completely, more naturally, than Joe DiMaggio. Only a few baseball players have ever approached that exalted status. But in DiMaggio, the hero seems fully expressed. In virtually every story ever written about DiMaggio, or in every interview with other players where DiMaggio's name is mentioned, he is referred to as a hero as surely as he is of Italian ancestry, or was a New York Yankee.

DiMaggio was revealed to America just after the Great Depression, just before the agonizing experience of World War II. The era was ripe with heroes, yet at the same time the individual hero was almost invisible. The survivors of the Depression, the sons and daughters of immigrants, suffered and labored in anonymity. Their heroism was never adequately acknowledged. No one sang their praises.

Before Joe DiMaggio burst onto the public consciousness, America was dominated by the provincial segregation of its people by class and ethnic background. The Depression, more than any act of legislation, helped break down those barriers. The son of a fisherman, an Italian immigrant, Joe DiMaggio stood before America and was accepted with open arms. This could not have happened a decade before. In Ernest Hemingway's *The Old Man and the Sea*, the old Cuban fisherman Santiago talks about baseball with Manolin, a younger man. Santiago speaks of DiMaggio and says, "I would like to take the great DiMaggio fishing. They say his father was a fisherman. Maybe he was as poor as we are and would understand." That is precisely how America felt. DiMaggio became the man in whom these everyday heroes found recognition. His journey mirrored the journey millions of Americans had just completed on their own. In the figure of Joe DiMaggio, America saw its own face.

It helped that DiMaggio's personality never overpowered or contradicted his image; the public was not often distracted, as it was by Cobb, Ruth, or Williams, by the man himself. Whether DiMaggio liked it or not, his talent and mythic status overwhelmed his character. He was a hero, and heroes do not exist for themselves, but for others. DiMaggio gave of his own individuality to achieve that status.

That he was a ballplayer made it all work. When DiMaggio reached the major leagues in 1936, the common denominators of American culture were the movies, radio, and baseball. Movie stars were celluloid illusions, radio personalities distant and scratchy voices. Baseball players were flesh and blood, and depended on no technological trickery to display their talent.

He was something of a natural, or at least people thought so. As a young boy he wasn't at the playground from dawn to dusk playing ball. He enjoyed the game, but it was not his passion. Even after he reached the major leagues, it never seemed as if DiMaggio really needed baseball, at least not in the same sense a player like Ted Williams did. Baseball defined him, but it was not him. DiMaggio hardly worked out in the off-season. He didn't practice much. He smoked cigarettes and drank coffee incessantly. He dated starlets. He stayed out late in nightclubs, not really drinking, but to compensate for insomnia. Then he got up the next day, put on the Yankee pinstripes, and was the best player on the field for the best team in the game, the standard against which all others were measured.

A ballplayer is considered complete when he has five skills in profusion. Most players have only two or three, and those limited talents are sometimes enough to guarantee admittance to the Hall of Fame. DiMaggio was the first major-league ballplayer of the lively-ball era to have all five in abundance. He could hit, hit for power, run, throw, and field. And that wasn't the half of it. DiMaggio had a sixth quality. He played baseball with style and grace. Style was as much a part of his game as any of those other five qualities. That style included a host of intangible factors that set DiMaggio apart: he hit in the clutch; he played—and usually even better—when injured; he led by example, playing better when the team was in trouble or playing poorly, in the second half of the season when they were fighting for a pennant, in key games against their biggest rivals, in the World Series. He gave of himself for the team. He did the things heroes do.

DiMaggio's oft-cited physical grace is known today primarily through the memory and reminiscences of those who saw him play. Only a few brief snippets of film and a handful of still photographs remain that show DiMaggio demonstrating what many thought was his singular talent, his grace in the field. That photographic evidence is compelling. Dark and angular, the Yankee pinstripes defining his figure into perfection, DiMaggio looks like the archetypal ballplayer. He never appears awkward, never seems to be caught off stride or unprepared. He rarely was. His style was both elegant and utterly simple. In DiMaggio, the fundamental movements of the game seemed fully developed. The difficult looked easy when DiMaggio did it.

DiMaggio's contemporaries were the only witnesses to his deeds. Over forty years after DiMaggio's retirement his actual deeds either have been forgotten, reduced to a few time-worn examples, or translated into a series of often misleading anecdotes. DiMaggio's career ended just before baseball was widely broadcast on television. His fans knew him because they saw him at the ballpark. The contemporary fan knows him through some scratchy newsreel footage, a few occasionally spurious stories, endorsements he has done for a coffee-maker, and his accomplishment over one fifty-six-game period. But fifty-six games do not tell the whole story.

Joe DiMaggio contemplates Fenway Park's Green Monster prior to an old-timers' game in May 1955. DiMaggio socked 29 homers at Fenway during his career.
(Photograph courtesy of the Boston Globe)

The goal of this book is to chart DiMaggio's voyage from immigrant's son to icon. Its main focus is his career in baseball, those significant moments in his journey when the public perception anointed him a hero. What did he do that made him a hero to so many?

Yet DiMaggio did not cease to be important when he stopped playing ball. If he had, he would not have continued to be a hero; he would have become merely a legend, like Lou Gehrig, a man whose symbolic importance, in his tragic death, outstripped his accomplishments. DiMaggio kept going. He traveled outside the range of normal human experience and somehow returned. After baseball, what could possibly challenge the great DiMaggio? He had proven himself to be master of the American myth of baseball. What possibly remained?

DiMaggio avoided the real-life pitfalls that destroy so many ex-athletes. His stature actually increased. One can rightly say that in retirement Joe DiMaggio's occupation has been Joe DiMaggio, hero, celebrity, living American icon.

As America's best ballplayer, he had played for the best team and won the most championships. When it was over he went on to try to win the heart of the most beautiful girl in America, Marilyn Monroe.

Curiously, had their romance ultimately succeeded, it is doubtful that today DiMaggio would be held in such continuing regard by the public. He would have slipped into the netherworld of celebrity-hood. The average person would feel little in common with the former ballplayer. He would be admired, but he would have ceased to be a hero. Had the marriage worked, DiMaggio would have become as remote and distant and sympathetic as some sort of god.

But heroes are not gods. They are human. They are not perfect. They have flaws. They are ordinary people who somehow accomplish the extraordinary. When Joe DiMaggio married Marilyn Monroe, he tested the Fates. When the marriage fell apart the public could now see that he was not perfect, not superhuman. Just as the bone spurs in DiMaggio's heels revealed the limitations of his physical talents and allowed observers to stand in his shoes and empathize with his plight, the breakup with Monroe revealed a similar flaw in DiMaggio's emotional makeup—his feelings—and provoked a similar response. In a sense, that failure secured, for all time, his place as hero. DiMaggio seemingly never lost on the field. But when he lost the girl and mourned for her, he became human. That loss made his previous accomplishments more poignant, and is at least part of the reason that, some forty years after he retired as an active player, he occupies a place in the hearts of his fans that includes no other player.

*   *   *

The student of DiMaggio who has read other accounts of his life may be surprised by some of the details included in this one. The primary resource material in the creation of this biography has been in sources essentially untapped by previous biographers, namely newspaper reports in microfilmed editions of the *San Francisco Examiner*, the *San Francisco Chronicle*, the *San Francisco Call-Bulletin*, the *New York Herald Tribune*, the *New York Times*, *The Sporting News*, and various other newspapers from around the country. Only in the close and thorough analysis of newspaper accounts does one generally find the specific, day-to-day record of what actually happened and, just as important, what did not. Clipping files contained at the National Baseball Hall of Fame Library were also helpful. Those clippings reproduced in *The DiMaggio Albums*, despite their occasional chronological mistakes and lack of bibliographic data, were of some help. Jack B. Moore's *Joe DiMaggio: A Bio-Bibliography* deserves special mention for its insightful and comprehensive overview of DiMaggio's life.

The author spoke to only a few former ballplayers during the writing of this book, preferring to concentrate on the facts of DiMaggio's life beyond the anecdote. Fortunately, many of DiMaggio's teammates and contemporaries have been interviewed by others; when their comments have been necessary to tell DiMaggio's story, they have been included. The author did interview a select number of lesser-known ballplayers and baseball historians, not only for their contributions of fact, but to check my own perceptions and interpretations. In so doing, I sought out those whom other authors have ignored to fill in time previously overlooked, preferring the fresh perspective of those who have not told the same story time and time again.

The impressions of DiMaggio's teammates and DiMaggio himself have been gleaned primarily from the above sources and books and articles about DiMaggio, the Yankees, and major league baseball in mid-century. The personal reminiscences help illustrate the factual content of the text. These sources, and others consulted for the project, appear in the bibliography.

The author did not speak to either Joe DiMaggio or members of his family concerning this project. DiMaggio remains a private man. He grants few interviews. Likewise, his family respects his privacy.

When this project was in its infancy, I was often asked, "What is left to write about DiMaggio?" My answer is that I had admired DiMaggio for the myths that surrounded him. Now my admiration has increased, for what Joe DiMaggio actually did is even more compelling.

The Son of a Fisherman: 1914–32

Joe DiMaggio's journey begins, not in the outfield of Yankee Stadium or even on the sandlots and playgrounds of San Francisco, but in Italy, on the small islet of Isola de Femmine in the Golfo di Carini, northwest of the Sicilian city of Palermo. From there, his father, Giuseppe DiMaggio, and then his mother, Rosalie, emigrated to the United States.

An economic depression in Italy led to Giuseppe DiMaggio's decision to leave his home. Despite the ethnic prejudice and occasional poverty he encountered in America, Giuseppe DiMaggio persevered. Some thirty-five years later, the same forces that drove his father to leave the land of his ancestors for a better life also provided the motivation that led his son to become the most remarkable baseball player of his era. Joe DiMaggio abandoned the ways of his father and embarked on a journey of his own, against tremendous odds, in the midst of the Great Depression.

Both father and son emigrated from the known—a limited life on Isola de Femmine, and the narrow life of a fisherman—for a dream—America, and the game of baseball. For each man, the promise of that dream allowed him to survive, and thrive, in an environment that broke many others. Millions of Giuseppe DiMaggios believed in the dream of America and followed that fantasy. Millions were overwhelmed by the reality they found and succumbed to it, substituting

Bereft of a high school degree and in possession of near-limitless baseball talent, Joe DiMaggio began his career in 1932 as a seventeen-year-old shortstop on the San Francisco Seals of the Pacific Coast League. (Photograph courtesy of Dick Dobbins)

Following his stellar rookie season in New York, Joe made a triumphant return to his boyhood home in San Francisco, where his father and mother are joined by Marie DiMaggio (r) and a young girl named Betty Kron who is seated on Joe's lap. (Photograph courtesy of the *Boston Herald*)

one form of poverty for another, or returning to Italy. Millions of would-be Joe DiMaggios threw their heart and soul into baseball and found similar disappointment.

Joe DiMaggio's character developed from experiences common to both father and son. Giuseppe DiMaggio rarely spoke of life in Italy and developed few ties to anyone apart from his family and his peers among San Francisco's insular fishing community. Similarly, Joe Di-Maggio displayed a reticence about his own background and his friendship was extended only to a few men with whom he felt kinship, old friends from San Francisco, fellow ballplayers, and, as he became an American icon, celebrities and those who catered to celebrities.

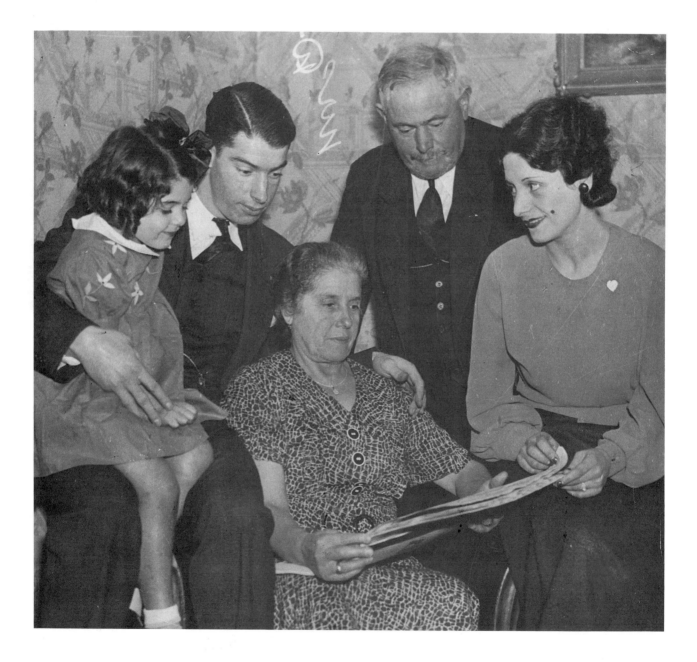

Joe DiMaggio and his brothers grew up between the old world of their father and the new world all around them. They wanted more from life than fishing, but were ill-equipped for anything else. The family's economic situation and the necessity of finding work precluded much formal education. Ethnic prejudice further limited their options. Initially, American culture was alien to them, but that made it all the more attractive. The adversity they faced as children left them distrusting of the outside world. Yet they were compelled to experience it. Baseball became the way.

When, almost too late, Joe DiMaggio discovered baseball, he found a way to overcome the awkwardness and innate self-consciousness he felt away from home. Baseball became his identity, the medium where he discovered who he was, and allowed him to become something more than the reserved, socially awkward son of an emigrant Italian fisherman. By his success on the field, and with the acknowledgment of that success by others, DiMaggio proved to himself who he was.

Giuseppe Paolo DiMaggio was born on Isola de Femmine in 1874, where he learned to take fish from the sea as had his father before him. The difficult work brought no hope of wealth, yet ensured a basic existence. By the time Giuseppe DiMaggio turned twenty, life on Isola de Femmine had begun to change. Italy was unified in 1870, and unification slowly brought change. The cultural and physical isolation that characterized Sicily began to erode. Her people were increasingly dissatisfied with the prospect of lifetimes of unceasing labor. An agricultural depression in the 1880s resulted in widespread poverty and occasional famine. While the rest of western Europe was moving toward industrialization, most Italians, particularly in the south, lived as peasants. Faced with a future of poverty, an increasing number of Italians began to emigrate to South America and the United States.

Italy's ill-conceived war with Abyssinia (Ethiopia) in 1896 exacerbated the problem. Giuseppe DiMaggio was conscripted into the Italian Army and fought in the failed war, earning a citation for valor. Upon his return to Isola de Femmine, he married Rosalie. By then, almost everyone was talking of going to America. Most emigrants from Isola de Femmine headed to California, to San Francisco Bay, which had a climate similar to Italy's and where the fishing was good. Even Rosalie's father left for America, settling in Collinsville, a small town north of San Francisco, on an island at the confluence of the Sacramento and San Joaquin rivers. Giuseppe DiMaggio followed his father-in-law to Collinsville in 1898, first living in a ramshackle house raised up on slats to protect it from recurring floods. Rosalie, for the time being, stayed behind, and several months after Giuseppe's departure, gave birth to a daughter, Nellie.

Most emigrants from Isola de Femmine went first to the city of San Francisco, but many discovered they were locked out from the fishing fleet by the more established Genoese. Collinsville was a second destination. Giuseppe soon resettled in the nearby town of Martinez and found work as a section hand for the railroad at ten cents an hour.

By 1902, he had saved enough money to bring Rosalie to America and resume his life at sea. His two brothers, one older, one younger, joined him in Martinez. Giuseppe's family grew quickly. Another daughter, Marie, was born in 1903, a son, Thomas in 1905, Michael in 1908, daughter Frances in 1910, and Vincent in 1912. Shortly after the birth of Joseph Paul DiMaggio on November 25, 1914, the family moved to the North Beach neighborhood of San Francisco, closer to the fishing grounds. Dominic was born in 1917.

They rented a small, four-room stucco house at 2047 Taylor Street for $25 a month, and Giuseppe tried to establish himself among the fishermen of nearby Fisherman's Wharf. Opportunities for young Italian immigrants were limited, and the Italian community in San Francisco suffered intense discrimination. Apart from fishing, farming, and domestic work, most Italians had a difficult time finding work, and many returned to Italy, frustrated and as impoverished as before. While the fishing community was almost exclusively Italian, those who found success did not welcome newcomers. The Italian community itself was stratified along regional lines. Northern Italians looked disparagingly on those from the south, who in turn regarded Sicilians with particular disregard. Even among the Sicilians, the fishermen of Isola de Femmine were accorded little respect. Newcomers often found their boats sunk, or nets mysteriously shredded. Groups of fishermen formed protective associations to safeguard their interests. Giuseppe DiMaggio was probably able to stake out his position on the wharf only through membership in a group like the Crab Fisherman's Association, a monopoly that, in essence, controlled the crab market in exchange for providing protection from the Genoese and other competing groups. He named his boat the *Rosalie*, after his wife.

Giuseppe DiMaggio worked hard under difficult and sometimes dangerous conditions. While he was never wealthy, he was able to provide for his family. While the children wore hand-me-downs and the family was cash-poor, there was always enough food. The children's upbringing followed traditional patterns. When the boys reached adolescence, they worked with their father, while the girls helped Rosalie with household tasks. Italian was spoken at home, and the children learned English at school. By the time Dominic was born, the children talked to each other primarily in English, and spoke Italian only to their parents, who understood only a few English words.

Like the children of most immigrants, the younger DiMaggios quickly adapted to a culture their parents found alien. For the boys, baseball was an attraction like no other.

Despite its isolation from the major leagues, which didn't expand west beyond St. Louis until 1958, the San Francisco area supported a baseball community as strong as any in the country. Professional baseball was first established in San Francisco in the 1870s, and amateur baseball was played virtually everywhere. The growth of baseball in San Francisco benefited from a climate that allowed it to be played year-round. The Pacific Coast League was formed in 1903 and provided high-quality, professional baseball, nearly the equal of the major leagues. Most teams featured a number of ex–big leaguers. Major league scouts made regular forays to the West Coast, and talented younger players often attracted the interest of major league teams. By the 1930s, players like Harry Hooper, Harry Heilmann, Tony Lazzeri, Paul Waner, Joe Cronin, and Lefty O'Doul had gone from the Bay Area to productive major league careers.

When the DiMaggio boys were not fishing or going to school, they escaped to the streets, playgrounds, and empty lots to play baseball. Weekends were relatively work-free. The fishing fleet usually stayed in and the men tended to repairs and maintenance chores. All over North Beach, boys seized every opportunity to escape the cultural and physical confines of the home to head outside and play baseball.

First Tom, and then Michael, were drawn to the game. Both boys worked on the boat with their father at the age of ten or eleven. Giuseppe DiMaggio usually fished at night. As soon as each boy was old enough, he went directly from school to the wharf and spent much of the night fishing with his father, catching catnaps when they weren't hauling nets. By the time Michael DiMaggio was old enough to accompany his father, Tom, who was establishing himself as the head of the family and even had a room to himself in the house, worked a second boat. The boys quit school after junior high and went on fishing trips that sometimes lasted several weeks. In the late 1920s, when Michael was old enough to fish alone, Giuseppe DiMaggio retired, retaining ownership of both boats and receiving a percentage of the catch. Michael, in turn, soon brought young Vince on board. Joe and

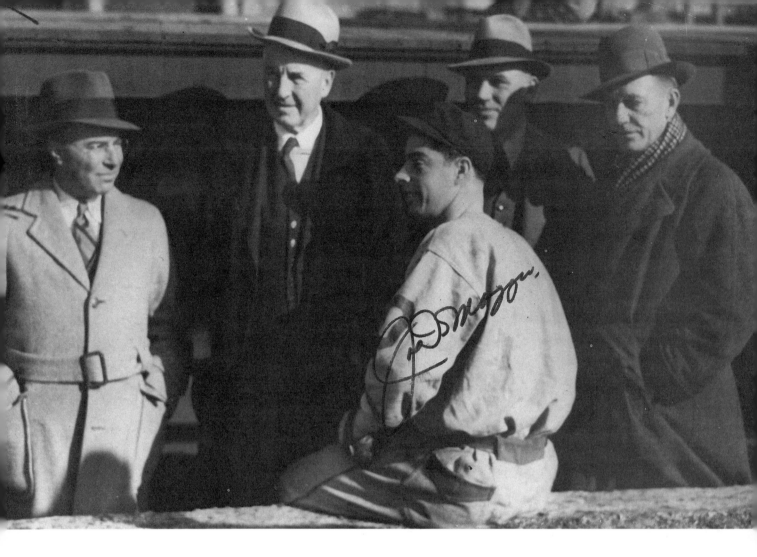

San Francisco Seals star Joe DiMaggio is the center of attention, surrounded by a group of unidentified gentlemen on a typical chilly early-season day at Seals Stadium. (Photograph courtesy of Dick Dobbins)

Dominic helped on shore, painting or cleaning the boat and keeping watch over the catch. The elder DiMaggio expected all his sons to follow him to the sea. He dreamed of buying a large boat so they could all work together.

Baseball got in the way of his plans. Giuseppe didn't understand the game, even confusing it with football, and resisted his sons' efforts to play, complaining that baseball cost "too many pants and too many shoes." But with Tom leading the way, each succeeding son of Giuseppe DiMaggio found baseball a stronger temptation than the sea. Giuseppe DiMaggio's resistance to the game wore down.

By the time Joe reached the age of ten, the pattern was well established. When work allowed, his older brothers Tom and Michael played on amateur and semipro teams. The occasional dollar earned playing baseball was a welcome addition to the DiMaggio household.

When Joe began to work on the boat, he also began to play baseball. With classmates from the Hancock Grammar School at Filbert and Taylor streets, Joe scurried off to the North Beach playground to play softball, or to an empty tract of land at the corner of Bay Street and Taylor the boys called the "Horse Lot," where a dairy company parked its wagons and there was room for a pickup game of baseball.

For Joe DiMaggio, baseball became, in effect, the only outlet from work, school, and the confines of home. He enjoyed other sports, such as touch football, and later, tennis, but he played baseball because other boys did, because his brothers did, and because playing baseball was not working on the boat. This apparently caused his father consternation, and Giuseppe sometimes accused Joe of being lazy and dodging hard work. As Tom took over as family head, Giuseppe's influence waned. Nellie married a non-Italian. Tom rejected an arranged marriage. Vince and Joe shunned the life of a fisherman.

Baseball came easily to the DiMaggio brothers. Even among their peers their talent was obvious, though they didn't play as often as other boys. While still in grammar school, Joe was expected to find a job in addition to his work on the boat, and to contribute to the family finances. He and Dominic hawked newspapers in downtown San Francisco, opposite a bank. One of Joe's regular customers was Jerry Donovan, an outfielder on the San Francisco Seals, who worked at the bank during the off-season. Donovan, who later served as president of the Seals and business manager for the San Francisco Giants, became one of DiMaggio's first athletic heroes.

At Francesco Junior High, Joe played third base on the school's 130-pound team. Vince, two years older, starred at third for the school's varsity team. The junior-high club was the first organized team Joe DiMaggio ever played for. His contribution was undistinguished, and the team won no championships. Joe never played on the varsity team.

When Vince graduated from junior high in 1928, he claimed hardship and dropped out of school, landing a job in a fruit market and turning his back on fishing. His baseball skills didn't go to waste; semipro teams sought his services. They knew his reputation from junior high and from his two older, baseball-playing brothers.

The Bay Area was a hotbed of semipro and amateur baseball. Small manufacturers, canneries, and markets sponsored teams in industrial and semipro leagues, while ethnic organizations, boys' clubs, and various neighborhood groups supported teams in recreational leagues. The semipro leagues were organized into increasingly competitive B, A, and AA divisions. The Pacific Coast League San Francisco Seals, San Francisco Missions, and Oakland Oaks sponsored teams in winter leagues that served as training grounds for young recruits and a forum for veteran players to stay in shape. Unpaid scouts, so-called "bird dogs," ran the better winter teams and brought the most talented players to the attention of the PCL clubs. Skilled players quickly developed a local reputation and teams scrambled for their services.

While the leagues were termed "semipro" owing to their sponsorship, few could afford to pay players during the Depression. Any money usually came from a hat passed around the crowd or from a pot created by contributions from the players, the winners dividing the take among themselves. Still, the money provided added incentive to play. During the Depression, few questioned the source of a dollar.

Tom DiMaggio played third base, Michael first, and Vince both second and third. Tom was even offered a tryout by the Missions, but his family responsibilities and an arm injury prevented him from taking advantage of the offer. But while Vince turned increasingly to baseball, Joe drifted away from the game for a time.

He became temporarily consumed by tennis. The exploits of court stars like Maurice McLoughlin, Bill Johnston, and Helen Wills competed with baseball coverage in the local sports pages, and Joe dreamed of becoming a court star.

The young athlete's brief flirtation with tennis came at a critical time in his life. Joe abandoned baseball for tennis at about age fourteen, at the precise time when his body was changing from boy to man. At this awkward stage, most adolescents go through an extended period of clumsiness. Up to this time, there is no evidence to suggest that Joe's baseball skills were anything but ordinary, and he apparently wasn't playing enough to fine-tune what talent he had. Had he continued his dispassionate pursuit of baseball, he might have grown increasingly uninterested as his changing body betrayed him.

But Joe took tennis seriously and practiced for long hours on the San Francisco playgrounds. His sudden immersion in the game allowed his coordination to keep pace with his changing physique. Moreover, the physical requirements of tennis are similar to those of

The brothers DiMaggio are shown in their minor league days with the Seals. Note the misspelling of their last name, a common error among sportswriters until Joe made the majors. (Photograph courtesy of Dick Dobbins)

Frank Crosetti was one of DiMaggio's early mentors as a veteran teammate and fellow San Franciscan. They would share the cross-country drive to spring training with Tony Lazzeri for the first few years of DiMaggio's career. (Photograph courtesy of Dick Dobbins)

baseball: one follows a ball moving at great speed, moves quickly toward it, then strikes with a racket in a movement not unlike swinging a baseball bat. When Joe stopped playing tennis and started playing baseball again, he was a young man and a much-improved athlete.

Tennis was hardly the sport for a young, poor, Italian-American. Whether Joe was aware of the social barriers that likely would have blocked his progress in the game, or whether he simply grew tired of the sport, is unclear, but by age sixteen Joe DiMaggio was no longer a tennis player. He was also no longer a student.

After junior high, he briefly attended Galileo High School, the only school he ever attended outside his own neighborhood. At Galileo he was surprised and embarrassed to see how much better dressed most other students were. He wanted to take a physical education class, but

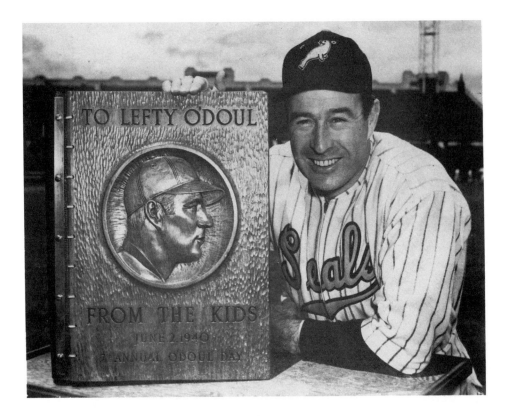

Frank "Lefty" O'Doul was DiMaggio's last minor league manager with the San Francisco Seals and a lifelong friend. (Photograph courtesy of Dick Dobbins)

it was filled and he was assigned to ROTC. He didn't like it, and simply stopped going to school, a fact he kept hidden from his parents for nearly six months. Joe left the DiMaggio house at eight o'clock every morning, and instead of going to school, hung around the wharf, fishing, until three, when he returned home and left again to sell newspapers. His parents finally learned of his deception and sent him back to school, but when the principal failed to show up for a meeting with the young truant, Joe left school again, this time for good. His parents didn't try to stop him. It was 1930, the Depression; he'd just turned sixteen years old, and had a junior-high-school education and no marketable skills.

According to the DiMaggio myth, which has been sustained over the years, Joe resumed playing baseball when Vince signed a professional contract with the San Francisco Seals, figuring that if Vince could earn money at the game, so could he. Joe played briefly for the San Francisco Boys' Club and two semipro teams, and it was soon evident he was blessed with natural hitting ability. Soon after Vince joined the Seals, a local scout named "Spike" Hennessey spied Joe peering under a fence at Seals Stadium and brought him to the attention of Seals owner Charley Graham. Joe got his chance to play for the Seals when Vince recommended Joe at the end of the 1932 season to fill in at shortstop. Based on his encouraging performance, the

Seals signed Joe to a contract and asked him to spring training the next season. Early in the 1933 season, Joe entered a game as the late-inning replacement for a veteran outfielder and never left the lineup. Vince was cut from the squad due to his brother's emergence.

That mythical story was later embellished to provide perfect support for the popular conception of Joe DiMaggio as a hero. Such a miraculous genesis appears to reveal the mysterious workings of fate. Joe DiMaggio was blessed with an innate ability to hit and was destined to succeed. Such an origin is mandatory for the creation of a hero. Yet this oft-repeated story, as attractive as it is, is *inaccurate*.

The truth about Joe DiMaggio's early career reveals a precocious young man of tremendous talent and confidence. Vincent DiMaggio didn't begin playing professional baseball until the spring of 1932, while Joe resumed his interest in the game in the summer of 1931. A little over a year later, Joe was one of the best players in San Francisco and had made his professional debut. Three years after that he was heralded as one of the best players in all of baseball, and perhaps one of the best ever. Not bad for a high school dropout who five years before hawked newspapers and dreamed of playing tennis. Baseball saved him.

Joe DiMaggio's older brothers sparked Joe's return to baseball, and their support allowed his talent to flourish. When Vince DiMaggio quit school, he went to work in a fruit market, played pickup baseball, and was sought by a number of semipro teams. By the fall of 1930, he was playing third base for Jack's Haberdashery in the M & M Winter League. His older brother Tom sometimes filled in at second base or in the outfield.

By the spring of 1931, Vince was playing for Crystal Palace, an "A" team, as well as Jack's. His reputation grew, and soon Vince was bringing home the occasional extra five or ten dollars from semipro play. At a time when most men felt lucky if they earned ten dollars a week, if they even had a job at all, an extra five or ten dollars made an impression.

After leaving school, Joe tried to get a more lucrative job than selling papers. But after a day or two of crating oranges, picking crabmeat, or loading trucks, he would inevitably slink off to the playground or the Horse Lot, to play tennis or the odd pickup game of baseball, or go to the San Francisco Boys' Club.

In the spring of 1931, the Boys' Club sponsored a team in an amateur recreation league. Joe already knew most of the boys on the team, and they'd seen him play in sandlot games, yet initially he wasn't invited to play. A year before, he'd feuded with Frank Venezia, one of the boys who'd organized the team.

In a 1975 interview with author Maury Allen for his book *Where Have You Gone, Joe DiMaggio?*, Venezia provided a unique look at the young Joe DiMaggio and his family. Venezia was, he claimed, "the only friend Joe had. He was really shy then. . . . If his brothers weren't around, he'd sit in the playground and not talk to anybody." After the feud, which Venezia recalls started when he failed to accompany Joe on a trolley ride to pick up newspapers to sell, leaving DiMaggio to make the trip alone, "we passed each other in the street, played in the playground, and sat in school together and never talked. . . . He didn't have any other friends. He didn't need any. He had his family." And of the DiMaggio family, Venezia remembers, "His parents were hermits. They didn't come out of the house much . . . [and] nobody ever got invited into their house."

By this time Vince DiMaggio was attracting favorable notices in Jim Nealon's weekly column on semipro and amateur baseball in the *San Francisco Examiner*, and Mike DiMaggio was playing first base for the Avalons, a semipro team whose roster included two brothers, the Gelardis, whose younger brother played for the Boys' Club. The Di-Maggios' reputation on the ball field, as well as Mike's friendship with the Gelardis, likely paved the way for Joe's inclusion on the Boys' Club team. In mid-summer, at the prodding of another player, Frank Venezia approached Joe and asked if he wanted to play. Joe said yes.

The three DiMaggio brothers—(l–r) Vince, Dom, and Joe—are reunited at Fenway Park on Old-Timers' Day in 1986. The trio not only were honored at Fenway Park that day but also planted a tree on Boston Common. Vince would die of cancer in October 1986. (Photograph courtesy of the Boston Red Sox)

It didn't hurt that the club had a doubleheader scheduled and was short a few players due to the July 4 holiday. Joe DiMaggio made his debut for the Boys' Club on Sunday, July 5, 1931.

In the first game, a 10–5 victory over Willoh Dry Goods, Joe played shortstop and hit second. He failed to collect a base hit in three tries. In game two, Joe again hit second and played short. His brother Mike batted cleanup and played first, as the Boys' Club reaped the benefits of the talented DiMaggio clan. In a 9–7 win over the San Francisco Market, Joe was 2 for 3 and scored two runs, while Mike went 2 for 3 and scored once.

The wins earned a headline in the *Examiner*. Joe's performance earned him a permanent place in the teams' starting lineup, and the Boys' Club team, which previously had struggled, ran off a succession of wins by lopsided scores. They easily won the club league championship, and by the end of the summer were playing against semipro teams composed of much older players, losing only to the more experienced Avalons, 8–4. In Joe's first-ever contest against a team that included another DiMaggio, he went hitless, while brother Mike earned the family honors with a 1-for-5 performance.

In effect, Joe became a full-time baseball player. While his father still hoped he would become a fisherman, Joe spent less time working on the boat and more time working at baseball. Over the next year and a half, he played hundreds of games for at least six different ballclubs, plus an undetermined number of sandlot games, something he could have done only with the tacit approval of his older brothers. They too wanted to play baseball, but the family's economic plight demanded they follow their father to sea. But by the time Joe started to play ball, the older DiMaggio sisters had married and moved out of the house, and though the Depression made every dollar count, the family was more secure. The family's improving financial situation also allowed Vince to escape from the wharf and develop his talent, which was increasingly paying off in cash. It was obvious that, Joe, too, had talent, and his older brothers encouraged him to play. They probably took vicarious pleasure in their younger brothers' success. Giuseppe DiMaggio, who hardly understood the game, probably did not. If Joe or Vincent wanted to play baseball, they played.

Joe DiMaggio quickly learned that once he set foot on a baseball field, he was no longer considered a shy, directionless teenager. His talent brought him immediate respect among peers, and, just as important, from his own brothers. The social awkwardness at school and the prejudice he might encounter due to his Italian heritage didn't matter on the diamond. Baseball pulled Joe from his insular home life and delivered a vital course in self-esteem.

That fall, as Joe turned seventeen, a man named Rossi, who owned an olive oil company, recruited the best players from the Boys' Club team and sponsored them in the McNamara B Winter League, a semi-pro circuit. Instead of playing against boys, Joe was now able to test his ability against some of the best young men in the Bay Area.

At the same time, Vince DiMaggio moved up to play with the Castro Natives in the Seals Winter League. Jointly sponsored by the Seals, Missions, and Oaks, the league was one way the Bay Area PCL clubs found talent. Each fall, they'd invite the best young amateurs to play in the four- or six-team league. During the week, they held clinics and practices at Seals Stadium under the auspices of scouts and the Seals' coaching staff. On Sundays, they played regular games. Veteran players sometimes participated in order to stay in shape for the upcoming season, so the Winter League provided an effective way to develop and evaluate young players. At the end of the season, the best young talent was invited to spring training and signed to contracts. Although the 1931–32 Winter League season was cut short when torrential rains flooded Seals Stadium, Vince DiMaggio's performance earned him an invitation to spring training from the Seals and a contract for the upcoming season.

Only twenty years old, Vince technically needed his parents' signature to play. But when he approached his parents and asked them to sign the contract, they refused. As Vince revealed to author Jack B. Moore in an interview for Moore's book *Joe DiMaggio: A Bio-Bibliography*, he told his father, "Do you want me to go with your will or against your will? I'd rather go with your will, but if you don't give it to me, then I'm going to go anyway." Vince had already given up on his aspiration to become an opera singer. He wasn't about to abandon yet another dream. When his parents still refused to sign the contract, Vince signed it himself, and left.

Joe continued to play for the Rossi team throughout the winter of 1931 and 1932. Vince attended spring training with the Seals, played in a few intrasquad games at shortstop, and was sent to Tucson in the Arizona State League to learn to play outfield and gain experience. When Jim Nealon printed a notice in the *Examiner* on May 3, 1932, reporting on Vince's progress, he added "[Vincent DiMaggio] has a young brother playing with the Rossi Olive Oils, champions of the McNamara Winter League, who looks like a coming hitter. Dimaggio [*sic*] is a shortstop, and in the final championship game cracked out two homers that came in the nick of time." It was Joe's first press notice.

While Vince battered Arizona State League pitching with a slew of home runs, Joe filled in on his old Boys' Club team, then was snapped up by the Sunset Produce club, an A division semipro club for which brother Tom also made an occasional appearance. Joe's powerful bat was earning him a citywide reputation, and he also played for the Avalons, his brother Mike's old team. Neither squad had much pitching and lost more than they won. The Sunsets even dropped a game to Joe's old Rossi team. Yet DiMaggio was facing much better pitching, better fielding, and playing against players with more experience. Playing nearly every day of the week, he managed to keep up, and even star, against older and better players. As the competition level increased, his skills kept pace.

In mid-summer, the Arizona League disbanded and Vince was called up to join the Seals. While in Arizona, he had saved nearly every dollar he earned. Coupled with a modest bonus he received from the Seals, Vince had $1,500. When he returned to San Francisco, he immediately went to see his father.

As Vince related it to Jack Moore, Giuseppe DiMaggio was relaxing in the kitchen, eating peaches dipped in wine, when his prodigal son

"If anyone wants to know why three kids in one family made it to the big leagues they just had to know how we helped each other and how much we practiced back then. We did it every minute we could."—Joe DiMaggio
(Photograph courtesy of the Boston Red Sox)

returned. He glanced up and asked Vince in Italian, "What are you doing home?"

Vince responded by dumping $1,500 dollars in cash on the table. His father first thought he had stolen the money, but Vince took Giuseppe DiMaggio to meet Seals owner Charley Graham the next day, and Giuseppe came away convinced that baseball wasn't such a bad thing after all. Vince was welcomed back into the family home, and no son of Giuseppe DiMaggio ever again faced resistance to playing baseball. Vince spent the remainder of the summer with the Seals.

In late summer, Joe began to play for the Baumgartens, a AA club in the Recreation League. His reputation as a hitter was well-known, and the DiMaggio name made him anything but invisible. Many of the AA teams acted as virtual farm clubs for the Seals, Missions, and Oakland Oaks of the PCL. The managers of the clubs, usually ex-players with ties to one or more teams in the PCL, received a commission if one of the players they recommended was signed to a contract. Major league baseball's minor league farm system was still in its infancy. Only a few major league teams sent scouts to the West Coast, and then usually to scout PCL talent. PCL teams signed their own talent, which they in turn hoped to sell to major league clubs. By the fall of 1932, it was apparent that Joe DiMaggio was a prospect.

Near the end of the 1932 PCL season, star Seals outfielder Henry "Prince" Oana, a native Hawaiian, received permission to miss the team's last three games in order to return to Hawaii and embark on a lucrative barnstorming trip to the Far East. Oana invited Seals shortstop Augie Galan to accompany him on the trip. After the grueling PCL schedule, which in 1932 totaled 186 games, such defections were common. PCL clubs often clowned around in the last few games of the season, or tried out new players.

As DiMaggio told Jack Moore in a 1984 interview, Galan asked Seals manager Jimmy "Ike" Caveney, a former shortstop with the Cincinnati Reds, for permission to join Oana. Caveney refused, asking, "Who am I going to play at shortstop?" Vince DiMaggio spoke up. "I got my kid brother, he's a shortstop and a good one." Caveney told Vince to bring him around, and gave Galan permission to go to Hawaii.

Vince DiMaggio did not believe Caveney knew of his younger brother, but this is unlikely. Most teams in the PCL were in financial trouble, and it was common knowledge that in 1933 they expected to trim their rosters of high-paid veterans in favor of younger and cheaper talent. A week earlier, on September 22, 1932, Jim Nealon reported in the *Examiner* that Mickey Schrader, the Seals scout who had signed Vince and was his manager earlier that season in Tucson, had recruited sixty players for the upcoming Winter League. Schrader had been scouting the amateur and semipro ranks in the Bay Area since the Arizona League folded, and he'd certainly seen Joe DiMaggio play. While the Bay Area PCL clubs cooperated in the Winter League, they were still in competition to sign those young players to a contract. Allowing Joe DiMaggio to play the final three games of the season in a Seals uniform gave the club an advantage over the Missions and the Oaks. In the same column, Nealon wrote, "We always could see where Vincent Demaggio [sic], now playing with the Seals, would be a ballplayer. Just tab Demaggio No. 2—a young brother of the Seal player, who can scamper through the short patch and do things in general around the ball field that makes him look like a comer."

Joe DiMaggio made his professional debut on October 1, 1932, when the Seals entertained the Missions. He hit second, behind his old hero Jerry Donovan, and played shortstop. Facing veteran PCL hurler Ted Pillette, DiMaggio tripled, drew the only walk off Pillette all day, and scored a run in four plate appearances. In the field, Joe handled four chances flawlessly. In what must have been a thrilling moment, he was on deck in the ninth inning when Donovan broke a 3–3 tie with a long home run to left field.

It was an impressive debut. The next day, in a 3–0 loss to the Missions in game one of a season-ending doubleheader, DiMaggio was hitless in four at bats. In five chances in the field, he made one error, throwing wildly to first, but also managed to start a double play. In game two, a 12–4 Seals victory that was cut to seven innings by the agreement of both teams, he again excelled, scoring one run and knocking in two with a double and a sacrifice in three plate appearances, and handling three chances in the field. In the short three-game stint, he hit .222. Although he was not paid by the Seals, he was, technically anyway, a professional ballplayer.

That same day in Chicago, the Yankees defeated the Cubs 13–6 to win the 1932 World Series in four games. The day before, in the fifth inning of game three, Babe Ruth had connected for his legendary "called shot," his last home run in World Series competition. It would be four years before the Yankees would win another pennant and return to the Series. When they did, batting third, in Ruth's old spot, would be Joe DiMaggio.

Vince DiMaggio is captured in this 1938 publicity shot eating spaghetti. Such shots promoted the stereotypical image of Italian-Americans at the time. (Photograph by Dick Thompson, courtesy of the Sports Museum of New England)

## CHAPTER TWO

The Quest Begins: 1933–35

DiMaggio's appearance with the Seals, brief as it was, did not go unnoticed. Jim Nealon wrote that Joe "took all to the merry . . . [and] in fact did everything in his appearance with the Seals that makes him look like a comer." Three days after the Pacific Coast League season ended, DiMaggio joined the Seals Winter League.

He was assigned to the Kenneally Seals, a team managed by veteran scout and former player Neal Kenneally, whose alumni included Yankee pitcher Lefty Gomez. The Seals dropped their first game on October 8, 10–9, but DiMaggio, batting third and playing short, went 3 for 5 and scored two runs. Three weeks later, with San Francisco manager Ike Caveney looking on, DiMaggio turned a triple off the left-field fence at Seals Stadium into an inside-the-park home run. By this time, Nealon was referring to DiMaggio as "Push 'Em Up Joe," a take-off on "Poosh 'Em Up" Tony Lazzeri, another Italian native of San Francisco who was currently a star with the Yankees.

While Kenneally's Seals struggled, DiMaggio's personal star rose, even as the spelling of his name took on a life of its own. At the end of November, Nealon wrote that "big gangling Joe DeMaggio [sic] . . . is easily the best looking batter in the Seals Winter League. Has a world of confidence and Holy Cow, how he can tag that onion! He is a cinch to make the trek to Monterey next spring."

The Seals shared Nealon's enthusiasm. They quickly signed Di-Maggio to a contract before either the Missions or Oakland Oaks beat them to it. Tom DiMaggio handled the negotiations, and Joe signed a contract worth $225 per month. Most other rookies were paid only about $150. The deal was still a bargain for the Seals—they planned to cut loose some costly veterans and rebuild anyway. If the Seals ever sold DiMaggio to the big leagues, the extra $75 or $100 a month would be recouped many times over.

While the Kenneally Seals failed to prosper in the Winter League, DiMaggio shined. Even in the best league in the Bay Area, facing better pitching and playing regularly for the first time on a groomed, fenced-in field, DiMaggio quickly discovered he could hit, and hit with power. During the week, the league sponsored clinics and held long practices. Major league stars like Cleveland third baseman Willie Kamm and Washington shortstop Joe Cronin, both native San Franciscans, offered advice, as did all-time great Ty Cobb. Under such sustained tutelage, DiMaggio made great strides. At the conclusion of the season, he was one of sixty Winter League players invited to join the Seals at spring training.

But the Depression nixed plans to train in Monterey. Instead, the Seals held camp at Seals Stadium, at the corner of 16th and Bryant streets in San Francisco, on March 1, 1933. That change of plans was the first of many that benefited DiMaggio in his first year of professional baseball.

Sixty rookies competed for a handful of open spots on the Seals'

The San Francisco Seals receive a "lecture" from pitcher Walter Mails (far left). His audience includes (l–r) Leroy Hermann, Larry Woodall, Joe DiMaggio, Jimmy "Ike" Caveney, Roy Frazier, and owner Charlie Graham. (Photograph courtesy of Dick Dobbins)

A teenaged Joe DiMaggio in the uniform of the San Francisco Seals. (Photograph from Transcendental Graphics, Mark Rucker)

roster. In an economy move, the Seals planned to carry only eighteen or nineteen players, and there were already more than twenty players returning from the 1932 squad. Mickey Schrader, who'd taken over as manager of Amarillo in the reconstituted Arizona-Texas League, would fill his roster from among the remaining prospects. Although DiMaggio was already under contract, his place on either team was still uncertain. He would have to play his way onto a team.

Physically, DiMaggio wasn't particularly impressive, even though he had broad, sloping shoulders, long legs, and strong arms. He stood just under six feet tall and weighed about 175 pounds, but he was still growing. DiMaggio wasn't mentioned in early press reports as among the best prospects in camp, although he did appear in an *Examiner* photograph with brother Vince. The Seals' shortstop position already was locked up by twenty-one-year-old Augie Galan, who later spent fifteen years in the major leagues. The odds were against DiMaggio making the Seals.

DiMaggio was not even the best rookie shortstop in camp. Tony Gomez was. He'd starred with Eddie Joost in semipro ball to form the Bay Area's best double-play combination, and excelled in the Winter League. He could hit, and was a much better fielder than DiMaggio. But Gomez didn't make it past the first cut.

Manager Ike Caveney pulled the young player aside and recommended he give up the game, despite his obvious talent. "Kid," said Caveney, "you're just too black." The Seals had hoped the Latino Gomez could "pass," but the dark-complexioned shortstop was cut loose, a victim of baseball's color line. Gomez was crushed. He later went on to play professionally in Mexico. DiMaggio inadvertently benefited from baseball's bigotry.

Caveney divided the youngsters into two "Freshman" squads that scrimmaged each other while he quickly winnowed down the number of players in camp. The veteran "Varsity," including Vince DiMaggio, trained separately.

The rookies had little time to impress Caveney, but Joe DiMaggio made the most of his chances, slashing out hit after hit in intrasquad contests. In the first meeting between the Freshman and Varsity on March 4, Joe played shortstop and hit cleanup, while his brother Vince played center field for the veterans. Joe collected one hit in four tries in the 5–2 Freshman win, but threw away a ball at shortstop.

He survived the first cut on March 6. San Francisco baseball writer Abe Kemp noted that "Caveney has a problem on his hands finding a spot for Joe DiMaggio. As a shortstop, this lad has little to commend him, but as a hitter he attracts attention. Caveney may decide to give Joe a trial at first base." (Kemp, whom *Chicago Tribune* sportswriter Jerome Holtzman interviewed in 1973 for his classic oral history of sportswriting titled "No Cheering in the Press Box," was an astute, experienced observer; he first covered the Seals in 1907. Kemp later told Holtzman he recalled sitting with Seals owner Charley Graham in the stands on the first day of camp. According to Kemp, "There were about eighteen kids on the infield, just an impromptu practice . . . some kid picks up a ground ball and he heaves it right past Graham's head. And Graham says, 'I'll say one thing about that kid, he's got a hell of an arm.' It was Joe DiMaggio.")

The next day, Caveney moved the erratic-throwing DiMaggio to first base. The Varsity spanked the Freshman team, 12–6. Joe collected two singles and an RBI from the leadoff spot, earning more praise from Kemp. DiMaggio's bat shined again the following day as he doubled off Seal ace Jimmy Zinn in another Freshman loss, but although he started a double play at first, he also errored. The first-base experiment ended.

The Seals opened their exhibition season on March 10 against the National League Pittsburgh Pirates. Joe DiMaggio didn't play in the first game of the series.

In game two, with the Seals trailing 8–3 in the ninth inning, they loaded the bases with no outs against veteran right-handed pitcher Waite Hoyt. Hoyt, a big leaguer since 1918, was already the winner of nearly 200 major league contests, including a league-best 22 for the 1927 New York Yankees. Eighteen-year-old Joe DiMaggio, barely two years off the sandlots, was called by Caveney to pinch-hit.

It must have been a heady experience for the youngster. The Pirates were second-place finishers in the 1932 National League pennant race and featured a lineup that included five eventual Hall of Famers: Hoyt, outfielders and brothers Paul and Lloyd Waner, shortstop Arky Vaughan, and third baseman Pie Traynor. All-time great Honus Wagner was a Pirate coach.

In front of such a star-studded crowd, DiMaggio lifted a lazy fly ball to the outfield, overmatched in his first look at major league pitching.

But Caveney did not lose faith in the rookie. DiMaggio's bat made him Caveney's pet. Despite his defensive shortcomings, Joe was one of only twenty-three men still on the Seal roster on March 15. A week later, the club played another exhibition series against another major league team, the NL champion Chicago Cubs. Appearing as a pinch hitter against Cub pitcher Lynn Nelson, DiMaggio failed to get a hit.

Seals manager Frank "Lefty" O'Doul claimed that DiMaggio had the best arm of any outfield prospect he had ever seen. (Photograph courtesy of Dick Dobbins)

The Seals met Chicago a week later and DiMaggio went hitless again, failing as a pinch hitter and in two full games at shortstop while Galan was sidelined with a minor injury. However, in the last appearance, DiMaggio did give observers a glimpse of his athleticism when he reached on a fielder's choice and scored on the front end of a double steal. But his two errors in the sixth inning led to a Cub run. Fortunately, the Seals still won, 5–2.

In the Seals' final two exhibition games, against the Missions, it was apparent that while DiMaggio's bat was PCL caliber, his glove was not. In a 17–2 drubbing, Joe collected one of only four Seal hits. But in the field, he was atrocious, committing four errors. Kemp bitterly observed that DiMaggio appeared "ill at ease at short, and not suited to the position . . . [he] is doing the best that he can, but appears bewildered." Although DiMaggio made no errors in the exhibition finale the next day, he also went hitless.

Yet he made the club. The myth is that Joe languished on the bench the first few weeks of the season, appeared as a pinch hitter for a slumping outfielder—usually identified as Al Stewart—then was sent to the outfield, where he immediately became a star and caused the Seals to release brother Vince. That's not exactly how it happened.

DiMaggio earned his spot on the Seals roster through a fortunate set of circumstances. Galan's injury certainly helped. The Seals were unwilling to start the season without a backup shortstop. Yet it was the Depression as much as anything else that won DiMaggio a place on the team.

Money was tight in the PCL in 1933. The preceding year, game attendance had fallen sharply. Before the 1933 season, all eight PCL clubs announced plans to sell beer and to roll back admission prices. They decided to trim rosters to a bare minimum, and cut salaries, which caused veteran players all across the league to grouse.

The situation was particularly dire in San Francisco. While the Seals were always more popular than the Missions, competition between the two clubs hurt both. Moreover, in the fall of 1929, Seals owner Charley Graham had announced plans to build a new stadium to replace decrepit Recreation Park, known as "Old Rec." Graham was confident he could afford the new park; after all, the Missions would have to pay him rent.

By the time the park opened in the spring of 1931, Graham was overextended. In the midst of a rapidly deteriorating economy, Graham built an expensive, state-of-the-art park, one of the best in baseball at the time. The new park cost over one million dollars and required the removal of over 84,000 yards of rock, while Graham still owed rent on Old Rec for another five years. As a result, Seals Stadium was heavily mortgaged.

By 1933, Graham was in trouble. Belt-tightening was the rule. He let several experienced players go during spring training, and after the regular season began, several more had to be cut loose.

Hawaiian native Henry "Prince" Oana was an obvious choice. Although the outfielder had been one of the PCL's premier power hitters in 1931 (leading the Seals to the PCL championship with a .345 average, 23 home runs, and 143 RBI), Oana slumped in 1932. In 1933, he arrived late at camp, complained about his contract, and suffered from some eye trouble. Then he and veteran pitcher Guidi Simoni, along with several other unnamed Seals, were charged by a young woman with assault. Oana was later exonerated, but the Seals cut him loose on April 6. He immediately signed with Portland, as Simoni had a few days before.

The same day, just two days into the season, Vince DiMaggio was also let go. He had hurt his shoulder tumbling to make a catch in spring training and just couldn't throw. Catcher Charley Wallgren suffered a similar fate. A severe case of jock itch was enough to precipitate his release. The Depression left little room for compassion.

The cuts surprised no one. Two days earlier, on Opening Day, April 4, the *Examiner* published Abe Kemp's season forecast, accompanied by photographs of nine Seals, mostly regulars. Neither Oana, Vince DiMaggio, nor Wallgren was featured in the pictures. Joe DiMaggio was; his position was listed as "utility."

The Seals opened at home against Portland and won their first two games. Joe and Vince didn't play in either game. In the series' third game, the Seals trailed 6–4 in the bottom of the eighth inning. With right fielder George Thomas scheduled to bat, Caveney called for Joe DiMaggio to pinch-hit. He flied out. The next two men reached base, and Caveney pinch-hit Vince, who made the second out of the inning. The Seals eventually loaded the bases, but failed to score.

In the top of the ninth, Caveney sent Joe DiMaggio to right field. Joe first thought Caveney was calling to Vince, but his brother couldn't throw. Joe also wondered why Oana wasn't sent in, but the Prince was already persona non grata. Caveney saved his only other outfielder, Joe's old hero Jerry Donovan, in case he was needed to pinch-hit in the ninth. So a somewhat bewildered Joe DiMaggio trotted out to right field, a position he had never played. He received no chances in one inning of work. The Seals went out in order in the ninth and lost, 6–4. Oana, Vince DiMaggio, veteran catcher Charley Wallgren, and infielder Julius Wera were released after the game. The cuts saved Graham and the Seals over $1,200 a month.

With only four outfielders on the roster, Caveney gave the rookie a chance to show what he could do. He already knew DiMaggio could run and hit. If he could find a position, he could help the team. If he couldn't, it was still early in the year. It was better to find out if DiMaggio could play. At $225 per month, the Seals didn't want to wait too long to find out.

In the fourth game of the season, DiMaggio started in right field and hit sixth. Although he was hitless in the 3–1 Portland win, he ranged far and wide in the outfield, collecting five putouts. He wasn't always pretty, but he got to the ball. Portland, aware of DiMaggio's lack of experience, gave his arm an early test.

The erratic shotgun that DiMaggio wielded in the infield proved more accurate from the outfield, and he gunned down two Portland base runners. Right field was his, at least until he stopped hitting or started dropping fly balls. Ironically, Jerry Donovan became the odd man out in the Seals' outfield.

Debuting with the Seals in the Coast League provided DiMaggio the best possible situation to begin his professional career. Playing for San Francisco allowed Joe to continue living at home. The existence of two other Bay Area teams in the league—the Missions and Oakland Oaks—kept road trips to a minimum. The weather on the coast was usually perfect for baseball, and night games were still a rarity. The PCL schedule, which at 26 weeks and 192 scheduled games was the most grueling in organized baseball, gave younger players ample opportunity to play and improve. Coast League teams could afford to wait a little longer in assessing performance than teams in other leagues. Each series lasted a week and consisted of at least seven games, which gave hitters a chance to learn the league's pitchers. If a pitcher gave a batter trouble, the hitter was reasonably sure he'd face him again soon. Moreover, most of Joe's teammates already knew his brother Vince, so Joe was spared the hazing endured by most rookies.

The Coast League was in transition in the early 1930s. Players tended to be veterans of great experience whose skills weren't quite major league caliber, or young recruits whose ability was tempered only by their lack of experience. Due to the Depression, players who fell into neither category had been let go. Youth rarely languished on the bench for long. You either played or were released.

The Coast League had a well-deserved reputation as perhaps the most offensive-minded circuit in baseball. The league used a ball livelier than that used in the major leagues or in many other minor leagues. As a result, a player's offensive performance was often considered suspect by major league scouts. One good year didn't automatically result in a big league contract. Over the years, a number of Coast stars had fizzled in the majors. The league favored place hitters who slapped the lively ball past infielders and minor league sluggers who took advantage of the ball and undersize dimensions of some parks. But the rabbit ball, and the general offensive reputation of the league, helped young hitters like DiMaggio build confidence.

The larger dimensions of Seals Stadium also helped DiMaggio. The park measured 385 feet down the right-field line, 365 feet in left. The left-field power alley was 404 feet, the right-field alley 424 feet. The outfield fence was 20 feet high. While the proportions discouraged power, any power displayed in Seals Stadium was genuine. The ballpark was seemingly built for the young DiMaggio. He hit line drives to the gaps, and hits off DiMaggio's bat had room to roll. Home runs in Seals Stadium were home runs almost anywhere.

The rabbit ball and the park's roomy outfield also allowed DiMaggio to show his two greatest assets as a fielder: his speed and throwing arm. Both would have been inhibited had he played in a smaller park or in a league with less offense. In short, DiMaggio and the Coast League were a perfect match.

According to the DiMaggio myth, once Joe was installed in right

At age eighteen, in his first full season with the Seals, DiMaggio compiled a remarkable 61-game hitting streak. (Photograph courtesy of Dick Dobbins)

field he became an immediate star and embarked on a Coast League–record 61-game hitting streak; attendance soared and DiMaggio saved the league from financial collapse. The reality is that his first season was not quite the one-way ticket to the Hall of Fame others have described. But the journey had begun.

DiMaggio did get off to a fast start. After his first appearance, he hit in eight of the Seals' next nine games, going 14 for 38, a robust .368. During the tear, he collected six doubles, and on April 16 he hit his first home run, off Portland pitcher Herm Pillette. In only his third start, on April 9, DiMaggio was moved from right field to center.

Although DiMaggio was hot, the Seals were awful. They were hit-

DiMaggio is shown in a publicity photo promoting his 61-game hitting streak in 1933. (Photograph courtesy of Dick Dobbins)

ting (Galan, third baseman Leo Osterberg, and second baseman Art Garibaldi all flirted with .400), but the pitching was terrible and the Seals were having a difficult time deciding on whom to pair with Di-Maggio in the outfield. Jerry Donovan and Ernie Sulik were troubled by nagging injuries, while George Thomas and Al Stewart had failed to hit. The Seals ended April in last place, a pitiful 9–18.

After his quick start, Joe cooled, hitting only .250 for the remainder of the month. The Seals, desperate to stop their slide, re-signed Vince DiMaggio on April 26. Vince temporarily pushed Joe from the fifth spot in the batting order to second, and Joe moved back to right field as Vince took over in center.

With his brother alongside him, Joe regained some of the consistency and power he had demonstrated over the first two weeks of the season. It helped that the Seals played the first month in the Bay Area. In their first road contest, on May 2, Joe exploded for two home runs off veteran Hollywood pitcher Tom Sheehan. Two days later, both Di-Maggios homered off Hollywood's Archie Campbell. Although the Seals hit five home runs off Campbell that day, they still lost, 7–6.

The Sporting News took note of DiMaggio's auspicious start, and Joe soon received his first accolades from the "Bible of Baseball." "Joe Demaggio [sic], the 17-year-old outfielder signed by the San Francisco Seals is creating quite a furore [sic]," wrote an unnamed correspondent. "This hard hitting kid seems to have no weakness at the plate and he knows how to play the outfield much better than more experienced flychasers . . . He has a right wing that propels the horsehide like a bullet shot from a rifle . . ."

But when the Seals failed to improve, they decided that two DiMaggios were a luxury they couldn't afford. On May 8, Vince was again cut loose. Joe had hit over .300 with Vince in the lineup.

With Vince gone, Joe struggled. He bounced back and forth between right field and center and was inconsistent at the plate.

In mid-month, he slumped terribly. Beginning on May 14, the Seals played series against Hollywood and Portland. Over twelve games DiMaggio was a pitiful 6 for 48. Worse, in the previous three weeks he had gotten only one extra-base hit. His average fell below .250. That didn't count for much in the potent PCL. Of the league's eighty-two players who had played more than fifteen games, fifty-three were hitting above .300. DiMaggio was seventy-sixth, ahead of only six other hitters. The Seals were desperate, and even pressed good-hitting pitcher Jimmy Zinn into service in the outfield. Had the Seals had an alternative, DiMaggio might not have hung on much longer.

It is unclear whether DiMaggio started to believe his press clippings, worried over the release of Vince, had trouble adjusting to life away from home, or was falling victim to the league's pitching grapevine, but his slump was serious. He was in danger of playing himself out of the league.

One other factor may have contributed to his slide. In mid-month the PCL was rife with rumors of an impending shutdown. The Depression was wreaking havoc in the minor leagues, and the PCL was in trouble. A wet, cold spring kept fans away from the park. The Seattle field, which featured a dirt infield, was a quagmire. The club was forced to play at a high-school field and was sinking under debt. If Seattle collapsed, the remaining Coast League clubs could no longer afford to travel north just to play Portland. A six-team league was untenable. The Seals themselves were losing more money each day. According to *The Sporting News*, their wholesale release of veterans sparked complaints among other league members of the Seals' "indifference," a charge that struck at the integrity of the league.

The rumors couldn't have helped DiMaggio's confidence. He was a struggling rookie, and it appeared as if the league was about to fold. Established veterans might have been able to hook on with other clubs, but rookies hitting like DiMaggio faced an uncertain future.

PCL owners met on May 20 and tried to squelch the rumors. They

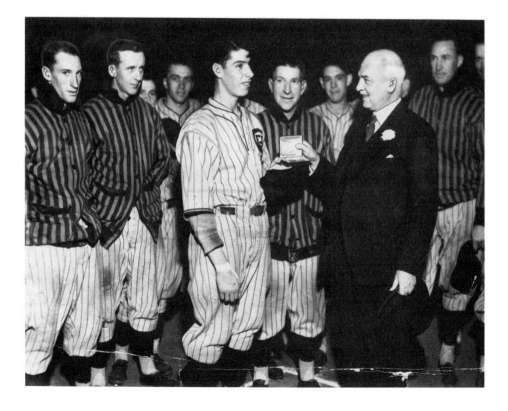

San Francisco mayor Angelo Rossi presents a medal from the City of San Francisco to Joe DiMaggio on the occasion of his then 50-game hitting streak in the Pacific Coast League. The streak would continue to 61 games before the end of the 1933 season. (Photograph courtesy of the *Boston Herald*)

wanted to disband, pay off players for the balance of the season, and re-form in 1934. But they dropped the idea when baseball commissioner Judge Kenesaw Mountain Landis ruled that if the league shut down, all players would become free agents, even if paid for the season. Landis's decision forced the league to keep going, albeit on a shoestring. The owners prayed for good weather. And a miracle.

They got both. As the weather warmed with the beginning of summer, something remarkable happened. Just as the league reached its nadir, and his own performance reached its low point, Joe DiMaggio did something extraordinary.

Beginning in the second game of a doubleheader against first-place Portland on May 28, he did the kind of thing heroes do. The eighteen-year-old DiMaggio, the youngest and arguably worst hitter in the league, smacked out at least one base hit in the next 61 games. When the streak ended, the future of Joe DiMaggio, the San Francisco Seals, and the Pacific Coast League was secure.

This singular ability is why Joe DiMaggio came to mean so much to so many. Beginning with his hitting streak in 1933, DiMaggio proved, over and over again, that he played best when all seemed lost.

After going 0 for 4 in the first game of the twin bill, a 10–2 Seals victory, DiMaggio smacked a double in game two. The Seals won that one also, 3–1. In the same game, Portland outfielder George Blackerby hit in his 36th straight game, a feat just beginning to attract attention in the press. In the offensive-minded PCL, hitting streaks of some duration were not uncommon. The league record was 49 games, set by Oakland's Jack Ness in 1915. Blackerby's streak ended when he went hitless his next game.

The Seals traveled to Seattle for a doubleheader on May 30. DiMaggio responded with his best day of the year, going 3 for 6 in the opener, including a tenth-inning double to cement a 10–8 Seals win. He was 3 for 4 in the second game, knocking in three runs and scoring three with a single, triple, and home run. He was off and running.

In four of the next five games he smacked out two hits, and homered twice during the stretch. When the Seals returned home to face Oakland, DiMaggio kept hitting. His streak coincided with a Seal turnaround, and the club began playing .500 ball. Ten games into his streak, on June 6, the Seals plugged the gap in their outfield. They signed center fielder Elias Funk, who'd hit .267 as a regular for Detroit in 1930 and the White Sox in 1932. The move allowed DiMaggio to return to the less-demanding challenge of right field, where he played the remainder of the season.

On that day, as the Seals played Oakland, DiMaggio likely received his first close look from major league scouts. Photographs in the *Examiner* showed eight big league scouts, including Bill Essick of the Yankees and Joe Williams of Cincinnati, seated in the stands with Seals owner Charley Graham. Graham was probably touting shortstop Augie Galan, but the scouts couldn't have helped notice DiMaggio.

Oakland catcher Billy Raimondi, who went on to play fifteen years in the PCL, was at the time a young backup catcher with the Oaks. He remembers that DiMaggio was "the best player I ever saw. He could do everything, run, hit, throw. Even then, he was the best player I ever saw." DiMaggio's hitting streak soon brought him to the attention of everyone.

There were still rough edges to DiMaggio's game. As his streak quietly reached 19 games on June 15, Abe Kemp, who had yet to make mention of the streak, remarked after two DiMaggio errors that "Joe appears able to drop fly balls and home runs with equal ease."

While Joe's streak continued, Dominic DiMaggio, the youngest of the DiMaggio children, received his first mention in the press. Jim Nealon noted that "from the house of DiMaggio comes another baseballer . . . Dominick [sic] playing shortstop for Galileo Post American Legion [and] second base for the San Francisco Boys' Club."

Joe DiMaggio's streak nearly ended five days later, as the Seals' Jimmy Zinn and the Missions' Johnny Babich squared off in a pitchers' duel. Entering the eighth inning, there was no score and DiMaggio was hitless. But Funk doubled and DiMaggio followed with a long drive off the left-field fence for a triple, knocking in the game's only run and extending his streak to 19.

Years later, in game 40 of DiMaggio's 1941 56-game hitting streak, Babich gained some notoriety when he publicly promised to stop Joe by not throwing him any strikes. In DiMaggio's second at bat, Babich worked the count to 3 and 0 before he was nearly castrated by a line-drive base hit between his legs on a pitch Babich meant to be ball four. Babich's pregame pronouncement might have been inspired by his recollection of the DiMaggio triple eight years before.

On June 21, 1933, DiMaggio's ninth-inning base hit again proved the difference in another Seals win. DiMaggio was now the big bat in the Seals' lineup. In the last twenty games, he had scored 18 runs and knocked in 21.

DiMaggio's streak was first mentioned in the press on June 25. After DiMaggio went 2 for 4 and 1 for 4 in a doubleheader split with the Missions, Kemp noted that DiMaggio "hit safely in his 29th and

San Francisco Seals manager Ike Caveney (l) *poses with his prize pupil Joe DiMaggio.* (Photograph from Bettmann Archives)

30th straight game," then added, "Joe has a long and tortuous path to weave before he can approach the Coast League record of Jack Ness." But from that day on, DiMaggio's streak was public knowledge.

The following day Kemp offered a cautious analysis of the young player. He wrote: "Joe De Maggio [*sic*] is a greatly improved hitter. He now hits the ball where it is pitched, and that is the secret of collecting base hits, at least one of the secrets. Joe, however, gives fans heart failure the way he goes after fly balls. His position in the outfield reminds you of a quarterback squatting behind the lines barking the signals."

The streak nearly ended on June 30 in Los Angeles. DiMaggio's only hit was an infield ground ball he managed to beat out in the fifth inning. In the same game, Los Angeles outfielder Jim Oglesby hit in his 20th game in a row. The next day, DiMaggio waited until the ninth inning to collect a hit, doubling in a four-run Seal rally to secure a 10–5 win.

By July 3, DiMaggio had lifted his batting average to .321, although he still trailed league leader Ox Eckhardt of the Missions by nearly a hundred points. As pleased as he may have been with his own performance, he must have been doubly pleased to learn that Vince, his sore arm now healed, had returned to the PCL with Hollywood.

As Joe's streak approached 40 games, only nine games short of Ness's mark, he became the object of increased attention. Attendance at Seals games started to rise, particularly on the road, and the press started filling in DiMaggio's background. They called him "Dead Pan Joe" in reference to his demeanor and one-word answers to questions. In game 40 of the streak, DiMaggio received his closest call yet. Hitless entering the eighth inning against Hollywood pitcher Tom Sheehan, DiMaggio worked the count to 3 and 2 before whistling a letter-high fastball to left-center field. Brother Vince, playing center for Hollywood, tried desperately to cut the drive off, but it fell just out of reach and Joe pulled in at second for a double.

The hit probably provided the inspiration for a spurious anecdote in the DiMaggio myth concerning the 61-game streak. DiMaggio and others have often repeated the story that in DiMaggio's last at bat in game 43, Sheehan, known as the Grover Cleveland Alexander of the minor leagues, fell behind DiMaggio 2 and 0. He eschewed giving in to DiMaggio with a fastball or walking him to end the streak, so instead he threw his best pitch, a curve, which Joe hit for a double. Sheehan then allegedly walked to second and told the young hitter, "you hit my curve ball when I didn't want you to. A fellow who can do that belongs in the big leagues." But DiMaggio didn't face Sheehan in game 43, and in their next matchup, in game 45, he tripled off Sheehan in the first inning.

The buildup was intense as DiMaggio approached Ness's record, but Joe still wasn't very responsive to the press. Abe Kemp even published an interview with Joe in which DiMaggio's responses consisted only of shrugs and nods. The press publicly translated DiMaggio's reticence into such praiseworthy characteristics as humility and determination, but privately they were frustrated. No one, it seemed, could pull DiMaggio from his shell. His almost painful shyness led him to focus entirely on baseball. "Dead Pan" DiMaggio's silence led the press to become ever more inventive.

He tied Ness's mark on July 13 in Seals Stadium versus Los Angeles. In his first at bat, Joe blooped the first pitch off pitcher Fay Thomas into center field. His next time up he homered on the first pitch, then collected a single to go 3 for 5. The Seals still lost, 8–2.

The next night, Joe shattered the record to stretch the streak to 50. Ten thousand fans, the Seals' largest crowd of the season and more than five times the normal draw, turned out on "Joe DiMaggio Night" and saw DiMaggio single in his first appearance to set a new PCL record. Then he lashed out three doubles to finish 4 for 5 in a 7–6 Seal win. After the game, San Francisco mayor Angelo Rossi presented DiMaggio with a watch in commemoration of the record.

The following evening, DiMaggio was feted at the Milano Theater in North Beach. With *Examiner* sports editor Curley Grieve serving as master of ceremonies, DiMaggio received a silver loving cup from the theater in recognition of his achievement as a "Son of Italy." The Italian community in San Francisco was following DiMaggio's performance with tremendous fervor. The fisherman's son was becoming a hero, whether he wanted to be one or not. Abe Kemp wrote a rare feature in the *Examiner*, predictably linking DiMaggio to outfielder Ping Bodie and infielders Tony Lazzeri and Frank Crosetti, earlier PCL stars of Italian heritage, who later all starred for the New York Yankees. Of DiMaggio, Kemp reported that "hero worshipers do not get far with this unassuming lad who dismisses them with a blank look and a shrug of the shoulders . . . to most questions Joe answers yes or no," and stereotypically added, "Joe admits his fondness for spaghetti, but as yet has been unable to find any base hits in it."

With Ness's record out of the way, the press set its sights on the minor-league hitting-streak record of 69 games, set by Joe Wilhoit for Wichita in 1919. DiMaggio increased his streak to 53 games in a doubleheader on Sunday, June 18, before the Seals headed to Sacramento for a seven-game series against the league's best pitching staff.

DiMaggio had little trouble extending the streak to 55 in the first two games of the series. But in game 56, he reached first twice on errors before lining a clean single off former Seal pitcher Bill Hartwig.

Collecting a hit every game in relative obscurity was one matter, but doing so under the gaze of hopeful and adoring fans was something else. DiMaggio hadn't had an extra-base hit in a week and was having trouble making solid contact. Even so, on July 21 he stretched the streak to 57 games on an easy ground ball that eluded Sacramento shortstop Ray French. On July 22, DiMaggio lucked out again on another sixth-inning ground ball to French. French, normally a fine fielder and later selected as a member of the all-time PCL All-Star team, let the ball roll between his legs for DiMaggio's only hit of the day. The Associated Press reported that while the hit was "legitimate . . . [it] was of the variety which are questionable to the spectators."

During a doubleheader on July 23, DiMaggio's brinkmanship continued. In the ninth inning of game one, played in Stockton, DiMaggio took advantage of the fact that the Sacramento infield was playing back; he beat out a hit on a swinging bunt. The teams traveled back to Sacramento for game two, and DiMaggio again lucked out. Hitless in the ninth inning, he drove a hard grounder to deep short. Ray French once again failed to field the ball cleanly, and DiMaggio

San Francisco was home to three players who later became stars for the Yankees, namely (l–r) *Joe DiMaggio, Tony Lazzeri, and Frank Crosetti. Here they are shown prior to embarking on a cross-country drive to spring training.* (Photograph courtesy of Dick Dobbins)

reached first without drawing a throw. *Sacramento Bee* sports editor Steve George scored the ball a hit.

After each game with Sacramento, irate fans, some of whom wanted to see the streak continue—legitimately—and others who hoped to see it end, stormed the press box. Police were called to escort George safely from the park following the second game.

Kemp defended the calls the next day. He wrote that any accusations that DiMaggio was receiving a break were unfair, and "so far the boy has honestly earned everything he has been credited with."

But the scorers were not entirely to blame for DiMaggio's specious performance over the previous week. Ever since DiMaggio's streak passed 40 games, Seals games had been drawing larger and larger crowds. Opposing players were well aware of DiMaggio's importance to the financial health of the league, so they had reason to want the streak to continue. A little help was not out of the question.

Of all DiMaggio's opponents during the final days of the streak, the performance of Ray French appears most suspect. French may have nonchalanted a play or two, though probably not deliberately. Even out-of-town newspapers failed to indict French for his miscues; each was described in numerous press accounts as "difficult plays." Late in the streak some opposing infields did give DiMaggio a break by playing deeper than normal, a strategy that gave DiMaggio a chance but didn't hand him a base hit. DiMaggio still had to hit the ball. He was skilled enough to turn the small allowance to his advantage.

Back in San Francisco on July 25, DiMaggio was hitless entering

Yankee owner Colonel Jacob Ruppert (r) *meets his newest acquisition as he greets Joe DiMaggio at an Elks Charity game in Oakland on October 30, 1935. In less than a year DiMaggio would help lead New York back to the World Series after a three-year absence.* (Associated Press photograph)

the eighth inning against Oakland. The Seals led 6–4. It was unlikely that DiMaggio, who'd failed to get a hit in the seventh, would receive another at bat. But in the eighth inning, the Seals rallied, fortuitously exploding for eight hits, including a clean single up the middle by DiMaggio, and eight runs. The streak was at 61 games.

Oaks catcher Billy Raimondi remembers the Oakland series well. "Everybody wanted Joe to get a hit," he recalls. "We even played the infield deep, and told him, 'Joe, why don't you just bunt?' But Joe wouldn't bunt." The incident in Sacramento the week before apparently had made him determined not to give the appearance of taking advantage of a cooperative opponent.

The next day, July 26, Caveney moved DiMaggio from the cleanup position to leadoff, hoping the change would give the young slugger an additional opportunity to hit. It didn't matter that the strategy might not have been the best for the ball club. DiMaggio's streak was far more significant than the Seals' record.

Facing Oakland pitcher Ed Walsh Jr., son of eventual Hall of Famer Ed Walsh Sr., a star for the Chicago White Sox three decades earlier, DiMaggio rolled out to shortstop in his first at bat. The Seals then touched Walsh for two first-inning runs, and DiMaggio next came to bat in the second with two out. He bounced out to third.

In the fourth inning, he stepped to the plate again with two outs, this time with runners on first and third. But he grounded to Cookie Lavagetto at second for a force-out. In the seventh inning, all he could manage was a lazy fly ball to left field.

With the score tied 3–3 entering the ninth inning, DiMaggio was scheduled to hit fourth. Seal first baseman Frank Fenton opened the ninth inning with a hard ground ball to shortstop, but it rolled suspiciously between the infielder's legs and Fenton dashed all the way to second, conveniently removing the possibility of a double play. Frank Bottarini carefully sacrificed Fenton to third. Walsh then intentionally walked pitcher Jimmy Zinn to set up the double play.

DiMaggio stepped to the plate, and the Seals Stadium crowd rose and gave him a long ovation. Walsh wound up, threw, and DiMaggio lifted a fly ball toward right field.

The crowd started to roar, but their cheers faded as Oak right fielder Harlan Pool drifted back. He caught the ball thirty feet short of the fence, and Fenton tagged and crossed the plate with the winning run. The Seals won, 3–2. DiMaggio's streak was over at 61 games.

When the streak began on May 28, Joe DiMaggio was unknown to all but the most attentive fans of Coast League baseball. He was apparently overmatched, and in danger of being released. By the time the streak ended, DiMaggio was a household name on the West Coast, a bona fide PCL star, the greatest drawing card in the league, and publicly acclaimed as its savior. In two short months, DiMaggio's life had changed dramatically. Moreover, in those two months he learned lessons that would later prove invaluable in the midst of another streak.

The questionable calls during the last week of the streak do not really diminish DiMaggio's accomplishment or make it any less impressive. Given his batting performance immediately prior to the beginning of the streak, a streak of any duration was almost a miracle. Had his streak stopped at even 30 or 40 games, it still would have been a sturdy foundation for a stellar career in baseball, and his turnaround as a hitter still would have been dramatic. The fact that it lasted as long as it did speaks volumes about DiMaggio's emerging character. Until the very end, the pressure did not affect his performance. It never did again.

The streak had meaning beyond its statistical significance. It brought attention to DiMaggio far out of proportion to his actual performance. For while DiMaggio continued to play well for the remainder of the 1933 season, the aggregate of his actual performance was not quite so spectacular when considered in the context of the PCL. Apart from the streak, his performance was no better statistically than that of literally scores of other players in other PCL seasons.

But the streak set DiMaggio apart and made everything about him—his youth, his ethnicity, his personality, his other baseball skills—appear more distinctive and symbolic. His own reticence made the details of his life seem more meaningful to the press and fans.

The most significant aspect of the streak is that it coincided with a sudden, pronounced elevation in DiMaggio's level of play and probably saved him from being released. To later observers, the streak completely obscured the genesis of his semipro career and his first six weeks as a professional. What really happened was supplanted by more colorful tales and anecdotes that supported the image of the player DiMaggio later became. His hitting streak was a unique record. The press created, even demanded, a player equal to that distinction.

From the time of the streak, when the press first wrote stories about DiMaggio, he was made into someone special. Such stories allowed the public to identify with DiMaggio. He was not presented as a ballplayer with hundreds of games of semipro ball behind him, but

Yankee teammate and fellow San Franciscan Frank Crosetti visits DiMaggio at Fisherman's Wharf, San Francisco. DiMaggio's father, Giuseppe, and brothers Thomas and Michael were crab fishermen. (Photograph courtesy of Dick Dobbins)

as an overnight sensation who was given a chance by fate and won the lottery of natural gifts, a regular guy blessed with luck. He wasn't shy and afraid, and perhaps ill-educated, but quiet and reserved, determined and serious. He wasn't Sicilian, but Italian. Not even an Italian, really, but the Americanized child of an immigrant. Not the son of a retiree, but the son of a fisherman. Each of these characterizations made DiMaggio more agreeable to the public, and each has stayed with him until the present day.

In the fifty-three games he played before the streak, DiMaggio had hit .249, scored 24 runs, and hit 6 home runs. The Seals were twenty games below .500. During the 61-game streak, he hit .405 (18 doubles, 4 triples, and 11 home runs), scored 48 runs, and knocked in 54. The Seals went 26–34, with one tie. DiMaggio's average had risen to .337, not close to leading the league, but among the top twenty.

After the streak DiMaggio cooled, but he continued to hit well, knocking in nearly a run every game and maintaining his batting average. He finished the year at .340, with 28 home runs, 129 runs scored, and a league-best 169 RBI in 187 games. But DiMaggio's lofty batting average was only second best in his own family. Vince played well after joining Hollywood, and finished at .342.

The Seals played nearly .500 baseball over the bulk of the season and managed to finish a respectable sixth at 81–106. Attendance at Seals Stadium increased by 10,000 from 1932. League-wide, PCL attendance climbed by more than 100,000. Many credited DiMaggio for part of the rise.

Despite his fine season, Joe was not yet the Seals' best player, a fact that places his accomplishments in context. Seals shortstop Augie Galan led the team with 264 hits, 162 runs scored, and a .355 batting average. Moreover, his teammates selected him club MVP.

In the off-season, DiMaggio took time off from baseball for the first time in two and a half years. He lived at home, worked out a little at the playground with Vince and Dominic, and looked forward to the 1934 season.

In the spring of 1934, Joe DiMaggio picked up where he had left off the season before. He'd grown and was now over six feet and about 185 pounds. Whereas he had looked rangy in the past, he was now powerful. In the off-season, the Seals sold shortstop Augie Galan to the Cubs for a much-needed $25,000 and, more important, seven players, including four pitchers. Owner Charley Graham needed money but preferred players. If he received too much cash, the bank holding the mortgage on Seals Stadium would get more than he did.

Six weeks into the season, it was obvious that both the Seals and DiMaggio had improved. The Seals were above .500, in third place. DiMaggio was hitting well, but for the first time his defense began to attract attention. He had matured, and was now in full command of his physical skills.

In mid-May, the Seals faced Hollywood in San Francisco. The press ballyhooed the matchup between Joe and brother Vince. While the two clubs traded victories, Joe clearly outplayed his older brother, even going 4 for 4 in one contest. Local fans were interested in the matchup, and Vince and Joe made several joint appearances on KYA radio, giving baseball tips to Bay Area youngsters.

For the final game of the series, a daytime doubleheader on Sunday, May 20, the Seals cashed in on the brother act and held "Family Day" at Seals Stadium. The entire DiMaggio clan was invited to the park and news photographers snapped several photographs of Vince and Joe with the family. The clubs split, the Seals winning game one 3–2 in twelve innings, with the Stars capturing game two 6–4, in a contest cut short by darkness. Vince and Joe both went 2 for 7, although one of Joe's hits was a triple. It must have been a happy day for the DiMaggio family.

What happened next isn't precisely clear, but it nearly ended Joe DiMaggio's baseball career. According to the story in every DiMaggio biography, and told most recently by Joe himself in *The DiMaggio Albums*, published in 1989, "One evening in June 1934 after a doubleheader and a dinner at my sister's house in San Francisco, I took a jitney cab home. When I was getting out, I put all my weight on my left leg, and it suddenly buckled. There was no twisting, just sharp cracks at the knee. I couldn't straighten out the leg and when I took a step the pain was awful." He had torn cartilage and pulled tendons in the knee. In other sources, DiMaggio goes on to describe how, despite great pain, he appeared in the Seals' next game in Los Angeles and hit a pinch-hit home run in the ninth inning to win the game. Later "[a doctor] put my leg in an aluminum splint for . . . the longest six weeks of my life. After it was taken off, I tried to come back that season but couldn't." In most accounts of the injury, it occurred after Joe's leg fell asleep.

Major league scouts said they were prepared to offer Graham up to $100,000 for his young star but backed off after the injury.

The story that evolved surrounding DiMaggio's knee injury became an important part of the DiMaggio myth. All heroes need to triumph over adversity, and the knee was often cited as an example of one of the many difficulties DiMaggio, the hero, overcame. But the San Francisco press gave conflicting accounts of how the injury occurred.

The *Examiner* provided the most detail. On Monday, May 21, the day after the "Family Day" doubleheader, the *Examiner* printed a story that stated "Joe DiMaggio, ace slugger and outfielder of the Seals, suffered injury to his knee early this morning when he fell entering his automobile . . . DiMaggio, police reported, was getting into his car, parked at Fourth and Market Streets, when he suddenly lost his footing on the running board, grasped desperately to save himself, and fell . . . At the hospital it was said by doctors that several tendons were badly strained and the knee cap severely bruised." Other San Francisco papers gave the incident briefer mentions, more in line with DiMaggio's account, but still placing the incident well after midnight.

As described by the press, the injury seems more the by-product of some early-morning celebrating after the "Family Day" doubleheader. DiMaggio's account misrepresents the date of the injury, fails to mention any "Family Day" celebration, and completely distorts the effect the injury had on the remainder of his season.

If it was a result of celebrating, there is no mystery as to why it wasn't reported that way in most of the press. Abe Kemp told Jerome Holtzman that the only advice he ever received from an editor was "if you can't write something nice about a ball player, don't mention his name. . . . I pursued that policy the rest of my life. . . . Now, I don't recommend it. I don't say it was good . . . [but] Hell, I could have written some of the most scandalous stories of all time. But I didn't." Neither did other writers of Kemp's generation.

DiMaggio did accompany the team to Los Angeles, but didn't appear in another game until May 26, when he hit a pinch-hit home run in the ninth inning and limped around the bases to give San Francisco a 4–3 win. In a doubleheader the next day, he pinch-hit in each game, collecting a fifth-inning double in game two, but was immediately replaced by a pinch runner.

He returned to the Seals' starting lineup on June 5. Although he collected only one hit in the Seals' 5–4 loss to Los Angeles, Kemp made note of a "sensational running catch" contributed by DiMaggio.

But the leg still wasn't right, and DiMaggio left the lineup again several days later. The Seals replaced him with Joe Marty, but slumped badly. Forty-year-old Ike Caveney even had to insert himself as a pinch hitter on several occasions.

The Seals were reluctant to give DiMaggio the time he needed to heal. Before the injury, he had been hitting nearly .370 and averaging almost an RBI a game. Besides, major league scouts were now very interested. His performance during the first two months of the 1934 season proved he was no fluke, and his defense was even more impressive than his hitting. The Seals tried to downplay the severity of the injury and keep the scouts interested.

At the end of June, DiMaggio made several pinch-hitting appearances, then was pushed back into the Seals' lineup. Scouts began making a regular pilgrimage to Seals Stadium to fawn over the young star. An *Examiner* story of July 12, headlined "DiMaggio Stirs Ranks of Ivory Hunters," compared his skills to those of Earl Averill, Paul Waner, and Lefty Gomez, and called him "the most sought after rookie in the minor leagues." But a few days later Abe Kemp cautioned that "DiMaggio has not struck his full stride as yet, Joe being inclined to favor his left knee, which is still ailing, judging from the manner in which he walks stiff-legged." Furthermore, since returning to the starting lineup, he was hitting only .270, further indication that the injured leg was still causing discomfort.

But Caveney and Graham stubbornly refused to pull DiMaggio from the lineup, apparently believing it was better to play through the injury and prove the soundness of his knee to the scouts. Besides in the second half of the PCL's split season, the Seals were in contention for the pennant. Their impatience nearly cost DiMaggio his career.

On August 10, the Seals played host to Los Angeles in San Francisco. In the first inning, Angel outfielder Jim Oglesby drove a sinking line drive to right. DiMaggio raced in and slipped as his knee gave out. By the time Joe had hobbled to the ball, Oglesby was on third with a triple.

When DiMaggio returned to the dugout, Caveney asked if he was hurt. DiMaggio said he was OK. Batting third, he grounded out weakly and then returned to the bench and sat down. When the inning ended, as he started to rise from the bench and take the field, the knee buckled. DiMaggio sprawled in the dugout. Scouts and fans watched DiMaggio struggle to his feet, unable to support his own weight. His season, if not his career, was over.

Seals' doctors diagnosed the injury as pulled tendons, and recommended that DiMaggio take the rest of the season off. Graham and Caveney had no choice but to agree.

Examiner sports editor Curley Grieve wrote what might have been DiMaggio's baseball obituary the next day: "As he hobbled to the dressing room, the muscles of his face were drawn tight, his eyes expressed the fear and grief that weighed down his heart. He seemed to sense that this hour and day was a critical one in his life. Joe was a $50,000 bundle of ivory to the Seals. His sale seemed definitely assured. And leading the pack of bidders was the impressive checkbook of Colonel Jake Ruppert, part-owner of the New York Yankees."

New York was indeed the most interested of bidders. The Yankees had the most active contingent of scouts on the West Coast in Bill Essick and Joe Devine, and enjoyed a close relationship with the Seals. Graham had even tried to pry Babe Ruth away from the Yankees for the 1934 season. Essick, the Yankees' southern California scout, lived near the DiMaggios and had watched Joe for years. Devine had been responsible for signing Joe Cronin and Paul Waner while a Pittsburgh scout, and had worked for the Yankees as their top western scout since 1929. While other major league clubs were sending more and more scouts to the PCL, the Yankees' prolonged presence gave them a distinct advantage.

The Yankees were not averse to Italian ballplayers, although most clubs were biased against them. By the early 1930s, fewer than two dozen Italians had played major league baseball. There was still some prejudice against Italian ballplayers, who were labeled as hotheaded and excitable, often described in the press as greasy and smelling of olive oil.

The Yankees exhibited no such bigotry toward Italians. Italian outfielder Ping Bodie played successfully for New York in 1920 and 1921, and in the 1930s the Yankees had signed Tony Lazzeri and Frank Cro-

"DiMaggio seldom showed emotion. One day, after striking out, he came to the dugout and kicked the ball bag. We all went, 'Ooh.' It hurt. He sat down and the sweat popped out on his forehead and he clenched his fists without ever saying a word. Everyone wanted to howl. But he was the god. You don't laugh at gods."—Yankee infielder Jerry Coleman as quoted in Baseball's Greatest Quotations *by Paul Dickson*   (George Burke photograph from the National Baseball Library & Archive, Cooperstown, N.Y.)

setti, both native San Franciscans, from the PCL. The city of New York was home to the largest Italian community in the United States, and Lazzeri and Crosetti, apart from their skills as players, were gate attractions in New York. To the Yankees, DiMaggio's Italian background was a plus.

While other clubs claimed that had DiMaggio not been injured, they were willing to pay upward of $100,000 for his contract, such assertions are dubious. The Depression cut into the amount teams were willing to risk on rookies, and there is no evidence to suggest that any team was willing to offer more than $50,000 for DiMaggio.

Even if they had, Graham would have been unable to accept the offer.

The mortgage on Seals Stadium made players more valuable to Graham than cash. The Yankees were prepared to make such an offer, but DiMaggio's injury put the deal at risk. Other clubs backed off, but the Yankees remained patient. Through Bill Essick they kept tabs on DiMaggio over the remainder of the season.

When the season ended, Joe Devine arranged for DiMaggio to visit a specialist in Los Angeles to have his leg examined. The specialist reported that the injury wasn't serious, and that with rest DiMaggio could expect a full recovery. Armed with the doctor's reports, the Yankees approached Graham.

They moved quickly. Graham's financial situation had worsened. PCL attendance in 1934 had fallen nearly 230,000 from 1933. On November 23, 1934, the Yankees offered Graham $25,000 and five players—first baseman Les Powell, outfielder Ted Norbett, third baseman Ed Farrell, and pitchers Jim Densmore and Floyd Newkirk—for DiMaggio. None was a prospect. Graham accepted.

But the Yankees both protected themselves and sweetened the deal for Graham by adding an interesting contingency. DiMaggio would play for the Seals in 1935, and Graham would receive the five players, but the cash would be forthcoming only if DiMaggio's knee held up. If it did, not only would Graham be paid, but he would reap the benefits, financial and otherwise, of having DiMaggio another season. It was a brilliant offer. If DiMaggio held up, the Yankees received a bargain and Graham a windfall. If DiMaggio broke down, Graham still had DiMaggio and five players.

When the deal was announced on November 24, San Francisco papers helped Graham save face and announced the sale price as $75,000. Kemp reported that when DiMaggio heard the news, he was in the kitchen of his parents' home, peeling potatoes, the day before his twentieth birthday. "It's hard to believe," he was quoted as saying, "but it's a fine birthday present."

The doctor was right: DiMaggio's injured knee healed during the off-season. But when the Seals broke camp in the spring of 1935, DiMaggio was not the same player who showed such promise during the 1934 season. He was better.

In the off-season, Charley Graham had let manager Ike Caveney go and spent 4,000 precious dollars to secure the release of New York Giants outfielder Lefty O'Doul, whom Graham made manager. Graham wasn't being cavalier with his cash. O'Doul was worth it.

A San Francisco native, O'Doul broke in as a pitcher with the Seals in 1918 before being drafted by the Yankees; he became a phenom in New York's 1919 spring training camp. O'Doul impressed observers as much with his bat as his arm, and writers covering the camp even petitioned New York manager Miller Huggins to start O'Doul in the outfield.

But the phenom flamed out. O'Doul developed a sore arm and hardly played, but when Babe Ruth joined the Yankees in 1920, the flamboyant, fun-loving O'Doul became an instant member of Ruth's crew, playing the good-natured imp to Ruth's irrepressible gargantua. Although he remained with the team all year, O'Doul's arm still wasn't right and he pitched only four innings. The Yankees sent him back to the Seals.

O'Doul starred for a season with the Seals, went back to the Yankees in 1922, played for Boston in 1923, then returned to the Coast League. Over the next five years he was one of the greatest batsmen and most popular players in PCL history. O'Doul had a well-deserved reputation as a student of hitting, and worked endlessly to get the most from his talent. At age thirty in 1928, the New York Giants were impressed enough to return O'Doul to the major leagues. He hit .319, but was traded to the Philadelphia Phillies in the off-season.

He shined with the Phillies, and in 1929 had one of the greatest seasons in baseball history, hitting .398, smacking 32 home runs, and striking out only 19 times. But success came to O'Doul too late. Traded to Brooklyn a year later, his skills began to erode. After spending the 1934 season back with the New York Giants, O'Doul was brought back to San Francisco.

DiMaggio was his project, and O'Doul was uniquely equipped to help the young player. Although O'Doul later said of DiMaggio that "I never taught him anything about hitting. He knew," the results speak otherwise. For while O'Doul didn't tamper with DiMaggio's stance or swing, the youngster undoubtedly benefited from listening to the old veteran talk about hitting, life in the big leagues, and life in New York. O'Doul whet DiMaggio's appetite for major league baseball. Playing for O'Doul prepared him for everything he would later face in his rookie season with the Yankees. He flourished under O'Doul.

So did the Seals. Reinforced by the players acquired in the DiMaggio deal, the Seals finished second to the defending champion Los Angeles Angels in the first half of the split season. But the Angels slumped in mid-season and the Seals surged, beating out the Missions to win the second half and finishing the year with the league's best record, 103–70.

DiMaggio's knee stayed healthy, except for a slight injury in early September that caused the Yankees to hold their breath and Joe to miss two games. While the knee never gave out completely, it was occasionally troublesome over the remainder of DiMaggio's career.

DiMaggio was superb all season, finishing with 34 home runs, 18 triples, 48 doubles, 173 runs scored, 154 RBI, and 24 stolen bases; he had 270 hits in 679 at bats, for an average of .398. Moreover, DiMaggio's defense was nonpareil, as he ran down virtually every fly ball and collected 34 outfield assists. For much of the year, he played right field, but in September the Yankees asked the Seals to play him in center. They were intrigued with DiMaggio's defensive potential. Joe was becoming a bigger part of the Yankees' plans for 1936.

DiMaggio's only disappointment came in the PCL batting race, which he lost to the Missions' Ox Eckhardt by one point. The manner of that loss has been embellished to enhance the DiMaggio image. As the story goes, on the last day of the season DiMaggio benefited from the indifferent play of an outfielder to get a hit. Unwilling to win the batting title on a spurious hit, DiMaggio subsequently asked the official scorer to change his decision. The scorer refused, but the request is exemplary of DiMaggio's inimitable class. What actually happened reveals something different.

Entering the last day of the season, DiMaggio trailed Eckhardt .395 to .393. Eckhardt, helped out by the opposition, went 4 for 5 in the first game of a season-ending doubleheader to raise his average to .399, then sat out the second game of the contest.

The same day, the Seals faced Seattle in another doubleheader. In the first game, DiMaggio, too, went 4 for 5, but as Abe Kemp later noted, "From our vantage point and observation, he was given three of them by indifferent fielding." In his first at bat, he laced out a legitimate single, but on two other occasions, the Seattle infield played deep. DiMaggio cooperated and bunted for base hits. In the ninth, according to Kemp's description, "DiMaggio hit an easy fly to center field which Lawrence [the center fielder] could have caught with his teeth, figuratively speaking, but he chose to play hobby with the ball, permitting it to drop for a double." DiMaggio complained to the scorer about the hit, but the scorer refused to change the call, leading Joe to remark that "I didn't want to leave this league under any cloud," a cloud that apparently didn't include the two bunts.

In game two, DiMaggio cracked two home runs and a double, but it wasn't enough to catch Eckhardt. Abe Kemp railed against the clowning that went on in both contests, as players on both sides failed to take either game seriously. In the last inning of the second game, with the Seals leading 10–1, flamboyant San Francisco pitcher Walter "The Great" Mails, who sometimes paraded around the park in a cape and offered ladies a "valuable" prize for the best chocolate cake, waved his fielders off the diamond before striking out the last hitter on three pitches.

Yet DiMaggio's season wasn't over. The Seals and the first-half-champion Angels squared off in a championship series. DiMaggio did not disappoint. In his first taste of postseason play, he provided a remarkable demonstration of the five baseball skills, proving he had all of them in abundance. The Seals won the best-of-seven series in six games, and DiMaggio was magnificent.

In game one, a 5–0 Seal win, DiMaggio used his speed to beat out an infield hit to score the Seals' first run, then scored again after dropping a surprise bunt. In the outfield, he chased down eight fly balls to preserve pitcher Sam Gibson's shutout. In game two, DiMaggio's power was on display as his long two-run homer to left broke a fifth-inning tie and proved the margin of victory. In game three, in his last appearance in San Francisco as a Seal, DiMaggio homered, doubled, knocked in two runs, and threw out two base runners in a 4–3 loss. In game four, DiMaggio managed only a single in a 10–7 San Francisco loss, but in game five, the first of a doubleheader, DiMaggio singled in the midst of the Seals' four-run eighth-inning rally in a 6–3 win. The Seals won the series in the second game, 4–2, although Joe went hitless and didn't have a ball hit to him in the outfield all day. All he did was demonstrate another attribute, one that would set him apart from other players in game after game, year after year. His team won.

At the end of the year, DiMaggio was voted PCL MVP. But he received perhaps an even greater kudo from Abe Kemp of the *Examiner*. On October 1, at the end of a story applauding O'Doul for his performance as manager, Kemp, who was usually grudging with his praise of DiMaggio, concluded his piece with an understated nod to Joe. "In passing," he wrote, "just a word about Joe Di Maggio [*sic*], who has finally convinced me that he is the greatest ballplayer I have ever seen graduate from the Pacific Coast League. And I have seen all of them since 1907."

DiMaggio now belonged to New York, who picked up their option, paid off Graham, and took possession of their prize. He didn't come a moment too soon.

## CHAPTER THREE

Carrier of the Torch: 1936–40

The Yankees had not won the American League pennant since 1932, Babe Ruth's last big season. As his skills diminished, so did the Yankee dynasty. In 1933, the Yankees finished second, seven games behind Washington. In 1934, Ruth's last year in pinstripes, the Yankees again finished seven games out of first, this time losing out to Detroit. In 1935, they fell short again. Detroit pushed the Yankees from the top spot in July and held on to win the pennant over New York by three games.

It was not simply the fact that the Yankees lost that galled New Yorkers, but the way they lost. Yankee fans were accustomed to cheering "the Bronx Bombers," the most powerful team in baseball. But from 1933 to 1935, the Yankees lost their standing as baseball's foremost home-run-hitting team. In 1934, the Philadelphia A's hit more home runs. In 1935, Detroit out-homered the Yankees, as did the National League Giants.

The Yankees missed not only Ruth's bat, but his charisma and gate appeal. First baseman Lou Gehrig was now the Yankees' big star, but he didn't have Ruth's presence. Besides, most observers considered Detroit first baseman Hank Greenberg to be Gehrig's superior, both as a power hitter and as a first baseman. Although fans appreciated Gehrig for his character and stamina, his reputation suffered during New York's slide simply because he wasn't Babe Ruth.

DiMaggio shags flies at Yankee Stadium during his rookie season of 1936. He was one of the first athletes about whom it was said "He made everything he did look easy." (Photograph from the National Baseball Library & Archive, Cooperstown, N.Y.)

Lou Gehrig and Joe DiMaggio cavort at Yankee spring training camp in St. Petersburg in 1936, DiMaggio's rookie season.   (Photograph from the National Baseball Library & Archive, Cooperstown, N.Y.)

The old Yankees, Ruth's Yankees, had aged. Only Gehrig and second baseman Tony Lazzeri remained from the historic 1927 team. While shortstop Frank Crosetti, catcher Bill Dickey, third baseman Red Rolfe, and pitchers Lefty Gomez and Red Ruffing were excellent players, too many at bats and too many innings were given over to nonentities like outfielder Jesse Hill and pitcher Vito Tamulis. In 1935, Gehrig walked a career-high 135 times; the opposition knew no other Yankee was likely to drive him home. "Murderer's Row" had apparently been caught, convicted, and was quietly adjusting to life in second place.

Attendance at Yankee Stadium tumbled. The "House That Ruth Built" was just another ballpark without the Babe. The Yankees drew only 657,508 fans in 1935, their lowest total since 1919 and fewer than the National League Giants drew.

The Yankees, and the New York press, looked to DiMaggio for help from the very beginning. They expected, and almost demanded, that DiMaggio lead the Yankees back to glory. No other New York rookie to date had faced greater expectations.

DiMaggio proved he was not just another rookie early on. He turned down the Yankees' first contract offer, and brother Tom eventually talked the Yankees into a contract worth $8,500, the largest New York had ever offered a first-year player.

DiMaggio left San Francisco in mid-February for spring training,

When DiMaggio joined the Yankees in 1936 he became a teammate of childhood idol Lou Gehrig (l). Despite batting .323, the young outfielder still was outhit by veterans Bill Dickey (.362) and Gehrig (.354).
(Photograph courtesy of Mike Andersen)

catching a ride with fellow Yankees Frank Crosetti and Tony Lazzeri. Several days into the trip, Crosetti and Lazzeri asked DiMaggio to share driving duties. They were shocked when Joe told them he didn't know how to drive. DiMaggio was in awe of his traveling partners and hardly spoke during the trip. Despite his recent accomplishments, DiMaggio remained shy and ill-at-ease around strangers. As a local hero in San Francisco, he still lived at home and spent most of his time away from the ballpark with his family. While DiMaggio's baseball skills improved exponentially, his social skills had yet to develop. In many ways, DiMaggio was still the same kid who had quit school a little over three years before.

The Yankees provided DiMaggio the best possible situation in which to begin his major league career. Teammates Lazzeri and Crosetti, fellow San Francisco Italians, took care of DiMaggio and helped him with his adjustment to the big leagues. Crosetti was DiMaggio's roommate, and DiMaggio himself had cousins that lived in the Bronx. A number of other players on the Yankees' roster, such as former Seal pitcher Lefty Gomez, had West Coast connections. They had heard glowing reports on the outfielder and made DiMaggio's transition to the major leagues easy.

Most Yankee players knew the club needed help and welcomed DiMaggio's presence. Finishing second three years in a row left them unsatisfied, as New York owner Jacob Ruppert was his usual penurious self at contract time. Yankee players didn't just want to win, they

Joe DiMaggio is pictured at his locker in his rookie season of 1936.   (Photograph from *The Sporting News*)

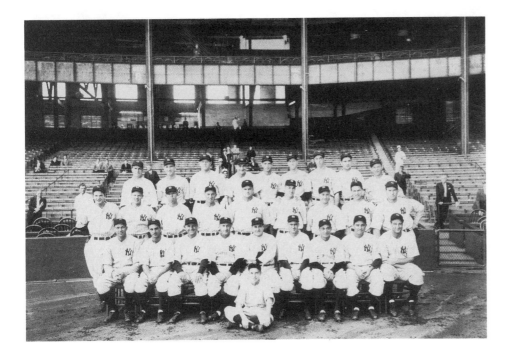

The 1936 Yankees, featuring a talented rookie named Joe DiMaggio, would win 102 games, capture the American League pennant by a 19¹/₂-game margin over the Washington Senators, and defeat the New York Giants in five games to win the World Series.   (Photograph from Transcendental Graphics, Mark Rucker)

When the young DiMaggio arrived at his first spring training camp at St. Petersburg Florida in 1936, the headlines concentrated more on the $75,000 paid by Yankee owner Jacob Ruppert to the Seals for his prospect than on the player himself. In fact, the Yankees had paid only $25,000 for DiMaggio. It would take only a few days before writers forgot his price tag and realized the Yankees had snared another wunderkind.   (Acme photograph from The National Baseball Library & Archive, Cooperstown, N.Y.)

needed to win in order to squeeze money from Ruppert. DiMaggio could help.

Yet at the same time, the Yankees were a veteran club. DiMaggio wasn't expected to be the whole show. He was under no more pressure to excel than any other player, except from the New York press.

The writers who covered the Yankees could hardly wait for DiMaggio. They spent the winter touting him as the best young player in the game. The writers missed Ruth desperately, and looked to DiMaggio to provide good copy. If he proved to be half the player they hoped, the New York press was ready to make him a star.

DiMaggio made an immediate impression upon his arrival at Yankee spring training camp at St. Petersburg, Florida. While the Yankees experimented with Joe in both left and center field, using DiMaggio to put pressure on holdout center fielder Ben Chapman, the instant DiMaggio picked up a bat he confirmed the hysteria that preceded him. In intrasquad games, DiMaggio hit third, Ruth's old slot, and lined out hit after hit. Yankee manager Joe McCarthy was as impressed as everyone else, and before the exhibition season even began, it was a foregone conclusion that DiMaggio would make the Yankees' starting lineup.

In the Yankees' first exhibition game, on March 18 against the Cardinals, DiMaggio first hit a long triple over Joe Medwick's head, then lined three singles, including one to right field on a curveball low and away. As Dan Daniel of the *World Telegram* commented, "DiMaggio had been the hot story of the New York Camp for more than a fortnight," but after this performance "the San Franciscan became a veritable Vesuvius of fire and action." Virtually every spring training story in the New York newspapers focused on DiMaggio.

He followed with two hits against the Cardinals the next day, including another triple, then went 4 for 6 in the Yanks' third exhibition game, against the Cincinnati Reds. Curiosity over DiMaggio drew three times the usual crowd to the game. In his fourth game, against the Boston Bees, DiMaggio went 2 for 5. He was hitting .600 and was the most talked-about player in baseball.

But on a force-out at second, Boston infielder Joe Coscaret stepped on DiMaggio's left foot. After the game, it swelled, and the next day DiMaggio could neither run nor hit. Yankee trainer Dr. Earle Painter prescribed diathermy treatment for the injured foot.

After only twenty minutes of the heat therapy, DiMaggio, unfamiliar with the process, noticed something was wrong. His foot was severely burned, and DiMaggio was unable to walk. Afraid of infection, Yankee doctors did what they could to treat the burns and confined DiMaggio to bed. They expected the phenom to return to action in ten days.

Even with DiMaggio out of the lineup, the New York press kept up an incessant din about the young prospect. Like their brethren in San Francisco, they soon learned that Joe rarely had more than a few words to say on his own behalf. But DiMaggio's silence did not slow the New York writers. They were experienced in concocting stories about their heroes.

While covering Babe Ruth, the New York writers learned valuable lessons in embellishment, hyperbole, and exaggeration. Ruth's on-

field talent was exceeded only by the excesses of his private life. Since the two didn't necessarily agree, the press created a sanitized hero in line with the champion of the batter's box. The fairy tales proved popular, pleased both Ruth and the Yankees, and assured the writers of continued access to both.

DiMaggio's reticence, far from hindering their efforts, actually allowed the writers' hero-making machine to shift into high gear. While DiMaggio recovered, the press continued to tout his ability. Increasingly, their stories had less to do with anything DiMaggio actually did, or who he really was, and more to do with an image of who they wanted him to be. DiMaggio was a hero-in-waiting.

With DiMaggio sidelined, the New York press fleshed out his biography, unconcerned whether their stories were wholly accurate or not. Readers soon learned the tale of the humble immigrant's son. In New York, a city of immigrants, it was like reading about the success of your kid brother.

No writer had a greater role in the promotion of the young DiMaggio than Dan Daniel of the *New York World-Telegram*. Daniel, who first covered baseball in 1909, was the best-known and most influential baseball writer of his day, covering the Yankees for the *Telegram* and contributing 5,000 words a week to *The Sporting News*. Like most baseball writers of the era, Daniel worried little about journalistic ethics and saw himself as an indispensable part of the game rather than an objective observer. On several occasions, he even interjected himself into Yankee contract talks and helped the club sign Babe Ruth and Red Ruffing. Daniel's stories in *The Sporting News* about DiMaggio made Joe a household name before he ever played an official game. By mid-May, Daniel had ghost-written DiMaggio's biography for the *Telegram*. Over the next few years Daniel and other New York writers soft-pedaled a public image beyond reproach. Many of the errors of fact that taint every subsequent DiMaggio biography originate with Daniel and other members of New York's sporting press.

To his credit, DiMaggio seemed blissfully unaware of what was happening. He later claimed that when a writer first asked him for a quote, "I thought it was some kind of soft drink." His personal reserve protected him, and ex-phenom O'Doul had undoubtedly warned Joe about believing press clippings. The young ballplayer just wanted to play.

Fortunately for DiMaggio, his talent was equal to the fanfare. When the regular season finally began, DiMaggio's performance increased the acclaim and reinforced the image created by the press.

His foot was slow to heal, and as the Yankees worked their way north in early April, DiMaggio was sent ahead to New York for hospital treatment. Joe accompanied the Yankees to Washington for the season opener on April 14 but didn't play in the 1–0 loss. The season was two weeks old, and the Yankees' record 11–6, second behind Boston, when Joe DiMaggio made his debut.

To make room for him, the Yankees sold outfielder Dixie Walker, hitting .350 at the time, to the White Sox. They were that confident.

More than 25,000 fans, the most since the Yankees' home opener, ignored a threat of rain and turned out at the Stadium for DiMaggio's first game. Joe wore number 9. Manager Joe McCarthy put DiMaggio in left field, bumping Roy Johnson, and batted him third. In his first at bat, with Frank Crosetti on third and Red Rolfe at first, DiMaggio bounced a pitch from St. Louis Browns pitcher Jack Knott to third baseman Harlond Clift. Crosetti got caught in a rundown off third, but a throw got away and Crosetti scored, while DiMaggio made it to second. After Gehrig walked and Dickey popped out, Ben Chapman's double scored Rolfe and DiMaggio. Gehrig later scored, and the Yankees led 4–3.

DiMaggio batted again in the second and collected his first hit, a looping single to center off Browns pitcher Earl Caldwell, as New York

DiMaggio is shown (top) *in his Boston hotel room in the early forties. Note the ever-present pack of cigarettes on the bedside table alongside a candle.* (Photograph from the Maxwell Collection)

Always a stylish dresser, DiMaggio was as elegant off the field as he was swinging a bat or gliding under a fly ball on the field. (Photograph from the Maxwell Collection)

DiMaggio is shown with Yankee manager Joe McCarthy at Fenway Park in 1939. Together they would contribute to seven Yankee pennant wins and six world championships from 1936 to 1943. (Photograph from the Maxwell Collection)

erupted for three runs. After Red Rolfe doubled to lead off the sixth, DiMaggio teed off on a pitch from Elon Hogsett, the third St. Louis pitcher, and drove the ball deep into the gap in left-center field. It bounced all the way to the wall in front of the bleachers, and DiMaggio raced to third. Rolfe scored, giving DiMaggio his first RBI. In the eighth, DiMaggio collected a third hit, a single to right off left-handed pitcher Russ Van Atta. The Yankees won in a rout, 14–5, and DiMaggio ended the day 3 for 6, with three runs scored and an RBI. In left field, he easily handled his only chance.

DiMaggio gave the Yankees a scare in his second game the next day. In the seventh inning, after his third hit in five at bats, he scrambled back to third to avoid being doubled off, then sat on the ground for several minutes, rubbing his troubled left knee. But the injury passed, and Joe was on his way.

Over the next two weeks, DiMaggio played well and the Yankees kept winning. Against Detroit on May 7, he threw out outfielder Pete Fox at the plate for the last out to preserve a 6–5 win. DiMaggio meant to bounce the ball to the plate, but it arrived on the fly and sent the crowd home buzzing over his arm. On May 10, when the Yankees beat Philadelphia 7–2 and the Red Sox lost to Washington, New York slipped into first place. DiMaggio, hitless in his previous ten at bats, cracked a two-run homer, his first round-tripper, down the right-field line off pitcher George Turbeville in the first inning to key the win. The victory was New York's tenth in twelve games, including six of seven with DiMaggio in the lineup.

DiMaggio received more credit with each Yankee win. The press virtually ignored the fact that, as a team, the Yankee offense was producing at a rate equal to the mighty team of 1927, and that Detroit, pennant winner in 1934 and 1935, was hampered by the loss of both Hank Greenberg and Mickey Cochrane to injuries. DiMaggio was good, but his perceived value exceeded his actual worth.

Yet even DiMaggio's teammates jumped on the bandwagon. Gehrig told reporters that he thought DiMaggio was going to become one of baseball's all-time greats. The ninth inning of a 10–4 win over Cleveland on May 19 provided a particularly telling moment.

DiMaggio singled, then Gehrig hit a ground ball. On a similar play the previous day, DiMaggio went into second hard and wiped out Cleveland second baseman Billy Knickerbocker. This time, DiMaggio again went in hard. Knickerbocker was knocked off balance and threw the ball at DiMaggio's head, intending to teach the upstart a lesson.

He missed. DiMaggio was oblivious to the situation and stood up and looked around, seeing the ball on the ground and wondering if he was out. Knickerbocker glowered at DiMaggio and tried to goad him into a fight as the third-base umpire dashed over to restrain the upset infielder. Tony Lazzeri raced from the Yankee dugout, followed by the remainder of the Yankee bench, to protect their young teammate. After considerable jawing, the incident passed with no punches, but it showed the respect the Yankees already accorded DiMaggio. He was the man.

On June 14, All-Star center fielder Ben Chapman, long a thorn in the side of Yankee management, was traded to Washington for outfielder Jake Powell. Some biographers have claimed the trade was made to accommodate DiMaggio's transfer to center field. It was not. Powell, who hit .312 in 1935 and knocked in 98 runs, moved into center field. At about the same time, DiMaggio was, in fact, shifted from left field to right field, while veteran George Selkirk moved from right to left. The move was predicated on the strength and accuracy of DiMaggio's arm, and besides, right field was Ruth's old spot, and the Yankees saw DiMaggio as Ruth's heir. Playing center field for the Yankees had no historical cachet. Had the Yankees planned on moving DiMaggio to center, they would have done so at the time of the Chapman trade, but they had already decided right field would be

DiMaggio poses for photographers in May 1936. Such photo sessions were uncomfortable for the rookie, and few similar shots were ever taken after his rookie season. His admonition to most photographers was "Just one, boys, just one." (Photograph from the National Baseball Library & Archive, Cooperstown, N.Y.)

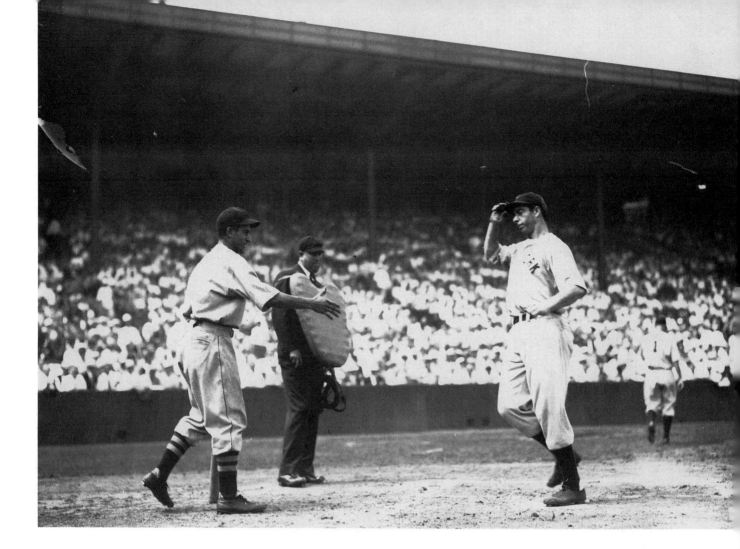

Joe DiMaggio crosses home plate in Boston following one of 29 career home runs at Fenway Park. Note that he tips his cap to the ovation that greeted most of his Fenway performances. (Les Jones photograph courtesy of the Boston Public Library)

DiMaggio's permanent home. The Yankee outfield was set. Backup outfielder Myril Hoag occasionally spelled both Powell and Selkirk.

Due primarily to DiMaggio, attendance at Yankee Stadium jumped by 200,000 in the first half of the season. The press noted an increasing number of Italian fans at Yankee games both at home and on the road. DiMaggio was easily the most popular player in the league. As the All-Star Game approached, DiMaggio, a rookie, led the voting, outpolling more established stars like Gehrig, Dickey, and Detroit second baseman Charlie Gehringer.

DiMaggio had his best day at the plate just over a week before the All-Star Game. In an 18–11 Yankee victory over Chicago, DiMaggio was 4 for 6, with two doubles and two home runs. Both home runs came in New York's ten-run fifth, as DiMaggio knocked home five runs in the inning. The victory increased the Yankee lead to 5 1/2 games over second-place Boston.

But DiMaggio's All-Star performance at Braves Field in Boston proved he was not immune to failure. Although he entered the game with a gaudy .356 batting average, DiMaggio went hitless in five at bats and played like the rookie he was.

In his first All-Star at bat, in the first inning, he grounded into a double play off Cardinal pitcher Dizzy Dean. In the second, playing right field, he misplayed Gabby Hartnett's drive into a triple. In the fourth inning, Carl Hubbell induced him to pop up to shortstop Leo Durocher. In the fifth, after DiMaggio's old teammate Augie Galan homered for the National League, Chicago second baseman Billy Herman singled sharply to right, but DiMaggio fumbled the ball for an error and Herman made second.

Down 4–0, the American League rallied in the seventh. With three runs in and two out, pitcher Lon Warneke intentionally walked Gehringer to load the bases. Up came DiMaggio. The fans at Braves Field greeted him with jeers and a smattering of boos. With a chance to win the game, DiMaggio hit a line drive to Durocher for the third out. Then, with two out in the ninth, DiMaggio came to bat for the last time. He popped out to end the game, and the NL had its first All-Star victory, 4–3. Rud Rennie of the *New York Herald Tribune* accurately summed up DiMaggio's performance as "the big shot that did not go off."

If anyone expected DiMaggio's All-Star performance to color his second half, they were wrong. Two games after the All-Star debacle, DiMaggio cracked one of the longest homers to left field in Yankee Stadium history in an 18–0 pasting of Cleveland. A week later, he appeared on the cover of *Time* magazine. On July 19, DiMaggio was honored with his own day at Yankee Stadium, where he received a trophy from *The Sporting News* honoring him as 1935 PCL MVP.

The Yankees almost lost their star rookie a week later. Instead, they gained a legend.

On July 28, in the sixth inning of a 16–6 Yankee win in Detroit, Tiger outfielder Goose Goslin drove the ball to right center. Myril Hoag, playing center field in place of a slumping Jake Powell, raced over to make the catch. So did DiMaggio.

The two men collided in full stride, striking heads, as Goslin's drive eluded both for an inside-the-park home run. The two outfielders dropped to the ground and, for a moment, neither moved.

DiMaggio was first to rise. He stood dazed, hands on hips, as his teammates hovered around Hoag. In a moment, Hoag also rose. Each appeared unhurt and finished the inning.

When Hoag returned to the bench, he was still groggy, and Jake Powell finished the game in center. The next day Hoag returned to the lineup, apparently fine; he singled, and made up for the previous day's miscue by robbing Goslin of an extra-base hit with a leaping catch in front of the screen in right-center field at Tiger Stadium.

But after the game, Hoag spent a sleepless night. On the morning of July 30, he collapsed in his room at the Yankees' hotel. Reserve outfielder Roy Johnson discovered Hoag unconscious on the floor, his eyes open in a blank stare. Johnson called for help and applied ice packs to Hoag's head. Hoag momentarily regained consciousness, stood up, then toppled over again. He was rushed to Detroit's Harper Hospital.

The Yankees fell to Detroit 5–4 that afternoon as Powell replaced Hoag in center. Hoag's life hung in balance. At 7:00 P.M., an hour after the Yankees left Detroit by train for Cleveland, Hoag underwent emergency surgery for a blood clot in the brain.

Brain surgery was an unusual and dangerous surgical procedure in 1936. Hoag was suffering from a hematoma caused in the collision with DiMaggio. Doctors drilled three holes in Hoag's skull to relieve pressure and held their breath. Had they waited any longer to operate, Hoag would likely have either died or suffered irreparable brain damage. But when the Yankees arrived in Cleveland, pitcher Johnny Broaca, whom the Yankees had left behind with Hoag, called Joe McCarthy and told him Hoag had survived the operation. The operation had worked. Hoag was conscious, and was expected to recover.

The collision was almost certainly DiMaggio's fault. The center fielder has the right of way on hits to the gap. Although Hoag missed the remainder of the season, he made a full recovery and eventually played another eight seasons, even making the All-Star team in 1939 after being traded to St. Louis.

Both Hoag and DiMaggio were extremely fortunate. By the narrowest of margins, DiMaggio escaped both injury and the stigma of being the scapegoat for the "what could have been," after Carl Mays's fatal beaning of Ray Chapman in 1920, only the second death of a major league ballplayer from an injury suffered during a game. Mays's career accomplishments should have earned him election to the Hall of Fame. Instead, Mays was blamed for Chapman's death and his reputation was forever tarnished.

DiMaggio was an inadvertent beneficiary of Hoag's injury. On August 1, the Yankees reshuffled their outfield lineup. DiMaggio was moved from right field. For the first time as a Yankee, DiMaggio played center. The change was barely noted in the press at the time. While the incident had a dramatic impact on DiMaggio's career, it passes without mention in any previous account of DiMaggio's career. Center field remained DiMaggio's throughout the balance of his Yankee career. The position provided DiMaggio with the perfect setting to display his myriad skills and was a huge factor in his growing reputation.

DiMaggio and the Yankees rolled through the remainder of the season, clinching the pennant on September 9, at the time the earliest date a team had ever clinched, and finishing 102–51, 19½ games ahead of Detroit. As a team, the Yankees hit an even .300, paced by Bill Dickey's .362 and Gehrig's .354. Five Yankees collected over 100 RBI, and seven hit 10 or more home runs. Red Ruffing won 20 games, Monte Pearson 19, and four other Yankee pitchers won more than 12. The team ERA of 4.17 was the best in the American League. The Yankees outscored their opponents by more than 300 runs.

Joe DiMaggio begins his second season in the majors at spring training camp at St. Petersburg, Florida, in March 1937. (Associated Press photograph, courtesy of the *Boston Globe*)

DiMaggio slumped over the last two weeks of the season, dropping his average from around the .350 mark to .323. He finished with 29 home runs, 125 RBI, and a major-league-best 15 triples. His 22 outfield assists led the American League. Although Lou Gehrig was later voted American League MVP, DiMaggio was widely believed to be the difference between the second-place club of 1935 and the juggernaut of 1936.

In the end, his performance had justified the accolades of the New York writers. Few players, and certainly no rookies, had ever before demonstrated such command of the five baseball skills. High-average hitters like Cobb, Napoleon Lajoie, Honus Wagner, and others played in an era before the home run. High-average home-run hitters like Ruth, Gehrig, Rogers Hornsby, and Jimmie Foxx lacked DiMaggio's defensive and baserunning skills. While some players had developed a well-rounded game, none demonstrated it so dramatically in their rookie year. It would not be incorrect to say that DiMaggio was the first ballplayer in the majors in whom those five skills—the ability to hit, hit with power, run, field, and throw—were made obvious. At age twenty-two, Joe DiMaggio was already the best all-around player in the game, not including those consigned to the Negro Leagues.

In the National League, the New York Giants won the NL pennant by five games over St. Louis and Chicago. Interest was high in the "nickel series," so called because the cost of the subway ride across the East River from Yankee Stadium to the Polo Grounds was five cents.

Led by outfielder Mel Ott and pitcher Carl Hubbell, eleven Giants had previously played in the Series. While only six Yankees remained from the pennant-winning 1932 team, the Yankees were 8 to 5 favorites. The Series opened at the Polo Grounds on September 30. In the crowd were DiMaggio's mother and his brother Tom, seeing Joe play in the major leagues for the first time.

Carl Hubbell started game one for the Giants, while the Yankees countered with their own ace, Red Ruffing. In the third inning, George Selkirk's home run gave the Yankees a 1–0 lead. Later in the inning, DiMaggio singled off Hubbell for the first of his 54 career Series hits.

The Giants scored single runs in the fifth on a Dick Bartell home run and in the sixth on a single by Gus Mancuso that scored Mel Ott, who had doubled. Entering the eighth, the Giants led, 2–1.

Crosetti led off for the Yankees with a double. Red Rolfe tried to sacrifice Crosetti to third, but Hubbell slipped while fielding the ball and both men were safe.

DiMaggio stepped to the plate. In the sixth, he'd struck out against Hubbell's signature screwball. This time Joe timed a pitch perfectly and sent a low line drive to the gap between second and first. But Giant second baseman Burgess Whitehead stretched to his left and snagged the liner, then flipped to first base for a double play as Crosetti scrambled back to third. Hubbell then hit Gehrig with a pitch and Dickey grounded out to end the Yankee threat.

The Giants erupted for four runs in the eighth off a tiring Ruffing, and the Yankees went quietly in the ninth, to give the Giants a 6–1 win. After the game, a reporter noted that "DiMaggio was surly . . . He was asked what he thought of Hubbell. . . . DiMaggio had snapped, I didn't think he was so tough. He wasn't invincible anyway."

A day of rain pushed back game two to October 2. In the first, Crosetti singled and Rolfe walked. This time, DiMaggio made sure there was no double play. He dropped a surprise bunt down the third-base line and caught Giant third baseman Travis Jackson flat-footed, loading the bases. Gehrig drove in a run with a sacrifice fly, and Rolfe took third. DiMaggio then moved to second on a wild pitch by Giant pitcher Hal Schumacher. Dickey flied out to center fielder Hank Leiber and Rolfe scored, but DiMaggio foolishly took off for third and was thrown out. Still, the Yankees led 2–0.

In the fourth, New York erupted for seven runs to blow the game open, four on a Lazzeri grand slam, only the second in Series history. The Yankees rolled to an 18–4 win as DiMaggio contributed an eighth-inning double off the left-field wall and a ninth-inning single to the same location.

In the bottom of the ninth, all three Giant outs came on fly balls to DiMaggio. His last catch, a drive off the bat of Giant outfielder Hank Leiber, may have been the best of his career. But hardly anyone saw it.

With the Yankees way ahead, much of the crowd had already left. Leiber hit the ball on a line to dead center field. DiMaggio turned and ran back and to his left after the ball, catching it over his shoulder in front of the monument to Eddie Grant in the slot in front of the clubhouse, some 475 feet from home plate.

After making the catch, DiMaggio slowed but never broke stride. When he reached the stairs leading to the clubhouse, he simply took a hard left and ran up, not stopping until he reached the top. Only then did the crowd realize he had caught the ball.

DiMaggio stopped only because he remembered that President Roosevelt was at the game, and the Giants had asked fans and players

Vernon "Lefty" Gomez was a teammate of DiMaggio for seven seasons. Gomez once re-marked that the depth of Yankee Stadium's center field was never fully realized until he was pitching with DiMaggio snaring fly balls in its farthest reaches. Gomez observed, "The only time I saw his face was in the club-house." (Photograph courtesy of the *Boston Herald*)

not to leave after the game until the president's car left through a gate in center field. DiMaggio waited patiently for the president's car to pass, and as it did, Roosevelt turned and gave DiMaggio a wave and nod of acknowledgment.

To put the catch in perspective, Leiber's ball was hit about forty feet *farther* than the ball Willie Mays caught in front of the bleachers in center during the first game of the 1954 World Series off the bat of Vic Wertz. While that catch is widely hailed as "the greatest ever," Mays did not think so himself. Its notoriety is due to its importance in the game and to the famous photograph that shows Mays making the grab. No such photo exists for DiMaggio's catch, and it is nearly forgotten today.

Rosalie DiMaggio kisses a photograph of her son on the eve of his first World Series appearance with the Yankees in 1936. (Photograph courtesy of the *Boston Herald*)

Despite collecting only four hits off Giant pitcher Freddie Fitzsimmons in game three at Yankee Stadium on October 3, the Yankees won 2–1 to go ahead in the series. DiMaggio collected a meaningless double, but made a fine running catch on a Bill Terry drive to center in the sixth.

DiMaggio went hitless in game four as the Yankees beat Hubbell 5–2 behind a two-run homer by Lou Gehrig, and Joe contributed a double but didn't figure in the scoring as the Giants came back in game five to win 5–4 in ten innings. Still, DiMaggio was proving to be perhaps the most popular player on the field. The *Herald Tribune* reported that an Italian flag was raised each time DiMaggio came to bat or touched the ball, and that the right-field bleachers were filled with Italian-American fans.

Back at the Polo Grounds, game six was the best of the series as the Yankees and Giants traded runs. In the seventh, with the Yankees leading 5–3, Bartell doubled, then Terry singled to center. DiMaggio charged the ball, but let it bound past him for a costly error, Bartell scoring. Entering the ninth, the team from the Bronx clung to a 6–5 lead. DiMaggio, whose error had allowed the Giants to stay close, led off.

He singled sharply over third, then moved up two bases on Gehrig's single. Bill Dickey then bounced to Bill Terry at first. DiMaggio broke for home, and as he later told writer Al Silverman, "I stopped, waiting to see what move Terry would make. I figured he would come right at me and force me to make the break. I thought I was gone."

But Terry gunned the ball behind him to third baseman Eddie Mayo, and DiMaggio broke for home.

Mayo threw home, well ahead of DiMaggio. Catcher Harry Danning blocked the plate, but DiMaggio dove headfirst over the tag, then twisted in the dust and touched the plate with his hand, scoring the insurance run. His daring baserunning rattled the Giants, and the floodgates opened. The Giants self-destructed as six more Yankees crossed the plate, the last on DiMaggio's second hit of the inning. New York won, 13–5, to win the Series four games to two.

DiMaggio hit .346 in the Series, the best mark of his career, and second only to Rolfe and Powell among Yankee regulars. But he also struggled, as his baserunning and fielding gaffes belied the notion of his perfection. Yet at two critical moments, in the first inning of game two and the ninth inning of game six, he stole runs with his athletic skills and he keyed rallies. While he'd disappointed in much of the Series, he'd excelled at its most critical moments.

Following his spectacular rookie season in 1936, DiMaggio returned to San Francisco in the off-season and often participated in exhibition games played by major and minor league players residing in the Bay Area. Here he is shown in the uniform of the Oakland Oaks prior to one of these games. (Photograph courtesy of Dick Dobbins)

In light of his later postseason achievements, the nature of his performance at crucial junctures in this Series was telling. DiMaggio was not perfect, but failure did not stop him. His occasional breakdowns only pushed him to reach deeper into his bag of talent. If he didn't hit, he could still run, throw, and catch.

DiMaggio never really had a standout World Series at the plate, one in which his bat alone powered the Yankees to victory. Yet his performance in his inaugural World Series provides a measure of his greatness and insight into his play in subsequent Series. In the World Series, DiMaggio's contributions were not confined to his bat. His most pronounced contributions came from other parts of his game and were still recognized as major factors in Yankee wins.

While his mother and brother returned home after the game, Joe remained in New York a few days. When he arrived in San Francisco, he was a bigger hero than ever before. He was met by a mob at the train station, which swept him from his father's arms and dumped him in the mayor's car. He was brought to city hall, then carried on the shoulders of his admirers into the mayor's office, where he received a key to the city. *The Sporting News* accurately reported that "the success of Joe DiMaggio has fired the imagination of many of the young Italian boys." Yet he still lived at home, and when the furor over his return died down, he was sighted on the docks at Fisherman's Wharf, helping his brothers with their fishing boats.

* * *

DiMaggio is shown returning to the visitors' dugout at Fenway Park with his teammates. (Photograph courtesy of Mike Andersen)

The Yankees quickly tried to sign DiMaggio for the 1937 season. Brother Tom, who handled Joe's finances, was onto the Yankee strategy. The Yankees had already announced plans to expand seating in right field at Yankee Stadium. Joe was the reason, and Tom wanted to make sure Joe received what he deserved. He and Joe turned down a contract identical to that of his rookie year.

The Yankees and the DiMaggios dickered all through the off-season. DiMaggio initially requested $25,000, but finally settled for $17,000, double his rookie salary, in mid-March.

DiMaggio reported to spring training in St. Petersburg, Florida, in fine shape. He had filled out in the off-season and gained nearly twenty pounds. He now stood a full six feet two, and weighed 195.

Joe was no longer the only DiMaggio in the major leagues, as the Boston Bees had purchased Vince's contract and invited him to spring training. Dominic, four years Joe's junior, was showing promise with the Seals and appeared on his way to the major leagues, too.

DiMaggio's right shoulder started giving him trouble. In an exhibition game in Tallahassee on April 2, he left the lineup after uncorking a long throw. For the next two weeks DiMaggio suffered with the sore arm, then was finally diagnosed with tonsillitis, the sore shoulder the result of inflammation. On April 14, a week before the season opener, DiMaggio's tonsils and a bad tooth were removed, but for the second consecutive year, he missed Opening Day.

The 1937 Yankees were much the same as the 1936 edition, with one significant difference. On April 18, the Yankees outbid seven other clubs and for $20,000 purchased outfielder Tommy Henrich, a Cleveland prospect who had been declared a free agent when the Indians tried to hide him from other clubs and prevent Henrich from being drafted. Henrich's arrival was fortuitous. Although he was later injured and spent some of the 1937 season with minor league Newark, over the next several seasons the development of Henrich, outfielder Charlie Keller, and second baseman Joe Gordon allowed the Yankee offense to accommodate the loss of Lou Gehrig. In less than a year Gehrig would begin to show signs of the illness that would force him from the lineup.

DiMaggio made his first appearance of the year on April 30, collecting a pinch-hit single in a 4–1 loss to Washington. In his first start, the next day against Boston, he blasted out three consecutive hits in a 3–2 Yankee win. DiMaggio was 4 for 4 and the Yankees were off and running. Another pattern was becoming clear: when DiMaggio returned from injuries, he immediately produced.

In first place with a 17–10 mark on May 25, the Yankees received a

Spurgeon "Spud" Chandler and Joe DiMaggio stroll toward the visitors' dugout at Fenway Park. Chandler, who pitched for the Yankees from 1937 to 1947, crafted a remarkable .717 lifetime winning percentage with a record of 109–43.
(Photograph from the Maxwell Collection)

tragic boost to their pennant hopes in a 4–3 win over Detroit. In the fourth inning, Yankee pitcher Bump Hadley beaned Detroit manager and catcher Mickey Cochrane, fracturing his skull and effectively ending his career. While the Tigers played well the remainder of the season, they were unable to head off the Yankees, and finished second.

The reason was DiMaggio. The extra weight he'd gained translated into power. On June 13, in St. Louis, in the second game of a doubleheader against the Browns, DiMaggio spanked three consecutive home runs. The last, with two out in the ninth, tied the contest at eight, but the game was called with the score still knotted after eleven innings. The three homers were DiMaggio's seventh, eighth, and ninth in the last nine games.

DiMaggio had changed his stance. When he played in the PCL, he stood with his feet relatively close together, only about fourteen inches apart. Now DiMaggio spread his feet farther apart, which allowed him to wait longer on the ball. He also now knew the pitchers in the American League, and was starting to tee off.

DiMaggio wasn't just hitting soft flies that barely made the fence; he was crushing the ball. In a doubleheader sweep of Boston at the Stadium on July 5, Joe came to bat in game two with the bases loaded and the score tied, 4–4. With two outs and two strikes, he drove pitcher Rube Walberg's pitch deep to left, where it landed in the Yankee bull pen between the left-field stands and the bleachers. Dan Daniel recalled that only the Athletics' Jimmie Foxx had ever hit a ball farther to the same location. The blast was DiMaggio's 20th of the year, and his first grand slam in the major leagues.

Two days later, at the All-Star Game in Washington, DiMaggio started in right field instead of center in deference to Cleveland outfielder Earl Averill. The game was all New York, as the five Yankees in the starting lineup accounted for seven of the AL's thirteen hits and five runs in the 8–3 American League victory. In the third inning, DiMaggio singled off Dizzy Dean and scored on Gehrig's home run. Later, Gehrig's sixth-inning double plated two more. DiMaggio made the play of the game in the top of the sixth. Pinch runner Burgess Whitehead tried to score from second on Rip Collins's single to right, but DiMaggio's throw nailed Whitehead at the plate.

After the game, columnist Richards Vidmer of the *Herald Tribune* summed up the feelings of many when he wrote, "I was only fooling a few days ago when I suggested that Joe McCarthy might as well select the Yankees en masse for the All-Star game . . . There were other players filling in other positions, but their names might as well have been Stanislaus. It was the Yankees who turned in the 8–3 victory."

After the All-Star break the Yankees won eleven of twelve, as DiMaggio ran a hitting streak to 21 games that began on May 29. On July 8, Joe hit for the cycle, plus an extra home run, in a 16–2 rout of Washington. DiMaggio was so hot that the next day one observer noted with sarcasm that "DiMaggio has a boil on his neck, he hit only one double." But as DiMaggio shined, the expectations that surrounded him grew. The remarkable was now expected, and occasional mistakes were magnified. After DiMaggio errored in a 9–6 Yankee win over Cleveland on July 17, the *Herald Tribune* noted, "There is no doubt about DiMaggio's powerful arm, but five wild tosses he made today are useless."

The next day in Cleveland, DiMaggio faced phenom Bob Feller in the most eagerly anticipated matchup of the season.

Feller burst upon the scene in 1936 in mid-season as a seventeen-year-old rookie, striking out fifteen St. Louis Browns in his first major league start. Now in his sophomore season, baseball's best young pitcher squared off against baseball's best young hitter.

It was no contest. While the other Yankees struggled to keep up with Feller's fastball, DiMaggio pounded him like a batting practice pitcher. In the first inning, DiMaggio welcomed Feller with a long triple. In the third inning, DiMaggio's double plated Crosetti for the first run of the game. But DiMaggio's teammates weren't so proficient. Entering the ninth, the score was tied at one apiece.

Red Ruffing led off with a single, then Crosetti dropped a bunt. Fel-

In 1940, Joe DiMaggio made headlines apart from those in the sports pages when he was named one of the ten best-dressed men in America.
(Photograph courtesy of the *Boston Herald*)

ler fielded the ball cleanly but threw low to first. Then the young pitcher walked Red Rolfe.

Up came DiMaggio with the game on the line. After two Feller fastballs, DiMaggio was down two strikes. DiMaggio ripped the third fastball on a line to left field. Outfielder Julius Solters started back, then stopped as the drive sailed over his head for a grand slam. DiMaggio won, 5–1.

Over the next month DiMaggio went on a power tear, socking his 31st home run on August 2 in a 14–5 win over St. Louis. The *Herald Tribune*'s Arthur Patterson led his description of the game by noting, "They said there would never be another Babe Ruth. And for the indefinite thing called color they were right. But for the Babe's chief

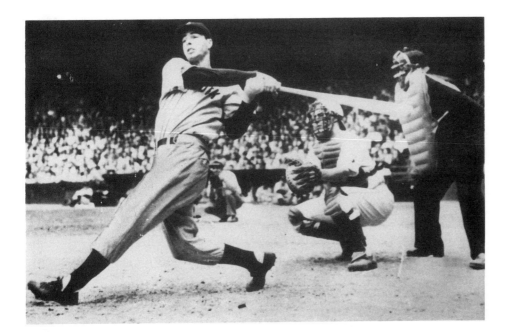

The classic image of DiMaggio at bat, arms fully extended in full stride, driving the ball. (Photograph from Transcendental Graphics, Mark Rucker)

stock in trade, home runs . . . there is another babe at Yankee Stadium, and this babe, Joe DiMaggio, right now is ahead of Ruth's pace for the Babe's peak year in home run production." DiMaggio's pursuit of Ruth, not the American League pennant race, fired the writers for the remainder of the season.

Of course, on his way to 60 home runs in 1927, Ruth cracked a Ruthian 17 in the month of September. It wasn't realistic to expect DiMaggio or anyone else to do the same, and he did not. Yet the fact the writers risked such a comparison demonstrates the regard with which they held Joe DiMaggio.

Over the course of the 1937 season, DiMaggio became more than just a ballplayer. He became a celebrity. The nature of his life changed. DiMaggio was pursued at every step by a public that couldn't get enough of him. Most other ballplayers could appear in public and remain virtually anonymous, but DiMaggio's singular appearance made him immediately recognizable. Teammate Lefty Gomez introduced DiMaggio to the high life, as did fight manager Joe Gould, who lived at the same hotel, the Mayflower, as DiMaggio.

They introduced DiMaggio to the crowd at Toots Shor's, a restaurant that catered to New York's biggest sports stars, entertainment figures, journalists, and politicians. At Shor's Joe was protected from the public. The crowd at Shor's respected his privacy. The writers who covered DiMaggio—Daniel, Jimmy Cannon, Louie Effrat of the *Times,* and others—were regulars at Shor's. Once inside, they stopped being reporters and became DiMaggio's friends, a relationship that worked to their mutual advantage. For even among the luminaries at Shor's, DiMaggio was on a pedestal, the man everyone wanted to meet. In exchange for the social cachet of DiMaggio's occasional company, the writers willingly suspended their journalistic responsibilities. Over the course of a single season Joe went from being a wide-eyed, unsophisticated, son-of-a-fisherman-rookie-ballplayer to an accepted member of New York's celebrity elite.

That acceptance came with a certain price. By placing himself in custody of the crowd at Shor's and entrusting them with his privacy, he gave up a certain freedom and accepted a certain isolation. Whether DiMaggio knew so or not, he allowed himself to be set apart from his fans, his fellow ballplayers, and, to some extent, even his family. Aside from Gomez, he was no longer close to any of his teammates.

Both everyday fans and big shots looked up to him. His individuality was lost in their expectations. He became responsible for more than his own performance on the field or his personal happiness. When America looked for a hero, it found DiMaggio. It was a terrible responsibility, and one that marked the remainder of his career. He felt the pressure. He couldn't let anyone down, ever.

Amid the high-powered egoists at Shor's, DiMaggio was something

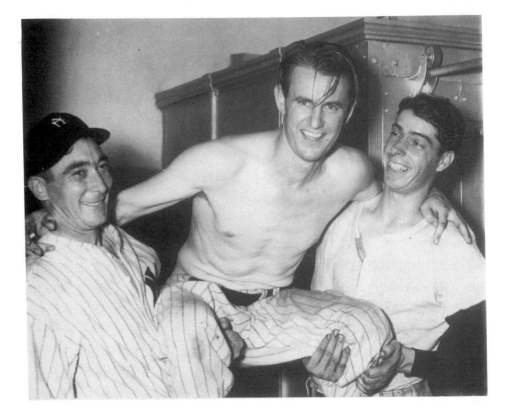

The 1937 Yankees celebrate the World Series win over the rival New York Giants. From left are Tony Lazzeri, Lefty Gomez, and Joe DiMaggio.   (Photograph from Transcendental Graphics, Mark Rucker)

DiMaggio crosses home plate following his home run in the third inning of game five of the 1937 World Series versus the New York Giants. The Yankees would win the game by a score of 4–2 to clinch the world championship.   (Photograph from Bettmann Archives)

of an anomaly. He was younger, less sophisticated and glib than his companions. While he held an honored position in their company, he was also an outsider. His newfound status was in some ways temporary. Heroes-of-the-moment passed through Shor's all the time. Few retained the rank. DiMaggio's prestige was entirely dependent upon his ability on the baseball field. Absolutely everything in his new life— his friends, his salary, his growing role within his own family— everything depended on it. He could not risk failure.

But not even Joe DiMaggio could do more than what was physically possible. Playing in Yankee Stadium robbed him of any chance to break Ruth's record. Like Ruth, DiMaggio pulled the ball. Unlike the left-handed-hitting Babe, the right-handed-swinging DiMaggio had no short porch in Yankee Stadium. While it was only 301 feet down the line in left, the wall veered sharply back, and a drive to straight left had to carry at least 400 feet. It was even deeper toward center. Joe could never hit enough home runs at Yankee Stadium to challenge the Babe. DiMaggio later told a reporter that he felt he hit so well in 1937 that "I could have hit 70 [home runs] in a field which favored right-handers. . . . I hit 15 triples that could have been homers. It seemed that every long ball I got ahold of that season was a 400-footer, even the outs."

He finished the season with 46 home runs, best in the major

Joe DiMaggio is shown easing back in a westbound Pullman car in February 1938. He is discussing with reporters his demand for a $40,000 contract from the Yankees after a season that saw him sock 46 home runs while batting .346. (Photograph courtesy of the *Boston Herald*)

leagues and still a Yankee record for a right-handed batter. At the Stadium, he hit a career-best 19. On the road, he hit a Ruthian 27. DiMaggio hit .346 for the year, with 167 RBI and a league-high 151 runs scored. The Yankees rolled to their second consecutive pennant with a record of 102–52, thirteen games ahead of Detroit.

In the National League, the Giants won the pennant for the second year in a row, but not even Giant manager Bill Terry seemed to expect a Giants win. When a reporter asked if he would bet on his own club in the series, Terry responded fatalistically, "I'm no sucker."

The Series opened at the Stadium on October 6, and the Yankees rolled to an 8–1 win on Lefty Gomez's six-hitter and a seven-run sixth. DiMaggio's bases-loaded single off Hubbell knocked in the first two runs and provided Gomez with the only runs he needed.

It was more of the same in game two as the Yanks won again 8–1 behind Ruffing's seven-hitter and the hitting of George Selkirk. Di-Maggio contributed two hits but didn't figure in the scoring until the game was out of reach.

In game three at the Polo Grounds, Yankee pitching shut down the Giants with just a single run for the third game in a row, as Monte Pearson scattered five hits. DiMaggio's infield single in the third helped move a runner along, and the Yankees won, 5–1.

The Giants avoided a sweep in game four when Carl Hubbell stopped the Yankees on six hits and the Giants shelled Bump Hadley for six runs in the second inning on their way to a 7–3 win. DiMaggio went hitless off Hubbell, but narrowly missed a home run and gave the Yankees a temporary 1–0 lead with a first-inning sacrifice fly.

Again, the last game of the series was the best. With New York leading 1–0 in the third, DiMaggio turned on a pitch from the Giants' Cliff Melton and drove it high and deep to left. The ball nearly left the Polo Grounds, striking a flagpole atop the stands on the stadium roof, just fair, to increase the Yankee lead to two. But the Giants' Mel Ott responded with a home run of his own in the Giant half to tie the score.

The Yankees got the lead back with two runs in the fifth, keyed by a Lazzeri triple that hit the fence in front of the right-center field bleachers, and a double by Gehrig, sandwiched around a Gomez single, a walk, and a DiMaggio foul pop. Gomez went the distance in the 4–2 win, and the Yankees were world champions for the second year in a row.

While DiMaggio hit only .273 for the series, his bases-loaded single and home run were key blows in two Yankee wins. Coupled with his performance during the season, DiMaggio was poised to cash in on his newfound fame.

Late in the season he took a small part in a movie, *Manhattan Merry-Go-Round,* a musical starring Phil Regan and Leo Carillo, designed as a showcase for stars like Cab Calloway, Jack Benny, and DiMaggio, who played himself and delivered a self-conscious monologue on baseball. During filming in Astoria, Queens, DiMaggio met a young chorus girl named Dorothy Arnold. Although he told an interviewer that "the smart thing I do is never fall in love, I just talk a good game with women," Arnold soon became DiMaggio's first serious love interest.

After the season, the New York Jewels professional basketball team offered DiMaggio a job playing basketball for $500 a game plus $50

Following his spectacular 1937 campaign, DiMaggio refused to sign a Yankee contract for anything less than $40,000. He is shown during his holdout clowning for photographers. (Photograph courtesy of the *Boston Herald*)

The 1938 baseball season was already under way and Joe DiMaggio was still conducting a futile long-distance contract negotiation with Yankee owner Colonel Jacob Ruppert. (Photograph courtesy of the *Boston Globe*)

for every minute played. The Yankees, fearing he might get injured, blocked his appearance, although DiMaggio did appear in some publicity photos carefully dribbling a basketball.

DiMaggio narrowly lost the American League MVP Award, as Charlie Gehringer edged him for the honor by four votes, 78–74. But DiMaggio won a public opinion poll for the same honor, and baseball writers in Philadelphia and New York voted him player of the year, as did *Baseball Magazine*, and he collected the most votes of any player for *The Sporting News* annual major league All-Star team.

DiMaggio also earned a nickname. In mid-season Yankee radio broadcaster Arch McDonald, impressed with the stylish way DiMaggio appeared to glide across the outfield in pursuit of fly balls, started referring to Joe as "the Yankee Clipper," in reference to the great sailing ships that once gracefully filled the North Atlantic. The name stuck.

Joe returned to San Francisco for the off-season but made several trips to the East Coast to appear at banquets and, presumably, court Dorothy Arnold. He played the dutiful son and bought his parents a new home in the Marina district, and opened a restaurant on the Wharf, DiMaggio's Grotto, managed by his brother Tom. Joe whiled away the hours in a corner of the bar, drinking coffee and occasionally seeing well-wishers, but just as often scurrying away when approached.

As was Yankee custom, Ruppert and business manager Ed Barrow offered DiMaggio a contract for 1938 identical to the one he signed in 1937. DiMaggio sent it back. He wanted $40,000.

While Tom DiMaggio still advised Joe on many financial matters, DiMaggio was depending more and more upon the counsel of Joe Gould. In mid-January, DiMaggio returned to New York to attend the James Braddock–Tommy Farr heavyweight championship fight, pick up a few awards, and talk contract with Ruppert and Barrow. He was confident of his own ability and his worth, telling Dan Daniel that "it seems to me I can win the Triple Crown."

On the afternoon of January 21, Ruppert and Barrow forced DiMaggio to cool his heels in an outer office for nearly an hour before agreeing to see him. DiMaggio left an hour later.

During the meeting Barrow argued that $40,000 was more money than the Yankees paid Lou Gehrig, to which DiMaggio replied, "Then Mr. Gehrig is a badly underpaid player." The negotiations quickly deteriorated.

DiMaggio told the press he hadn't signed a contract, but refused to disclose his asking price, saying, "I promised the colonel [Ruppert] I wouldn't mention any of the amounts we were discussing." But after DiMaggio left, Ruppert felt no such obligation to secrecy, and told the press he had offered DiMaggio $25,000, "A very fair salary."

Whether the offer was fair or not was open to question, but DiMaggio felt betrayed by Ruppert's tactics. Neither party budged, and both embarked on a verbal war in the press. Ruppert called DiMaggio "an ungrateful young man," and claimed the Yankees "would win the pennant without him." But DiMaggio didn't give in. Talking tough at contract time was a family trademark. Both Vince and Dominic, now a member of the Seals, were also holding out for more pay.

DiMaggio was particularly galled by the fact that the Yankees had taken out a $100,000 insurance policy on him, which he felt was indicative of his value. The Yankees, on the other hand, groused about the alleged influence of Joe Gould.

DiMaggio was surprised and hurt when most of the press either sided with the Yankees or remained neutral. But Joe refused to give in. He had no leverage in the negotiations except to hold out. When the Yankees opened spring training in Florida at the beginning of March, DiMaggio stayed in San Francisco.

Yankee second baseman Joe Gordon is shown with Di-Maggio in 1940. Gordon, who replaced Hall of Famer Tony Lazzeri, would star for the Yankees from 1938 to 1946. In 1942, he batted .322 and was named American League MVP. (Photograph courtesy of Mike Andersen)

For the next six weeks, DiMaggio stewed while the Yankees acted as if they didn't need him. Ruppert even claimed, "I've forgotten all about him. . . . Presidents go into eclipse, kings have their thrones removed under them . . . and great ballplayers pass on." Gehrig finally signed for the $39,000, and the Yankees were winning the war in the press. For the first time, DiMaggio's public image took a beating.

The Yankees opened the 1938 season sans DiMaggio but with much the same lineup as the 1938 club. Tony Lazzeri was the sole exception. After the World Series, he was released and allowed to sign with the Cubs, making room for rookie second baseman Joe Gordon.

The Yankees opened the regular season in Boston on April 18 and dropped three of four. Joe finally concluded that the Yankees were not going to capitulate to his demands, and reluctantly made the decision to sign the $25,000 contract. He returned to New York on April 23.

DiMaggio avoided a press throng at Penn Station by leaving his train at Newark, leading one writer to crack that "DiMaggio went slightly Hollywood." But when Joe was tracked down at Jim Braddock's new restaurant in the company of Joe Gould, he tried to make amends, saying one reason he decided to sign were the fifty or sixty letters he received each day from young fans begging him to play. But the Yankees weren't finished playing hardball. After DiMaggio signed on April 25, the club announced he'd be docked a day's pay for every game he missed while working himself into shape.

The Yankees rushed DiMaggio back into the lineup on April 30 in Washington. Gehrig wasn't hitting, catcher Bill Dickey was nursing a sore back, outfielder George Selkirk had a sore wrist, and New York was playing .500 ball. The Yankees nearly paid a dear cost for their impatience.

DiMaggio started off in mid-season form. Greeted by jeers from the partisan crowd in his first at bat, Joe silenced the fans by smacking a single to right field. In the bottom half of the inning, he made a stellar catch on a drive by Senator outfielder John Stone. In the sixth inning, with the Yankees leading 3–0, Washington outfielder Taft Wright lifted a lazy fly to center field, just to the left of second base. DiMaggio, left fielder Myril Hoag, and second baseman Joe Gordon all raced toward the ball.

But DiMaggio and Gordon had never played together, and neither Hoag nor Gordon deferred to the center fielder. DiMaggio pulled up at the last instant, but Gordon crashed into him at full speed while Hoag twisted out of the way of both men and somehow made the catch.

DiMaggio sat on the ground, tried to stand, then slumped back. Gordon lay almost motionless. An ambulance was called while Yankee trainer Doc Painter attended to the two men. DiMaggio finally rose to his feet and was helped off the field, but Gordon was carried off on a stretcher. Both players were taken to Garfield Hospital and remained overnight for observation. The Yankees won, 8–4, but everyone worried about the two Joes.

DiMaggio emerged with only a bump on the head and returned to the lineup the next day, but Gordon suffered a concussion and missed several games. DiMaggio cracked a home run in a 4–3 Yankee loss. The following day, manager Joe McCarthy, troubled by the slumping Gehrig, moved DiMaggio into the cleanup position and dropped Gehrig to sixth in the order. With DiMaggio collecting at least one hit every day, the Yankees won their next seven games and set their sights on another pennant.

In spite of the Yankee turnaround, the fans were slow to warm to DiMaggio again. Throughout most of the season he was booed by fans resentful over the holdout and his high salary. In the midst of the Depression, it was hard to feel sympathetic. Besides, he'd bumped Gehrig from the cleanup spot, and although he was playing well, DiMaggio's performance was nothing like that of his previous season. He trailed Detroit's Hank Greenberg in the American League home-run race, and the emergence of Joe Gordon and Tommy Henrich as premier power hitters served to diminish DiMaggio's role on the Yankees.

At the All-Star break, the Yankees still trailed Cleveland, but their first-half record was an acceptable 41–25. In the 4–1 American League loss at Cincinnati's Crosley Field, DiMaggio again played right field in deference to Earl Averill. Hitless in his first three at bats, Joe hit a single in the ninth and scored the American League's only run.

The Yankees resumed their familiar spot atop the American League in the second half, taking over first place for good following a double-header sweep of St. Louis on July 12. From there, it was just a matter of time until the Yankees clinched their third consecutive pennant. On August 28, New York buried Cleveland for good with a doubleheader sweep at the Stadium, 8–7 and 13–0. In the second game, Yankee pitcher Monte Pearson twirled a no-hitter, backed by three triples from DiMaggio, each of which carried over 400 feet in the air.

The Yankees clinched the pennant in their 140th game, on September 20, and finished the season 99–53, $9^1/_2$ games ahead of second-place Boston as Cleveland fell to third. Manager Joe McCarthy later claimed that the 1938 Yankees, despite winning fewer games than all but one of his pennant winners, were his best ball club. They were certainly the most balanced, and the addition of Joe Gordon provided a much-needed defensive boost. All but one member of the starting lineup finished with ten or more home runs and the Yankees led the AL in virtually every offensive category. The staff ERA was the best in the league.

DiMaggio's season was something of a disappointment. Although he hit .324 with 32 home runs and 140 RBI, all club highs, it was no

(l–r) Joe DiMaggio, Tommy Henrich, and Charlie Keller at Fenway Park, c. 1940. This trio formed perhaps the greatest outfield in Yankee history and one of the greatest in baseball history. (Photograph from the Maxwell Collection)

The many Joes of the 1939 Yankee lineup: (l–r) *Joe Gordon, Joe Gallagher, Joe Beggs, Joe DiMaggio, and Joe McCarthy.* (Photograph from Transcendental Graphics, Mark Rucker)

Triple Crown performance. He did not lead the AL in a single offensive category. The fans had turned against him, and DiMaggio was reportedly estranged from many members of his own team, who resented his posturing during the salary holdout and, like Ruppert, felt they could have won without him. DiMaggio didn't reach out to his teammates, but reacted to the boos and cold shoulders by retreating into a shell and spending more time with his friends at Shor's. After most games, DiMaggio sat alone in the locker room, sipping coffee and smoking cigarettes—a habit he adopted in the major leagues—waiting until the clubhouse was nearly empty before showering by himself and either going to Shor's or returning to his hotel room. He didn't lack female companionship, as he was still seeing Dorothy Arnold. In mid-season, columnist Dorothy Kilgallen produced a fawning profile that summed up the feeling of many women. She gushed, "Goodness, he's divine."

The Yankees met the Cubs in the World Series in search of their third straight world championship, something no team, not even Ruth's Yankees, had ever accomplished. DiMaggio was looking to redeem something of a wasted season.

He failed in game one in Chicago, going hitless, but the Yankees won, 3–1, on Ruffing's complete game and catcher Bill Dickey's perfect 4 for 4 at the plate. In game two, DiMaggio demonstrated his value to the Yankees.

Dizzy Dean started for the Cubs against Lefty Gomez. Only twenty-seven, Dean was no longer the intimidating fastball pitcher who had starred with the Cardinals. In the 1937 All-Star Game his toe was broken by a line drive. Dean came back too quickly, changed his motion,

Joe DiMaggio at bat in 1939. (Photograph from Transcendental Graphics, Mark Rucker)

and hurt his arm. His fastball was gone. Traded to the Cubs in 1938, Dean proved he was more than just a hard thrower, as he used a succession of slower stuff to fashion a 7–1 record in limited duty, with an ERA of 1.80.

The Cubs led 1–0 in the second when DiMaggio collected the Yanks' first hit, a single. Gehrig walked, and after two outs, Cub third baseman Stan Hack and shortstop Billy Jurges collided going after Joe Gordon's slow roller. The ball rolled into the outfield, and both DiMaggio and Gehrig scored.

The Cubs came back with two more in the third to lead 3–2. Dean then shut out the Yankees through seven innings, as New York's sluggers just couldn't adjust to his off-speed repertoire.

Light-hitting Frank Crosetti connected for a two-run homer in the eighth to put the Yankees on top, 4–3. In the ninth, after a Henrich single, DiMaggio timed Dean's soft delivery perfectly, driving the ball deep to center, into the teeth of a strong wind. It landed on Sheffield Avenue outside Wrigley Field for a home run. Gomez held on for a record sixth straight World Series win.

The Yankees rolled to workmanlike wins in the next two games in New York, winning 5–2 and 8–3 to capture a record third straight World Series. In each game, singles by DiMaggio led to rallies that keyed the Yankee wins, but his contributions went virtually unnoticed. The Yankees were now expected to win, and his role in winning was almost taken for granted.

While DiMaggio again lost out in voting for the American League's MVP Award, finishing sixth behind Jimmie Foxx of Boston, he was again selected to *The Sporting News* All-Star team, collecting more votes than any other player. In the off-season, he let it be known that he planned to ask for a $5,000 raise. He wanted the contract settled early. Entering his fourth year in the major leagues, he had yet to take advantage of spring training.

Jacob Ruppert died in the off-season, and Ed Barrow became Yankee president. He offered DiMaggio the same $25,000 Joe had earned in 1938, and warned DiMaggio against holding out. Although displeased that the Yankees felt he wasn't worth $30,000, DiMaggio wanted to attend spring training and didn't want to risk a repeat of the 1938 negotiations. Both sides compromised, and in mid-February DiMaggio signed for $27,500.

If possible, the Yankees appeared to be even better in 1939 than they were in 1938. They added powerful rookie outfielder Charlie Keller, and expected Lou Gehrig to bounce back from a disappointing performance in 1938, when he hit only .295 with 29 home runs, a career season for most players, even in the 1930s, but Gehrig's worst year since his rookie season in 1925. DiMaggio appeared content, and Dorothy Arnold let slip that she and Joe were planning to be married.

In spring training Keller proved to be what the Yankees hoped, and DiMaggio was healthy for the first time. But Gehrig moved in slow

Charlie "King Kong" Keller, a lifetime .286 hitter and member of seven American League championship Yankee teams, played alongside Di- Maggio and Tommy Henrich in one of the greatest outfield trios of all time. (Photo- graph courtesy of Mike An- dersen)

Joe DiMaggio is shown waiting on deck at Fenway Park in 1939. He would bat .381 for the season with 30 home runs and 126 RBI while playing in only 120 games. (Photograph courtesy of Mike Andersen)

motion. He had trouble hitting the ball, even during batting practice, and when he did, it was without his usual power. The Yankees were patient with the Iron Horse. He was thirty-six, and had gotten off to a similar slow start in 1938.

The season was scheduled to begin in Boston on April 17, but three consecutive days of rain pushed the opener to April 20. The Yankees won, 2–0, beating Lefty Grove behind Ruffing's seven-hitter. DiMaggio managed only a single, but Gehrig hit into two double plays. Starting in the Boston outfield for the first time was rookie Ted Williams.

The Yankees won five of six before another East Coast rainstorm caused rainouts on April 26, 27, and 28. Over the next few days, disaster struck.

On April 29, in the third inning of a 3–1 loss to Washington at Yankee Stadium, DiMaggio raced in after a line drive by the Senators' Bobby Estalella. He had taken only a few steps when he slipped and caught the spikes of his right foot in the Stadium grass. DiMaggio rolled over his leg, collapsed on his back, and writhed in pain as Estalella went to third.

Doc Painter and Yankee doctor Robert Walsh raced onto the field. It was five minutes before DiMaggio could bear being lifted to his feet and half-carried from the field, his right leg dangling beneath him. Walsh first thought the leg was broken and rushed DiMaggio to the hospital. Though the X rays were negative, DiMaggio was badly hurt, his calf muscles torn away from his ankle. Walsh optimistically estimated that it would be at least ten days before DiMaggio would return to the lineup. DiMaggio blamed the injury on a new pair of spikes.

The cover of *Life* magazine dated the next day featured DiMaggio. The accompanying story was hardly complimentary. In what can only be described as one of the most bizarre profiles to appear in print about any ballplayer, the story, written by Noel F. Busch, was apparently intended to be laudatory. Instead, it mocked DiMaggio for his Italian background, described him as shiftless yet successful in baseball only because of natural talent, called him "lazy, shy and inarticulate," claimed that "instead of olive oil or bear grease, he keeps his hair slick with water . . . [and] never reeks of garlic." As the article demonstrated, Italian-Americans still faced a great deal of prejudice in American society, and a certain level of intolerance was still quite acceptable. DiMaggio might have been able to date starlets and be a hero at Shor's, but some still felt obligated to put him in his place.

On May 2, the Yankees received more bad news. While DiMaggio was back in New York convalescing, Lou Gehrig approached Joe Mc-

Carthy before a game against Detroit and took himself out of the lineup "for the good of the team." Lou had collected only four hits in 28 at bats, and his teammates had noticed him stumbling. Gehrig later claimed he'd made the decision to pull himself from the lineup on April 29, in the Yankees' 3–2 loss to Washington. After making a routine play at first, several of his teammates rushed to congratulate him on his glovework. "They meant to be kind," said Gehrig, "but if I was getting wholesale congratulations for making an ordinary stop, I knew it was time to fold."

As Gehrig fulfilled his role as Yankee captain and carried the lineup card to home plate, an announcement was made to the crowd that Gehrig's streak had come to an end at an astounding 2,130 games. The Detroit fans burst into spontaneous, sustained applause. Gehrig returned to the bench, tears in his eyes, and buried his face in a towel. While Gehrig continued to travel with the club, in mid-season an examination at the Mayo Clinic revealed he was suffering from amyotrophic lateral sclerosis, a degenerative nerve disease for which there was no cure. Lou Gehrig played no more for the Yankees.

Despite the absence of both DiMaggio and Gehrig, the Yankees crushed Detroit, 22–2, demonstrating the depth of their talent. Charlie Keller knocked in six runs while Gehrig's replacement, Babe Dahlgren, homered and doubled.

The Yankees took over first place on May 11 and lost only four games the entire month as they adjusted to life without Gehrig and DiMaggio. By the time DiMaggio returned to the lineup on June 7, following two Yankee losses to Detroit, the pennant race was virtually over.

DiMaggio hit as he had in 1937, and New York rolled over the opposition. In a doubleheader sweep of Philadelphia on June 28, the Yankees hit 13 home runs and outscored the A's 33–2, winning 23–2 and 10–0. DiMaggio led the onslaught with three home runs, six RBI, and six runs scored.

The extent of Gehrig's illness became known at mid-season, and the Yankees held "Lou Gehrig Appreciation Day" on July 4. Gehrig provided one of baseball's most memorable moments when he spoke to the crowd, saying, "Today I consider myself the luckiest man on the face of the earth."

DiMaggio cried during the ceremony for the first time in his adult life. If he had a personal hero, it was Gehrig, who was one of the first players to welcome DiMaggio to the Yankees. DiMaggio admired Gehrig not only for his talent but for his grit, determination, and abil-

Joe DiMaggio celebrates the Yankees' four-game World Series sweep of the Cincinnati Reds in 1939 as manager Joe McCarthy (c) and pitcher Johnny Murphy (r) join him in the visitors' shower at Crosley Field. (Photograph by Gene Smith, courtesy of Kevin Grace)

ity to lead through action, all qualities others would eventually ascribe to DiMaggio. The emotionally exhausted Yankees then fell to the Senators, 3–2.

DiMaggio was again selected to the All-Star team, starting in center field for the first time. The game was played at Yankee Stadium, and DiMaggio delighted the crowd by hitting a solo home run into the left-field stands off Cub pitcher Bill Lee in the sixth inning, helping the AL to a 3–1 win.

With his average hovering close to .400, Joe was playing perhaps the best baseball of his career. He inadvertently became involved in a controversy when Tris Speaker, to whom DiMaggio was often compared, allegedly claimed there were fifteen outfielders in the major leagues he considered better than DiMaggio. While DiMaggio never commented on Speaker's outburst, his play in back-to-back games against Detroit provided an answer.

In a 5–2 loss to the Tigers at the Stadium on August 1, DiMaggio kept the game close by recording a remarkable ten putouts, one short of the major league record. Arthur Patterson in the *Herald Tribune* wrote, "Tris Speaker should have seen DiMaggio in centerfield yesterday. He may not play in close enough to suit 'Old Spoke,' but don't tell that to [Detroit batters] Averill, Higgins and Fox. He robbed each of a hit, coming in and going out."

The next day, DiMaggio made a catch that many observers believe was the best of his career. With the Yankees behind 7–2 in the ninth inning and Mike Higgins on first, Hank Greenberg drove the ball high and deep to left center. Playing the left-handed Greenberg to pull, DiMaggio stood in right center. At the crack of the bat, he took off on a full run toward the deepest part of Yankee Stadium.

Higgins ran for home, thinking that DiMaggio didn't have a chance to catch the ball, and the slow-footed Greenberg later admitted, "I figure it's going to hit the wall and maybe I can get an inside-the-park home run on it."

DiMaggio glanced once at the ball and kept running. Just to the left of the monuments in left center, behind the flagpole and in front of the "461" sign, he looked up, stretched out his glove, and somehow caught the ball.

Greenberg was nearing second and Higgins was rounding third when DiMaggio made the catch. But DiMaggio lost track of the outs and started to trot toward home before he realized he had a chance for a double play. He threw the ball in, but Gordon's relay hit Higgins in the back and he made it back to first. Greenberg's description of the play indicates that DiMaggio ran over 200 feet for the ball, and those who saw both DiMaggio's catch and Willie Mays's famous snag in the 1954 World Series at the Polo Grounds claim DiMaggio's was the better catch. Unlike Mays's catch, DiMaggio's grab was not captured on film, and exists only in the memory of those who saw it.

DiMaggio kept hitting in streaks of twelve or thirteen games, then going hitless for a game, then hitting in another ten or eleven straight, all the while keeping his average above .400. During a Yankee road trip in late August, he hit .509 in twelve games. On September 2, he ran a hitting streak to 18 games, best in baseball that year, and his

Joe DiMaggio and Dorothy Arnold announce their marriage plans to the press on May 18, 1939. (Photograph courtesy of the Boston Globe)

average was up to .408. Moreover, despite playing in only 92 games, 30 fewer games than AL RBI leader Ted Williams, DiMaggio had 113 RBI, only seven behind Williams. The next day, in a doubleheader in Boston, after going hitless in one at bat, DiMaggio wrenched his right knee and left the game, halting his streak. But he returned in game two and went 3 for 4 to raise his average to .410. His 25 home runs were only ten behind Jimmie Foxx. Despite missing thirty games, DiMaggio had an outside chance at the Triple Crown.

It was not to be. He caught a bad cold in the first week of September and instead of sitting out, kept playing. The cold bothered his eyes. He expected Joe McCarthy to sit him out a few games to recover, but McCarthy didn't offer and DiMaggio didn't ask. Joe slumped over the last three weeks of the season and his average tumbled below .400. He finished at a career-high .381, best in the American League, and the Yankees finished with a record of 106–45, seventeen games ahead of Boston.

Cincinnati won the National League pennant by 4½ games behind pitchers Bucky Walters and Paul Derringer, who won 52 games between them. Still, the Yankees were 3-to-1 favorites in the World Series.

Game four of the Series provided one of DiMaggio's signature moments, but in the first two games in New York, his contributions were undervalued. In game one, DiMaggio contributed only a fifth-inning infield hit to the 2–1 Yankee win. In game two, DiMaggio collected another infield hit after New York scored twice on their way to three runs in an eventual 4–1 win. The *Herald Tribune* cynically commented that "DiMaggio has revealed a new batting talent. He tops the ball with such a terrific spin that it drags slowly along the third-base line for a hit."

The two teams traveled to Cincinnati for game three. On October 6, an off day, DiMaggio stayed behind after the Yankees' morning workout and took extra batting practice. It helped. In game three the next day, DiMaggio demonstrated his more usual talents. His two-run third-inning home run to center off Junior Thompson provided the margin of victory in the Yankees' 7–3 win, but Charlie Keller garnered the headlines by hitting two home runs and knocking in four.

Game four was the best of the series, and DiMaggio's defense and alert baserunning proved the difference between the clubs. In the second, following a Frank McCormick double, DiMaggio ranged far back to snag Ernie Lombardi's drive to center with a one-handed catch to save a run. In the third, with pitcher Paul Derringer on first, DiMaggio ran to the center-field gate to pull down Billy Werber's fly and save another run.

Derringer held the Yankees hitless into the fifth and scoreless into the seventh. Then Keller and Dickey homered around a deep fly by DiMaggio to put New York up 2–0. But in the bottom of the inning, Cincinnati scored three times. DiMaggio nearly snuffed the rally with a shoestring catch of Willard Hershberger's Texas leaguer, but the ball trickled from his glove. The Reds added a run in the eighth to take a 4–2 lead.

In the Yankee ninth, with Bucky Walters pitching in relief of Derringer, Keller led off with a base hit, then DiMaggio singled him to third. Dickey grounded to Red second baseman Lonnie Frey, but with DiMaggio bearing down, shortstop Buddy Myers dropped the throw from Frey. DiMaggio and Dickey were safe and Keller scored on the play. Selkirk flied to deep right. DiMaggio smartly tagged up and made third.

Joe Gordon promptly chopped a ball to third. Werber ranged behind third base and flagged it down as DiMaggio broke for home. Werber gunned the ball to catcher Lombardi, but the throw was off-line and DiMaggio swept around the tag to tie the game. The Yankees failed to score again, and when Cincinnati was shut out in the ninth after DiMaggio made another catch against the wall off Bucky Walters, the game went into extra innings.

The Yankees didn't waste time. Frank Crosetti worked a walk and Red Rolfe sacrificed him to second. Keller proved the wisdom of McCarthy's move when he bounced the ball to second, but Buddy Myers bobbled the ball. Crosetti moved to third and Keller was safe at first.

DiMaggio came up with the game on the line. Joe took Walters the other way, lining the ball to right field. Red outfielder Billy Goodman charged the ball and it got past him. Crosetti scored and Keller kept running. The throw got to the plate just as Keller crashed into Ernie Lombardi. Lombardi dropped it and Keller was safe.

Lombardi sat on the ground, stunned, as the ball trickled away. DiMaggio kept tearing around the bases like some maniacal Little Leaguer. As Lombardi caught sight of DiMaggio rounding third, he woke from what observers later characterized as the big catcher's "snooze" and scrambled after the ball. Lombardi recovered it and threw himself at the plate, his glove blocking DiMaggio's path. But DiMaggio slid to the infield side of the plate, lifted his lead leg up in the air over Lombardi's mitt, then dropped it on the corner of the plate. The Yankees led, 7–4.

Cincinnati threatened in the bottom of the inning against Yankee relief pitcher Johnny Murphy but failed to score, and New York won its fourth consecutive World Series.

Talk after the game was all DiMaggio. His glove saved at least two runs, and maybe more, while his baserunning tied the game in the ninth, his bat knocked in the winning run in the tenth, and his baserunning put the game out of reach. As the Yankees celebrated madly in the visitors' clubhouse at Crosley Field, DiMaggio retired to the trainer's table, where Doc Painter treated Joe's thighs, which were covered with strawberries. In the Cincinnati clubhouse, one disappointed Red was reported to be muttering over and over, "How did DiMaggio get around those bases?"

To no one's surprise DiMaggio was named the Most Valuable Player in the American League on October 25, winning the honor by a wide margin over Jimmie Foxx of Boston. DiMaggio finally had the proof of what many had been saying since he first entered the league. Joe's attention turned to his wedding. The event provided a measure of the hero's soaring popularity.

DiMaggio and Dorothy Arnold were married on November 19, at the Saint Peter and Paul Cathedral in Joe's old neighborhood, North Beach, in San Francisco. Although the church seated nearly 2,000, all of Fisherman's Wharf would not have been sufficient to contain the throng that turned out for the wedding.

DiMaggio's wedding day seemed more a coronation than any ceremony of matrimony. To the Italians of North Beach, Joe was a king, and the entire neighborhood turned out to see him take his queen. Only seven years before, he had simply been another of the faceless masses scrambling for a dollar in the middle of the Depression. Now he was a god. San Francisco had never seen anything like it.

The DiMaggio family severely underestimated the appeal of North Beach's favorite son. They sent out nearly 800 invitations, but an hour before the ceremony, the Cathedral was filled with nearly 2,000 guests. In the close-knit Italian community, an invitation to one member of a family was extended to many. The wedding was front-page news in every San Francisco newspaper.

The ceremony was scheduled to begin at 2 o'clock, but the hour came and went without the main participants. Outside the church, police had to force their way through a mob estimated at 10,000 just to get the wedding party in the door. Hundreds of young men hung on the scaffolding of the still-under-construction cathedral for a better view. When police finally got Dorothy Arnold and her family inside, they locked the door, inadvertently locking Vince DiMaggio outside. He eventually gained admittance through a side door along with several dozen crashers.

Inside the church, the scene was chaotic, as babies cried, necks craned, and guests took on the character of a crowd at a baseball game. The priest who would perform the ceremony, Father Parolin, stepped to the pulpit several times and asked the crowd to "remember that you are in the house of the Lord. I ask you in His name to be silent." His pleas were in vain.

The wedding finally got under way at about 2:30, although many never heard a word of it. The bride wore a Grecian-style white gown with a V neck and sculpted bodice, and carried gardenias and orchids. Joe wore a tuxedo.

After the ceremony police again formed a flying wedge to help the couple escape, and the newlyweds went to a photographic studio for pictures, had a private family dinner, and then tried to make their way to DiMaggio's Grotto for the wedding reception.

The scene at the restaurant duplicated the scene at the cathedral. While a three-piece orchestra played swing music, occasionally supplanted by an operatic tenor, the crowd mobbed the bar. Joe and Dorothy were the last to arrive. They stayed long enough to cut the cake and beat a hasty retreat as the party continued without them. The

Dorothy Arnold and Joe DiMaggio cut their wedding cake in 1939. (Photograph from Transcendental Graphics, Mark Rucker)

Vince (r) and Dominic Di-Maggio meet as rivals in a spring training game in March 1940. (Photograph courtesy of the Boston Globe)

couple left for parts unknown, exhilarated and happy, but probably glad to have the day over with. If Dorothy Arnold, at twenty-one, three years younger than Joe, hadn't known what being Mrs. Joe DiMaggio entailed, she did now. She might belong to Joe DiMaggio, but Joe DiMaggio belonged to everyone.

If the wedding was an omen that the future might not be quite what they expected, the 1940 season fulfilled the prophecy. DiMaggio again asked for $40,000, but finally signed for $32,000 on March 5. After an uneventful spring training, the Yankees played the Dodgers in Brooklyn to end the exhibition schedule. With New York leading 5–3 in the ninth inning of the final game at Ebbets Field on April 14, DiMaggio hit a short fly to center. Playing hard, he tried to stretch the hit into a double. As he slid into second, he caught the spikes on his right foot and wrenched his knee.

Although initial reports indicated that the Yankees hoped DiMaggio would play in the season opener in Philadelphia on April 17, he did not. The strained ligaments kept him out for three weeks, and for the fourth time in five seasons, the Yankees started the season without DiMaggio.

The 1940 Yankees were in transition and could ill afford his loss, even for three weeks. Gehrig was gone, and old stalwarts like Red Rolfe, George Selkirk, Bill Dickey, and Red Ruffing were showing their age, while Frank Crosetti and most of the pitching staff slumped. Without DiMaggio, the Yankees started off poorly.

New York had lost three in a row and was 6–9, good for last place, when DiMaggio returned to the lineup on May 7. But not even DiMaggio could stop the slide, which stretched to eight games on May 11 following a loss to Boston.

No sooner was Joe back than he faced another distraction. Baseball commissioner Kenesaw Landis received reports that Joe Gould was acting as DiMaggio's agent and sharing his salary. Since Gould was connected to boxing, boxing to gambling, and baseball frowned on agents of any kind, Landis was concerned. While DiMaggio was able to reassure Landis about his relationship to Gould, the incident and subsequent investigation by the press may have contributed to Joe's slow start.

The Yankees started playing better in June, and by the All-Star break were only 6½ games out of first. The Classic was played on July 9 at St. Louis's Sportsman's Park, and DiMaggio started in center field. He went an undistinguished 0 for 4 as the NL shut out the American League 4–0.

Keyed by the addition of rookie pitcher Ernie Bonham, the Yankees finally went on a tear in August, winning 21 and losing only three from August 9 to September 3 to surge into the pennant race. But they couldn't keep up the pace, or catch Cleveland or Detroit. DiMaggio provided the offense during the streak, despite pulling a muscle while running out a game-winning ninth-inning triple against Cleveland on August 24 and missing nearly a week. He keyed a comeback win against St. Louis with a pinch-hit, three-run home run with two outs in the ninth on August 29. It wasn't enough. The Yankees briefly crept into first place by half a game on September 11, beating Cleveland in the first game of a doubleheader, then lost the second game and never regained the lead. New York finished the 1940 season in third place, a game behind Cleveland and two games behind Detroit.

Despite the Yankees' disappointing finish, DiMaggio had another good year; he won his second batting title with a .352 batting average, with 31 home runs and 133 RBI in only 132 games. He finished third in MVP voting to Hank Greenberg and Bob Feller. Still, for the first time in six seasons, one with San Francisco and five with New York, a team led by DiMaggio wasn't playing, let alone winning, a postseason series. For once, Joe DiMaggio had October off.

The Streak and the Emergence of an American Hero: 1941

D iMaggio began the 1941 season not only as baseball's best active player, but perhaps as baseball's best and most complete player to that date, a characterization that is not given lightly. In his first five seasons, averaging only 137 games per year due to injuries, his seasonal average was .343, sixth best all-time, with 33 home runs, 138 RBI, 123 runs scored, 194 hits, 12 triples, 34 doubles, 52 walks, and only 29 strikeouts. On average, in every game he played he was on base twice, collected three total bases, scored a run and knocked one in. His total of 168 home runs already placed him among the top-twenty list all-time. If he didn't hit for the average of Cobb or the power of Ruth, his combined achievement in both categories elicited comparisons to both.

Yet unlike Ruth and Cobb, DiMaggio was a right-handed hitter. As such, he was at a distinct disadvantage due to the predominance of right-handed pitching, and he played in a stadium that robbed him of power production. Of all other right-handed hitters, only Rogers Hornsby and Jimmie Foxx had previously demonstrated the ability to hit consistently for both a high average and power, but each had played in ballparks far more forgiving than Yankee Stadium, and both

DiMaggio's perfect batting form is captured in this game against Cleveland during his record-setting hitting streak. (Photograph courtesy of Mike Andersen)

In 1942, Ted Williams and Joe DiMaggio basked in the glory of the feats of the previous season while contemplating an inevitable interruption of their careers due to war. (Photograph from Transcendental Graphics, Mark Rucker)

lacked the combination of other skills DiMaggio had. DiMaggio was widely acknowledged to be one of the best outfielders in baseball. His baserunning ability, despite his lack of stolen bases, was obvious.

The fact that he played for the Yankees, in the nation's media capital, ensured that those accomplishments were not overlooked. Neither were they tainted by the bluster of boosterism. The New York press was becoming almost blasé about their star. What was left to say or write about Joe DiMaggio? After DiMaggio joined the Yankees the club won four straight pennants, by an average of almost 15 games, and four straight World Series, losing in the fall classic only three times in nineteen games. Even including the 1940 season, in DiMaggio's first five seasons, the Yankees' average record was a gaudy 99–53, a standard better than any five consecutive Yankee season records when the club included either Ruth, Gehrig, or both.

The performance was unprecedented in the modern era of baseball history. No player, from the moment he stepped onto the field for his first major league game, had been so proficient at the five baseball skills. Even including the Yankees' third-place finish of 1940, no team had ever been so good for so long.

To be certain, it helped that DiMaggio was surrounded by an outstanding supporting cast, but even among such luminaries as Lou Gehrig, Bill Dickey, Joe Gordon, Tommy Henrich, and Charlie Keller, DiMaggio's star still shone brightest. His Yankee teammates, his fans,

His hitting streak stood at 53 games when this photo of DiMaggio in his flip-up sunglasses appeared in July 1941. (Associated Press photograph)

and everyone else in baseball expected no less than the extraordinary to crack from DiMaggio's bat, gather in his glove, and flow through his golden right arm. But no one was prepared for the magic of the 1941 season, except, perhaps, DiMaggio himself. He had already been through it once before.

His achievements in 1941 would do much to create his lasting reputation. It helped that for the first time there was a challenger to DiMaggio's crown, another player whose performance and talent caused some to compare him with DiMaggio. Beginning in 1939, Boston's

Dom DiMaggio entertains the media by shoveling snow at Fenway Park. Note the advertising signs on the left-field wall. (Photograph by Dick Thompson, courtesy of The Sports Museum of New England)

Dom DiMaggio was considered nearly the equal of his brother Joe as a fielder and thrower. This photo, taken at Fenway Park in 1940, displayed the agility of the youngest DiMaggio brother. (Photograph by Dick Thompson, courtesy of The Sports Museum of New England)

Ted Williams had emerged as another great, young, precocious batsman who hit for both average and power from the moment he came into the league, and Williams did so at an even younger age than DiMaggio. While Williams didn't share in the bounty of DiMaggio's other skills, he was, at the very least, in the same class as a hitter.

Beginning in the 1941 season, the careers of Ted Williams and Joe DiMaggio would be curiously joined, like opposite poles of a powerful magnet, around which a nation of baseball fans gathered in wonder. In comparison to the other, the skills, and sometimes the failure, of each was brought into sharper focus. The public's continuing preoccupation with each player is due in part to the other. For at no other time in the history of baseball have two such magnificent hitters starred, for so long, and as such bitter rivals, in such heated contests for pennants and personal honors. Their individual battles and those of their two teams fired the imagination of the baseball world for much of the next decade and invited endless comparisons. What if Joe had played with Dom? What if Ted had enjoyed DiMaggio's surrounding cast? What if Joe had remained healthy? What if Ted had suffered DiMaggio's injuries?

Each man performed in a ballpark that seemed ideally suited for the other, and each possessed a personality that seemed more appropriate to the other's adopted city. In New York, DiMaggio's pronounced stoicism sometimes left him taken for granted. In Boston, Williams's tempestuous nature made him the occasional object of ridicule. The Boston press salivated over DiMaggio's intangible impact on a team. Their desire even led them to boost brother Dom as his equal. The New York press reveled in Williams's "color" and would have turned him into the equal of Babe Ruth.

In any dictionary of American baseball, under "1941" the definition should simply read "1: Fifty-six and .406. see also DiMaggio, Joe; and Williams, Ted." In that season their deeds eclipsed all others.

Nineteen forty-one was a year of great change. The Depression was over, but the war in Europe threatened to spread across the globe. Baseball was just beginning to feel the impact of the impending strife, as a trickle of players left the game for military service. Yet the 1941 season was still almost immune to the growing conflict.

DiMaggio spent much of the off-season in San Francisco with Dorothy. As usual, he returned the Yankees' first contract offer, which called for the same salary he earned in 1940. He wasn't worried, as many other players were, about being drafted. His marriage earned him Class 3 status, still exempt from service. The Yankees began

Ted Williams and Joe Di-Maggio are shown at Fen-way Park prior to a game in 1941. (Les Jones photo-graph courtesy of the Boston Public Library)

spring training without him, but on March 6 DiMaggio and Ed Barrow finally agreed to a contract worth $35,000. DiMaggio and Dorothy then drove to Florida. Joe even picked up a speeding ticket along the way.

The Yankees' third-place finish in 1940 caused manager Joe McCarthy to shake up his lineup. Shortstop Frank Crosetti, who had hit only .194, was moved into a backup role and replaced by rookie Phil Rizzuto, 1940 minor league Player of the Year. The Yankees traded away first baseman Babe Dahlgren and experimented with second baseman Joe Gordon at first. Another rookie, slick-fielding Gerry Priddy, supplanted Gordon at second. Tommy Henrich ended a long apprenticeship and replaced George Selkirk in the outfield. The pitching staff was basically unchanged, but received a boost by the return of Lefty Gomez, who had missed most of 1940 with a sore arm.

DiMaggio got off to a great start. After hitting in all nineteen exhibition games in which he played, he opened the season by hitting over .500 in the Yankees' first eight games. If one considered the previous year's World Series and the exhibition season, DiMaggio had hit in 31 consecutive games.

The Yankees stumbled a bit at the beginning of the season, winning only two of their first five, before taking off to win seven of eight. Then

Mr. and Mrs. Joe DiMaggio arrive at the Yankees' spring training camp in St. Petersburg, Florida, in March 1940. (Photograph courtesy of the *Boston Globe*)

DiMaggio went into into the worst slump of his major league career. From April 22, when he went hitless against junkball pitcher Lester Mc-Crabb of the Athletics, through May 14, DiMaggio hit only .194. His average tumbled from above .500 to .306. The only DiMaggio listed among the league leaders was brother Dominic, hitting just under .400 for the Red Sox.

As DiMaggio slumped, so did the Yankees. They won only four games in the first two weeks of May and fell to 14–13 on May 14, barely good enough for fourth place. Priddy wasn't hitting at all, Rizzuto was slumping, Gordon was uncomfortable and a defensive liability at first base, and the pitching was inconsistent. Manager Joe McCarthy was on edge; he wasn't used to losing. The Indians were streaking, and Boston was much improved. The Yankees were in free-fall and appeared lost.

But they still had DiMaggio. Once before in his baseball career DiMaggio had endured similar collapse. In his first full season with the San Francisco Seals, beginning on May 14, 1933, he went a pitiful 6 for 48 over twelve games, a slump that threatened to end his professional baseball career. But DiMaggio emerged from that lapse to embark on his PCL-record 61-game hitting streak. Incredibly, this slump would end with a similar streak, one perhaps even more extraordinary.

In his column in the *World-Telegram* on the morning of May 15, Dan Daniel, perhaps thinking of DiMaggio's earlier slump, made a prescient comment. "Slumps are overcome suddenly," he wrote, "and once the bellwether shows the way, a whole club will often follow him. It is possible when DiMaggio begins to hit again he will pull the other Yankees with him."

This situation was radically different. DiMaggio had been a minor league rookie in 1933. Now, he was the man the Yankees looked to for leadership. The concept of responsibility was one that DiMaggio was keenly aware of off the field as well. Dorothy was pregnant.

In 1933, with his baseball future hanging precariously in the balance, Joe had responded. Now, although his own status was secure, everyone expected DiMaggio to end not only his slump but that of the entire Yankee team. Again, Joe responded.

On May 15, the Yankees lost to the White Sox, 13–1, for their fifth straight defeat, leading Robert Cooke in the *Herald Tribune* to open his game story with the comment "The New York Yankees, who are currently going downhill at a great rate in the American League pennant race, continued their non-stop flight toward the second division

. . . the Yankees floundered before the crowd of 9,040 as though they were playing in complete privacy."

DiMaggio himself opened the gates to the White Sox win in the first inning. Chicago's Billy Knickerbocker, the same man who tried to goad DiMaggio into a fight five years before, singled, then Luke Appling followed with another single. DiMaggio charged the ball, and Knickerbocker decided to test DiMaggio's arm. DiMaggio's throw caromed off Knickerbocker's arm and he scored, Appling moving to third and eventually scoring himself on a sacrifice fly, giving the White Sox the only two runs they needed. DiMaggio was charged with an error, but the miscue may have woken him from his slump.

In the Yankee half of the first, Phil Rizzuto doubled off White Sox left-hander Edgar Smith. Then DiMaggio, hitless in his last two games, drove in Rizzuto with a solid single to center. Although the hit scored the last Yankee run for the day, DiMaggio was not finished. In two subsequent at bats he smashed the ball to third, where Dario Lodigiani, his old North Beach teammate, backhanded one behind the bag and deflected the other to Appling at short. DiMaggio was out on each play, but now he was turning on the ball and hitting it hard.

The next day McCarthy shook up his lineup again, sitting down Rizzuto and Priddy, moving Gordon back to second, and installing Crosetti at short and rookie Johnny Sturm at first. DiMaggio continued to hit the ball hard, homering into the left-field bleachers at Yankee Stadium in the first inning and tripling off the left-field fence in the ninth to key a Yankee comeback for a 6–5 win.

But the Yankees dropped two of the next three. DiMaggio managed hits in each game, even going 3 for 3 in a 12–2 win over St. Louis on May 18. But his perfect day at the plate was not without a struggle. According to the *Herald Tribune*, "DiMaggio was credited with three hits on drives that were manhandled by fielders," yet he received the benefit of the doubt from the scorekeeper. Had such a thing taken place later in the streak, he'd likely have faced criticism, but thus far DiMaggio's streak was only a modest four games and escaped notice.

The Yankees turned a corner on May 20 against St. Louis. New York fell behind early, rallied to take the lead, then fell behind again, trailing 8–6 after St. Louis scored three times in the top of the eighth. In the bottom of the inning, DiMaggio, hitless so far, stroked a leadoff single, then scored on Dickey's three-run homer. The Browns tied the game in the ninth, but the Yankees came back again to win 10–9 as Henrich scored all the way from second on a play at first.

The victory keyed a five-game Yankee winning streak, not including a 9–9 tie against Boston on May 23 in a game called because of darkness. The contest counted statistically, and DiMaggio's eighth-inning single stretched his hit streak to nine games. The Yankees climbed to third place.

DiMaggio's streak reached ten games the next day. In the sixth inning, Dominic DiMaggio, playing center field for Boston, twisted and turned under Joe's deep fly before dropping it for an error. (Joe DiMaggio would later mistakenly credit his brother with making a catch on a similar play in game 44 of the streak, when in fact no such play ever took place.) DiMaggio singled in the seventh to keep the streak alive.

Oddly, DiMaggio's streak was not reported in the press even after it reached double figures, although the shorter streaks of other Yankees were noted. On May 25, both Johnny Sturm and Frank Crosetti hit in their ninth straight contest, coinciding with their addition to the starting lineup. In previous years DiMaggio had routinely hit in streaks of eight or ten or twelve games. His performance wasn't news.

DiMaggio's streak ended the next day—sort of. But the game didn't count. The Yankees traveled to Norfolk, Virginia, and played an exhibition against their Class B farm club, the Norfolk Tars. The Yankees

"Baseball isn't statistics, it's Joe DiMaggio rounding second base."—Jimmy Breslin, as quoted by Herb Caen in the San Francisco Chronicle, *June 3, 1975. Editor's note: Ditto for first base!* (Photograph from Bettmann Archives)

came from behind to win, 7–4, as Tar pitcher Jimmy Halperin pitched six effective innings before being rocked in the seventh. DiMaggio played only the first seven innings, walking once and popping out twice. Halperin, who never played an inning in the major leagues, nevertheless managed to do something no pitcher in the American League would be able to accomplish for most of the summer.

DiMaggio's streak finally received a brief mention in the *New York World Telegram* on May 29, the first mention of the streak in the press. The same day, the Yankees played Washington and earned their second tie in a week. With the score knotted 2–2 after five innings, the Yankees exploded for five runs in the top of the sixth. But as the Yankees rallied, a storm washed out the game, wiping out the sixth inning and resulting in a tie. The sudden storm stopped Johnny Sturm's streak at 11 games, erasing his sixth-inning single. DiMaggio also lost a hit to the weather, but he had already run his streak to 14 games while beating out an infield hit in the fourth inning.

The Yankees next traveled to Boston for a Memorial Day doubleheader. In the midst of what would be considered his greatest accomplishment, Joe DiMaggio had his worst day as a major leaguer.

The Yankees lost both games, dropping the first 4–3 as a ninth-inning rally fell one run short, and getting crushed in game two, 13–0. DiMaggio managed a single in the ninth inning of game one, and a double in game two that outfielder Pete Fox lost in the sun in right field. Bothered by a cold and a stiff neck, Joe was atrocious in the field. In the eighth inning of game one, he dropped an easy fly ball, and in the first inning of game two, he muffed Ted Williams's single and threw a ball into the stands for two more errors. Later in the game, he threw another ball to the Fenway fans, his third error of the game and fourth of the day. The total was equal to the number of errors he made the rest of the season. Nevertheless, his streak had reached 16 games.

Ted Williams extended a streak of his own in the doubleheader. Also beginning on May 15, Williams had now hit in 17 consecutive games, batting an unreal .510 for a season average of .429, nearly sixty points ahead of Bill Dickey, second in the American League, and 98 points ahead of DiMaggio. Despite his streak, DiMaggio's average had risen less than thirty points. He was hitting only .331.

Although DiMaggio's streak was previously mentioned in passing in the press, it was not until he collected hits in both ends of a doubleheader sweep against Cleveland on the first day of June that anyone really took notice of his accomplishment. Rud Rennie, of the *Herald*

Tribune, was the first writer to give a daily update on DiMaggio's streak in his game story. Until then, the Yankees' resurgence after McCarthy's lineup changes and the batting streaks of DiMaggio's teammates had been the story. But now that the other streaks were over, DiMaggio's took center stage. As it did, writers began to look back at the Yankee record since the streak began on May 15. Correctly or not, DiMaggio soon received credit for the turnaround.

Beginning on June 2, the Yanks lost three in a row, yet still clung to third place with a record of 25–21, 3½ games behind Cleveland and 2½ games behind Chicago. The slump was understandable. Lou Gehrig died on June 2.

Before the Yankees played in Detroit on June 3, in the same ballpark where Gehrig had taken himself out of the lineup just over two years before and ended his consecutive-game streak at 2,130, the players stood somberly on the field for a moment of silence. After the 4–2 loss, manager Joe McCarthy and Bill Dickey left for Gehrig's funeral in New York. The rest of the Yankees remained in Detroit, and were rained out as Gehrig was laid to rest. Although DiMaggio remained with his teammates, his wife attended the services at Christ Protestant Episcopal Church in New York. Gehrig's illness had weighed heavily on the ballclub, and his passing, while saddening all who knew him, was seen as Gehrig's final relief from terrible suffering. Just as the

DiMaggio is pictured here in the game against the Washington Senators in which he broke George Sisler's American League record for consecutive games with a hit. The game of June 29, 1941, marked DiMaggio's 42nd straight game with at least a hit. (Photograph from the National Baseball Library & Archive, Cooperstown, N.Y.)

Yankees had responded with a streak of wins when Gehrig took himself out of the lineup in May of 1939, they now embarked on a similar tear.

Beginning on June 7, the Yankees won 41 of their next 47 games. Joe DiMaggio hit safely in all but one of those contests. He may not have been the reason for the Yankee's earlier turnaround, but he was certainly the determining factor in the club's record after Gehrig's death. His performance over the next six weeks spoke as eloquently as any eulogy for his teammate.

DiMaggio keyed the first win of the streak. In St. Louis, the Yankees took a 6–1 lead over the Browns on Charlie Keller's third-inning grand slam but couldn't hold on. Trailing 6–4 in the eighth, the Browns tied the game at six on pinch hitter Walt Judnich's two-run home run, then loaded the bases with none out. Roy Cullenbine drove a deep fly to center field to put the Browns up 7–6, but DiMaggio snuffed the rally by nailing George McQuinn going to third for a double play.

Rolfe singled and Henrich doubled him home to tie the score in the ninth. Then DiMaggio, who already had two singles to his credit, beat out an infield hit. The Yankees went on to score four more times and win by the score of 11–7.

DiMaggio's streak was at 22, and for the first time, he was stinging the ball. His teammates followed suit. On June 8, Joe accounted for four of the Yankees' 19 extra-base hits as New York swept St. Louis, 9–3 and 8–3. DiMaggio knocked in seven runs for the day and hit three home runs, the last over the right-field roof of Sportsman's Park.

Meanwhile, Ted Williams went hitless in the Red Sox doubleheader sweep of Chicago. His streak was over at 18 games, the longest of his career. Although Williams was hitting well over .400, with almost four months left in the season there was as yet little speculation he might hit .400. Attention turned toward DiMaggio.

The timing was perfect. Williams's streak ended just as the Yankees took off. With DiMaggio hitting in every game, the Yankees ripped off eight wins in a row. With each game, Joe received more attention, as writers took note of the Yankees' surge and DiMaggio's relentless drive to the record book.

On June 14 in New York, the Yanks halted first-place Cleveland's winning streak at six with a 4–1 win over Bob Feller. DiMaggio ran his streak to 27 and knocked in the winning run in the second. Henrich singled, and with the count 3–0, McCarthy gave DiMaggio the green light against Feller. DiMaggio always hit Feller well and did so again, stroking a double. When the Yankees edged Cleveland 3–2 the next day, DiMaggio's third-inning home run to the upper tier of the left-field balcony at Yankee Stadium was the difference. The Yanks beat Cleveland for the third straight time on June 16, 6–4, as DiMaggio contributed a double and ran his streak to 29, tying the Yankees' team record set by Roger Peckinpaugh in 1919 and Earle Combs in 1931.

DiMaggio broke the record the next day against Chicago, the same team he had started the streak against a month before. DiMaggio was hitless when he came to bat in the seventh, and grounded to White Sox shortstop Luke Appling. The ball took a bad hop and bounced off Appling's shoulder. Official scorekeeper Dan Daniel signaled a hit, and the record was DiMaggio's. He narrowly missed winning the game and collecting another hit in the ninth when Chicago outfielder Taft Wright snagged his drive over the low fence in left field. As it was, the White Sox halted the Yankee win streak with an 8–7 win on Myril Hoag's ninth-inning single. On the same day, Phil Rizzuto had replaced Frank Crosetti in the starting lineup.

The Yankees lost to Chicago the following day, 3–2, as DiMaggio returned Appling's favor and overran Appling's second-inning fly ball, leading to a Chicago run. But Appling also helped DiMaggio by failing to pick up his hard ground ball, which Daniel again scored as a hit, to

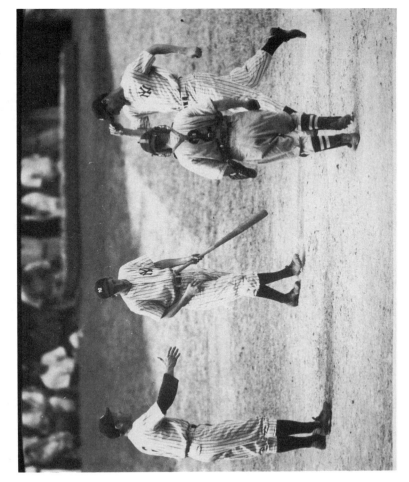

Joe DiMaggio tips his cap as his home run in game 45 of his 1941 consecutive-game hitting streak sets a new major league record. The old mark of 44 was held by Willie Keeler.   (Photograph from Transcendental Graphics, Mark Rucker)

run DiMaggio's skein to 31. Another streak continued as Charlie Keller homered for New York, marking the 14th game in a row a Yankee had hit a home run.

Daniel's role in extending the streak in games 30 and 31 has since been the subject of much criticism. While it is true that Daniel was DiMaggio's friend and that both hits could have gone either way, had DiMaggio not run his streak to the eventual 56 games, Daniel's calls would never have been questioned. Only DiMaggio's later accomplishments brought the calls under scrutiny.

The Yankees got back on track against the White Sox on June 19 with a 7–2 win. DiMaggio went 3 for 3, including a home run. The press now set sight on DiMaggio's pursuit of George Sisler's major-league-record 41-game hitting streak.

On June 20, DiMaggio got hits his first four at bats as the Yankees played host to Detroit on June 20, boosting his average to .354 with his seventh consecutive safety. The Yanks bombed the Tigers, 14–4. In the second game of the series, DiMaggio's first-inning single knocked in a run and helped New York beat Detroit, 7–3, but the big hit was Phil Rizzuto's seventh-inning home run, only the second of his career, which tied a major-league record as it marked the 19th consecutive game in which a Yankee had hit a home run.

DiMaggio continued his streak and broke the record the next day with a sixth-inning home run, his 15th, then helped win the game with a ninth-inning double as the Yankees scored twice to win, 5–4.

As DiMaggio approached Sisler's mark, his streak took on the character that has since dominated virtually every account of DiMaggio's pursuit. Only in its last weeks did the streak become something of an American obsession, for now DiMaggio was doing something wholly remarkable, testing the Fates, pushing the envelope of belief. Conversations around the country started with the question "Did he get one today?", and only now did the streak become the occasional topic of radio broadcasts and sandlot speculation. Behind each question was the knowledge that DiMaggio was destined to fail eventually. But to discover that fate had been put off for one more day made all things, for a moment anyway, seem possible.

The focus on DiMaggio increased in intensity. Soon, his every appearance was promoted like a prizefight. In a few weeks a popular song, "Joltin' Joe DiMaggio," was recorded by bandleader Les Brown and played on the radio.

Following a Yankee off day, columnist Richards Vidmer took stock of DiMaggio in the Herald Tribune on June 24, offering "Pals for performance—To Joe DiMaggio . . . who was being overshadowed by the spring sprinting of his brother Dom . . . Through the last month and more he has been hitting against every team he has faced, swinging the war club with a steady beat . . ." But Vidmer also took notice that it was not just Sisler's mark that stood before DiMaggio, but Wee Willie Keeler's 44-game streak set in 1896 when foul balls didn't count as strikes. DiMaggio's task would be just a little tougher.

Later that day, St. Louis Browns pitcher Bob Muncrief retired DiMaggio in his first three plate appearances, the last on a deep drive to left that caused Tommy Henrich to be doubled off base. In the eighth, with the Yankees leading 4–0, Henrich cracked a two-run homer, clearing the bases for DiMaggio. Muncrief pitched carefully. Joe worked the count to 2 balls and 1 strike, then slammed a line single to left, starting another rally that led to three more Yankee runs in the eventual 9–1 win. After the game, St. Louis manager Luke Sewell asked Muncrief why he hadn't walked DiMaggio. A weary Muncrief reportedly replied, "That wouldn't have been fair, either to him or me. Hell, he's the greatest player I ever saw."

On June 25, DiMaggio homered in the fourth inning to lead New York to a 7–5 win over the Browns and run the streak to 37 games. Moreover, the Red Sox beat the Indians, and for the first time since April, the Yankees were in first place.

DiMaggio had another exercise in brinkmanship the next day. The Browns' Eldon Auker again held DiMaggio hitless in his first three at bats. His first time up, McCarthy let Joe swing with the count 3 and 0 and DiMaggio flied to left, and in his second at bat, with the count 3 and 2, DiMaggio grounded ball four sharply to second baseman Johnny Berardino, who muffed it. Joe's teammates stepped from the dugout and looked up to the press box, awaiting the call from official scorer Dan Daniel. But this time DiMaggio received no assistance from the scorekeeper, who ruled the hit an error. In his next appearance, in the sixth, DiMaggio grounded to third.

With the top of the order due up in the eighth and the Yankees leading 3–1, DiMaggio, hitting cleanup as usual, needed help to get another at bat. Leadoff man Johnny Sturm popped up, but Red Rolfe worked Auker for a walk. Tommy Henrich came to bat, and DiMaggio waited on deck.

Henrich knew that if he hit into a double play, DiMaggio's streak was likely over. He stepped away from the batter's box, returned to the Yankee dugout, and asked McCarthy if he could bunt. The manager thought for a moment, weighing the strategy, then agreed. The

Yankees were only up by two, and the way DiMaggio was hitting, if Rolfe made it to second there was a good chance DiMaggio could bring him in. Besides, DiMaggio deserved every chance he could get.

Henrich bunted foul in his first attempt, and the New York crowd, now aware of what was happening, started to roar. Rolfe took off on the next pitch, and Henrich pushed the ball to first baseman George McQuinn, who fielded the ball and had no choice but to step on first. DiMaggio had one more chance.

He swung at Auker's first pitch and knocked it into the left-field gap for a double, driving in Rolfe. The Yankees won, 4–1.

The streak was still intact at 39 when the Yankees played in Philadelphia and faced A's pitcher Johnny Babich on June 28. In 1940, Babich had beaten New York five times and earned a reputation as something of a Yankee-killer. Before the game Babich passed word to the Yankees that he didn't intend to give DiMaggio anything good to hit.

Babich's pronouncement may have been inspired by events that took place some eight years earlier. Babich, pitching for the Missions against his old teammates on the Seals, had faced DiMaggio in the 19th game of DiMaggio's 61-game streak. On that day, Babich came close to ending DiMaggio's streak. He held Joe hitless into the eighth and was working on a shutout when Joe extended his streak and knocked in the only run of the game with a triple, making a loser of Babich. This time, Babich hoped for a different outcome. Revenge would be sweet.

Babich was true to his word. When Joe came to bat in the fourth inning, Babich threw three quick balls. But McCarthy gave DiMaggio the go-ahead to swing. Babich's fourth pitch was wide, but DiMaggio, looking for a ball off the plate, reached out and drove the ball straight back at the pitcher, nearly castrating him. Then DiMaggio added to the insult by stretching the hit into a double. He later collected another hit as the Yankees won, 7–4.

The streak was at 40, and Sisler's mark within reach, when the Yankees faced the Senators in a doubleheader in Washington on June 29. DiMaggio drew 31,000 fans to Griffith Stadium as he tied the mark in the sixth inning of game one, smacking a fastball from Washington pitcher Dutch Leonard into the gap in left center for a double. The Senators lost, 9–4, but few fans in Griffith Stadium cared. They were there to see DiMaggio.

One fan, in particular, set his sights on Joe. Between games, the anonymous Newark, New Jersey native slipped into the Yankee dugout and disappeared into the crowd with DiMaggio's bat. DiMaggio tried to downplay the theft, but his teammates knew he was upset. While no more superstitious than most ballplayers, DiMaggio still had his affectations, like stepping on second base while running on and off the field. More than anything else, the theft threatened to break his concentration.

DiMaggio borrowed a bat from Tommy Henrich, who had, in fact, borrowed the same bat from DiMaggio in the first place. In the seventh inning, DiMaggio broke the record, lining a clean single to left off pitcher Red Anderson. After the game, DiMaggio called the lost bat "just a piece of wood," but he was clearly happy to break Sisler's mark, admitting, "I wanted that record."

With the Yankees clinging to a two-game lead over stubborn Cleveland, Willie Keeler's 44-game record provided DiMaggio's next challenge. DiMaggio later claimed to be ignorant of Keeler's record when he broke Sisler's mark, but it had been mentioned in the press much of the previous week.

The Red Sox, only five games behind the Yankees, came to the stadium for a doubleheader on July 1. Over 52,000 fans, the largest of the season, packed Yankee Stadium to witness history. In the first game, a replay of the 9–9 tie of May 23, the Yankees won 7–2. In his first two at bats, DiMaggio was put out easily, but in his third time up, against relief pitcher Mike Ryba, DiMaggio grounded the ball to third

DiMaggio is hoisted on the shoulders of teammates Tiny Bonham (l) and Tommy Henrich (r) following his record-setting 45th game in his hitting streak that would stretch to 56 games. DiMaggio hit a home run for his only hit in five at bats as the Yankees beat the Red Sox by a score of 8–4.   (Wide World photograph)

baseman Jim Tabor. Tabor dropped the ball, then rushed his throw to first. The ball eluded first baseman Lou Finney and DiMaggio was safe. Up in the press box Dan Daniel signaled a hit, but many in the crowd missed the call. At the time, hit or error calls were not reflected on the scoreboard. Daniel was later criticized for the call. In an interview with Jerome Holtzman, Daniel later recalled that while he "scored about twenty-one games during DiMaggio's streak . . . there wasn't a hit he wasn't entitled to. I never favored him one iota and made him get his hits as I saw them." DiMaggio rendered the potential controversy moot when he singled cleanly off Ryba in his next at bat, earning a five-minute ovation from the crowd.

One streak did end in game one. For the first time in twenty-six games, since June 1, no Yankee hit a home run. During the streak they'd smacked 40 round-trippers—10 by DiMaggio—and won 18 games, losing only 7.

DiMaggio tied Keeler in game two. In the first inning against Jack Wilson he drove a single over Joe Cronin's head. The Yankees went on to score three runs and romp to a 9–2 win in five innings; the game was cut short by rain, and then darkness. Two errors by Ted Williams proved critical in the Red Sox loss. The Yankee victories dealt a serious blow to Boston's pennant hopes.

Keeler's record fell in the fifth inning the next day when DiMaggio unloaded his 18th home run of the year in the fifth off Dick Newsom, leading New York to an 8–4 win, dropping the Red Sox eight games off the pace and increasing the Yankee lead over Cleveland to three games. After the game, Lefty Gomez quipped, in reference to Keeler's maxim to "Hit 'em where they ain't," that "Joe hit one today where they ain't."

The streak was at 45 games, and in his first head-to-head matchup with Ted Williams in a series that meant anything, DiMaggio retained title over the young star, going 4 for 12, knocking in four runs, scoring three times, and leading his team to a sweep. Williams went 3 for 7, but with only two runs scored, no RBI, and no extra-base hits in the three Red Sox losses. After the game, even Williams seemed to admit he was not yet at DiMaggio's level. He marveled at the Yankee star, saying, "I really wish I could hit like that guy Joe DiMaggio."

DiMaggio was now in uncharted territory, on his way to a place where no other major league player, in any era, under any conditions, had gone before. Yet, no one was more prepared than he for the drama of the next several weeks, since only DiMaggio had hit in so many games and knew what it was like trying to extend such a record.

Cartoonist Willard Mullin captures one of the great moments of the 1941 season as DiMaggio greets Ted Williams at home plate at Briggs Stadium following the Red Sox slugger's dramatic game-winning homer in the All-Star Game. (Courtesy of The Sports Museum of New England)

Now the press began to recognize that DiMaggio was approaching his own personal record of hitting in 61 consecutive games, a magical number that threatened to supplant, by one, the mystical numerology of Babe Ruth's home-run record of 60. Oddly, DiMaggio's earlier hit skein received only cursory mention through most of his current streak. While it had been big news upon DiMaggio's arrival in New York six years earlier, his subsequent accomplishments had pushed it into the deeper recesses of memory. Few observers bothered to note that DiMaggio had been through all this before. He was in competition only with himself.

After an off day, the Yankees and Washington were rained out twice, giving DiMaggio a chance to rest. Now the pressure of the streak really took hold, and over the next two weeks much occurred that ended up part of the DiMaggio legend.

The Yankees played host to Philadelphia for three games before the All-Star break, and DiMaggio was on fire. He had reason to be. His bat had been returned.

After the theft DiMaggio had put the word out that he wanted it back. The thief apparently bragged of his take to his buddies in Newark, and before long a friend of DiMaggio's located the bat. A small ransom was paid. A courier delivered the bat to DiMaggio before the game on July 5, and he used it to homer on the first pitch he saw as the Yankees won 10–5.

In a doubleheader on July 6, as the Yankees honored Lou Gehrig and unveiled his monument in left-center field, DiMaggio upped the streak to 48 games. He went a combined 6 for 9, including a double and triple, and knocked in three runs as the Yankees won their eighth and ninth games in a row, 8–4 and 3–1.

DiMaggio didn't need a base hit in the All-Star Game to extend the streak. Like the exhibition game some six weeks before, his All-Star performance wouldn't count. But fans took the All-Star game seriously. Had Joe failed to get a hit, then extended the streak, the record would have lost considerable luster.

Before the game, played in Detroit's Briggs Stadium on July 8, DiMaggio quashed a rumor that he'd been hurt in an automobile accident. He came to bat in the first inning and popped out off Brooklyn pitcher Whitlow Wyatt. In the fourth, with the game scoreless, Cecil Travis doubled for the American League. DiMaggio came to bat against Paul Derringer and brought the crowd to its feet with a long drive to the deepest part of center field, but Pete Reiser pulled the drive down after a long run. Then Ted Williams doubled to right to score Travis and give the AL a 1–0 lead.

The National League tied the game in the top of the sixth. With one out, DiMaggio worked a rare walk. Williams flied out, then Jeff Heath walked, moving DiMaggio to second. Lou Boudreau singled to center, and when Reiser muffed the play, Joe came around to score and give the AL a 2–1 lead.

In the seventh, Arky Vaughan of the NL hit a home run to put the NL ahead 3–2. The AL failed to score, and in the eighth Vaughan hit another two-run homer and the NL lead increased to three. In the bottom of the eighth, with one out, DiMaggio doubled.

Williams then struck out and endured the jeers of the Detroit fans. But Dominic DiMaggio drove his brother home with a hit.

The score was still 5–3 when the American League came to bat in the ninth. With one out, Ken Keltner and Joe Gordon singled before Cecil Travis walked to load the bases for DiMaggio. The setting was perfect. He had already scored twice and now had the opportunity to cap his amazing first half of the season by winning the game for the American League.

Cub pitcher Claude Passeau got two quick strikes on DiMaggio. But Joe, the hero of the moment, became goat. He swung at the next pitch and bounced a perfect double play ball to National League shortstop Eddie Miller, who flipped the ball to Billy Herman at second as the crowd at Briggs Stadium started to rise and head home.

But Cecil Travis surprised Herman by going into second hard and breaking up the double play. Keltner scored and DiMaggio reached first. Ted Williams stepped to the plate, still wearing goat horns and hearing about it for his eighth-inning strikeout.

It was Williams who turned hero. He smashed a Passeau pitch deep

Joe DiMaggio collects an infield single to extend his consecutive-game hitting streak to 49 games on July 10, 1941. (Photograph from Transcendental Graphics, Mark Rucker)

into right field for a three-run home run to end the game, giving the American League a 7–5 win. It was a precious moment for Williams, and he fairly danced around the bases, jumping for joy and waving his arms. At the last possible instant, he'd one-upped DiMaggio, and for a day at least, Williams pushed DiMaggio off the headlines of sporting pages around the country. Ted's home run caused the press to take notice. DiMaggio had indeed hit in 48 straight games, but Williams was hitting .405. DiMaggio's .357 was only fourth best in the league.

DiMaggio resumed his relentless pursuit of history. He stretched the streak to 49 on July 10 versus St. Louis in his first at bat after the break by collecting an obvious hit on a ground ball in the hole that shortstop Alan Strange barely managed to knock down. The Yankees won the rain-shortened contest 1–0.

An interesting coincidence emerged. In 1933, the end of DiMaggio's streak was preceded by a series of games in which he collected single hits, many of them bobbled by shortstops, and some of questionable merit. On July 10, the pattern reappeared.

On July 11, DiMaggio increased the streak to 50 as the Yankees won their 11th in a row. Joe collected a hit in his first at bat for the fifth game in a row, and went on to collect three more, the last a home run off Jack Kramer, his 20th of the season. The next day, DiMaggio failed in his first at bat, then doubled off Eldon Auker his second time up to key a Yankee rally as New York went on to win 7–5, increasing the team's lead over Cleveland to five games. As the streak grew, so did the Yankee lead.

The Yanks next traveled to Chicago, and more than 50,000 fans turned out on Sunday, July 13, to see DiMaggio and the return of Chicago manager Jimmy Dykes who had recently been suspended for cursing out an umpire. DiMaggio singled off pitcher Ted Lyons in the second inning as Luke Appling muffed a ground ball. Joe collected another hit in the fourth and New York won for the twelfth straight time, 8–1. In game two, DiMaggio's only hit was a sixth-inning single off Thornton Lee, and the Yankees won in eleven, 1–0. The streak was at 53.

On July 14, the Yankees finally lost to Chicago, 7–1, but the pattern continued. In baseball parlance, Appling had been DiMaggio's "cousin" the day before. Today, it was Cub third baseman Bob Kennedy.

In the second inning, DiMaggio lofted a lazy fly behind second base. Billy Knickerbocker retreated, but the ball flopped out of his glove. DiMaggio stood on first, but the play was scored an error.

In a game at old League Park in Cleveland, Joe DiMaggio strokes one of tbe three bits be collected in tbe 56tb and final game of bis record-setting consecutive-game bitting streak. (Photograph from Transcendental Graphics, Mark Rucker)

Joe broke his bat on the swing. He'd already given away the replacement he'd borrowed from Henrich for use in a USO raffle in San Francisco. Using another bat, he walked in the fourth. In the sixth, he took a big swing at a pitch from the White Sox' Johnny Rigney, barely topping the ball, which rolled slowly down the third-base line. Bob Kennedy charged in, but DiMaggio easily made it to first. The hit pushed the streak to 54.

In the first inning of the final game of the series the next day, Joe grounded to Appling, who made yet another error. In the third, he hit the ball slowly to Appling's left. Both Appling and second baseman Knickerbocker dove for the bouncer behind second, but it squirted between them and the string was 55 games. DiMaggio later doubled, and New York won, 5–4.

The Yankees went to Cleveland for a three-game series leading the Indians by five games. New York had Cleveland on the ropes. Potentially, the 1941 American League pennant hung in the balance. Cleveland could ill afford to lose the series, and if they swept, they were back in the race.

The series was the most important played in Cleveland in years. The chance to stop the Yankees and DiMaggio had the entire city fired up. The Indians hadn't won a pennant since 1920. Before the series, the Indians upped their insurance policy on star pitcher Bob Feller, 18–4 so far in 1941, to $200,000.

The first game was played in Cleveland's League Park, where the Indians still played weekday home games. Cleveland pitcher Al Milnar had the task of trying to stop DiMaggio and the Yankees.

The drama concerning DiMaggio ended early. On the first day of the third month of his streak, DiMaggio came to bat in the first after two outs and a walk to Tommy Henrich. He singled sharply to center, sending Henrich to third and running the streak to 56 games. Joe Gordon, up next, smashed the ball to the Indians' Ken Keltner at third. Keltner ranged far behind third, backhanded the ball, and threw wide to first. Gordon slid around first baseman Hal Trosky's tag as Henrich scored easily.

DiMaggio went to second. Yankee catcher Buddy Rosar hit a ground ball to the right side that second baseman Ray Mack just managed to smother. Mack tried for the out at first, but Rosar beat the throw. DiMaggio just kept running, and a surprised Trosky threw home, but Joe slid around the tag to put New York up 2–0.

Cleveland scored single runs in the first and second off Yankee pitcher Atley Donald to tie the score. DiMaggio got another hit in the third on a single to center, then walked in the midst of New York's four-run rally in the fifth to put the game out of reach. In the ninth, DiMaggio doubled. He scored three runs in New York's 10–4 win, helping the Yankees increase their lead over Cleveland to six games.

The events of the next day, June 17, have since been retold a thousand times, from a thousand different perspectives, but always with the same result. Joe DiMaggio's hitting streak came to an end.

This game was played at night in Cleveland's enormous Municipal Stadium before 67,468 fans. A story says that when DiMaggio and Gomez took a cab to the ballpark, the cabbie told the men that today the streak would end, putting a hex on DiMaggio. Still another claims a shoeshine boy in the hotel lobby said the same thing, just to Gomez. No matter. It wasn't any hex or jinx that broke DiMaggio's streak. It was a matter of luck and the glove of Cleveland third baseman Ken Keltner.

The Yankees jumped out to a quick lead. In the first inning, after Johnny Sturm made an out, Red Rolfe singled off Cleveland left-hander Al Smith. Tommy Henrich cracked a double and the Yankees led 1–0.

Smith was struggling. He threw DiMaggio a curve in on his hands and DiMaggio pulled the ball sharply to third. Keltner, playing DiMaggio deep and to pull, backhanded the ball on the line and his momentum carried him into foul territory. DiMaggio had trouble getting out of the box, which was soft from rain the day before, and Keltner's long throw to Oscar Grimes at first just beat him.

DiMaggio next came to bat in the fourth, the score still 1–0 in the Yankees' favor. Keltner, taking note of the field conditions and DiMaggio's performance in the earlier at bat, inched back and closer to the line, figuring the soft ground of the base paths gave him that much more time. He also remembered a play he had made against DiMaggio six weeks before, when Joe hit one just off his glove toward the line. But Smith walked DiMaggio.

Cleveland tied the game in the bottom of the inning. In the seventh, DiMaggio faced Smith again. He again grounded to Keltner, who backhanded the ball, this time on a short hop, and gunned down DiMaggio. The plays were no matter of luck. Keltner was easily the best-fielding first baseman in the American League in 1941. Gordon followed with a home run to put New York ahead, 2–1.

DiMaggio came up for the final time in the eighth, after the Yankees had rallied to score twice and take the lead 4–1. With one out, the bases were loaded.

Cleveland manager Roger Peckinpaugh, whose Yankee record DiMaggio had broken, came out to the mound. Taking note of Joe's previous at bats against Smith, he waved right-handed pitcher Jim Bagby Jr. in from the bullpen. Bagby's father had starred for the Indians years before.

The hitting streak finally came to an end for DiMaggio on July 17, 1941, as the Cleveland Indians, sparked by fine fielding plays by Ken Keltner and Lou Boudreau, stopped the streak at 56 games. DiMaggio almost appears relieved as he signals twin zeros to indicate the streak's conclusion. (Associated Press photograph)

In 1941, Joe DiMaggio set his 56-consecutive-games hitting record, won the MVP Award, and led his Yankees to a world championship. (Photograph courtesy of the Boston Globe)

Eight years before, DiMaggio's 61-game streak had been stopped by the son of a former major league pitcher, Ed Walsh Jr., and now another pitcher's son had the task of trying to stop him.

DiMaggio took Bagby's first pitch for a ball, then swung viciously and missed, to even the count. The Cleveland crowd cheered madly, some in anticipation of seeing the streak stopped, some in the hope that the Indians could halt the Yankee rally, and some hoping to see DiMaggio's streak continue. No one in the crowd of more than 67,000 was indifferent. DiMaggio swung at the next pitch.

The ball bounded straight to Cleveland shortstop Lou Boudreau, who, incidentally, was celebrating his twenty-fourth birthday. At the last instant, the ball took a bad hop, but Boudreau snagged it at his chest, flipped to second baseman Ray Mack, and Mack gunned the ball to first baseman Oscar Grimes. DiMaggio was out, and the Yankee rally was over. New York still led, 4–1.

Joe's only chance to continue the streak rested in the hands of Yankee hitters in the ninth inning, or in Cleveland's powerful lineup in their last chance. Bagby, however, was equal to the task in the ninth and the Yankees failed to score.

In the bottom of the ninth inning, Lefty Gomez faltered. After giving up two singles, McCarthy replaced him with relief ace Johnny Murphy. Murphy gave up a triple to pinch hitter Larry Rosenthal that scored two and made the score 4–3.

If Rosenthal scored, the game would go to extra innings, potentially giving DiMaggio another at bat. The crowd was going crazy.

Pinch hitter Hal Trosky failed to plate Rosenthal as he grounded to Sturm at first. Then Soup Campbell bounced a shot to Murphy. Rosenthal inexplicably broke for home, and Murphy trapped him off base. Rosenthal was out, and Campbell made first.

DiMaggio's streak officially ended, not with a ground ball to Ken Keltner or a pitch from Jim Bagby, but on a weak ground ball from Roy Weatherly to Johnny Sturm, who stepped on first to end the game. New York won, 4–3, increasing the lead over Cleveland to seven games, but Joe DiMaggio's streak had ended at 56 games.

The Yankees entered the clubhouse after the game, happy with the win, but silent, waiting for DiMaggio's reaction. He finally cut the tension by commenting, "I'm glad it's over. Keltner was a little tough on me tonight." In Cleveland's clubhouse, Keltner was understandably disappointed in the loss, and snapped, "I hate to lose," but later took pride in his role in ending the streak. Immedi-

"I always try my hardest because there probably is a kid in the stands who is watching his first game." —Joe DiMaggio, as quoted on numerous occasions. (Photograph courtesy of Mike Andersen)

ately following the game, it was not Keltner who received attention from the press, anyway, but pitchers Smith and Bagby.

While DiMaggio was relieved, he wasn't particularly happy. He didn't want to leave the park by himself, and asked Phil Rizzuto to wait for him. After the two men walked in silence for several blocks, DiMaggio reached into his pocket. "Son of a bitch," he said, "I forgot my wallet. Phil, how much money have you got?" Rizzuto dug into his wallet and gave DiMaggio all his cash, eighteen dollars. DiMaggio turned to walk into a bar and Rizzuto started to follow, but DiMaggio put out his hand and told Rizzuto to go back to the hotel, saying, "I want to relax a bit." DiMaggio spent the evening drinking in a Cleveland tavern while word of the game spread across the country.

In Fenway Park as in every American League stadium, there was no autograph more coveted than that of Joe Di-Maggio. (Photograph from the Maxwell Collection)

The numbers tell only the partial story of DiMaggio's streak. From May 15, 1941, through July 16, 1941, DiMaggio hit .408 with 91 hits in 223 at bats. He scored 56 runs, drove in 55, hit 16 doubles, 4 triples, and 15 home runs. He walked 21 times and struck out only 5. Over the same time period, Ted Williams of Boston hit .412, but DiMaggio, by a slim margin, was more productive—Williams, playing in 55 games, hit 12 home runs, knocked in 50, and scored 61. Moreover, the Yankee record during the streak was 41–13, with two ties, and the club went from fourth place, playing barely .500 baseball, to first place, six games ahead of Cleveland (for additional statistical comment on the streak, see the Appendix).

Since 1941, much has been said and written analyzing the streak and pondering its meaning. Before DiMaggio, the hitting streak was one of baseball's more obscure records. The fact that DiMaggio, and not some other player, set the record, has contributed to the public's enduring fascination with the mark.

Some observers view the streak as symbolic of the capacity of American society to ignore the conflict in Europe in the months be-fore World War II and escape into something more pleasurable, an interpretation that is rarely attached to Ted Williams's pursuit of .400. Others see the streak as emblematic of DiMaggio the hero, while a handful of writers have consistently tried to deride the record and question its authenticity.

Before DiMaggio, other ballplayers had captured the attention of fans with their bids to break records. Most notably, in 1927, Babe Ruth's pursuit of a new home-run record received widespread attention in the final weeks of that season. In 1931, even Yankee outfielder Ben Chapman was the object of a short burst of intense publicity when it briefly appeared as if he might challenge Ty Cobb's stolen-base record.

Many people mistakenly believe that DiMaggio's streak was a public passion that lasted fully two months. In fact, like Williams's quest to hit .400, it went unnoticed by most fans until the final three weeks. The public's earnest devotion to DiMaggio's streak was unique in that it came about due to the increased role of print and radio in American life. The streak's popularity was in part a product of the growing efficiency of the media. Toward the end of the streak, nearly everyone in America knew the result of each of DiMaggio's at bats within minutes. Radio bulletins even enabled Boston's Ted Williams to receive reports from the scoreboard operator in Fenway Park in the middle of a game and relay the information to Dominic DiMaggio in center field.

The streak played a dominant role in the public's perception of DiMaggio as a hero, and has colored every subsequent account of his career. While many fans already looked upon DiMaggio as a hero, the hitting streak reinforced the notion and provided more evidence of what the press and the public were already feeling.

Yet some have sought to denigrate the streak as a fiction, attacking its authenticity primarily because of Dan Daniel's decisions as official scorer. While close scrutiny of the streak can call hits into question in four or five games, and one can even infer that DiMaggio may have been the beneficiary of Daniel's friendly scorekeeping, to conclude that this taints the record is misguided.

To be sure, were there any evidence of collusion between DiMaggio and Dan Daniel, the authenticity of the streak would be tarnished. But there is none. Daniel wasn't even involved in any of the scoring decisions that took place after game 44. A few earlier hits may have been less than genuine. That's speculation, not fact, but over the course of 56 games some hits were bound to be questionable. Judgment is part of the game. The streak, like any other record, is in some ways artificial, subject to circumstance, timing, and luck. To deride the streak as tainted because of a borderline scoring decision makes no more sense than penalizing DiMaggio for benefiting from a pitcher who refused to walk him, or from the positioning of an outfielder who played him deep to prevent a run, rather than shallow to prevent a hit, or because the Yankees played St. Louis twelve times and the Indians only seven. Day after day, DiMaggio faced the factual reality of the streak, with all its resultant pressures. And day after day, he succeeded.

Writing in *The Nation* in 1991, Gene Case tried to diminish the streak by noting correctly that a number of other hitters, including Williams, have outperformed DiMaggio over 56-game spans. DiMaggio's aggregate performance during the streak, good as it was, has been bettered by numerous other players. But none faced the public expectation to continue that level of production each and every day.

Each of these perceptions misses the point. What is most remarkable about the streak are not the details of its construction, but DiMaggio's response to its tangible existence and resulting pressure. Once the public became aware of the streak, DiMaggio performed under increasing pressure. As Stephen Jay Gould explains in his essay following this chapter, streaks like DiMaggio's, even including a few "lucky" breaks, push the boundaries of mathematical probability. When DiMaggio continued to collect hits game after game, beyond the point where the law of averages indicates it is likely, DiMaggio was doing something truly incredible, something that none of the thousands of others who had played major league baseball had come remotely close to doing. In fact, in professional baseball's modern era, only two men have ever bettered DiMaggio's streak of 56—Joe Wilhoit, who hit in 69 games playing for Wichita in the Western Association in 1919, and DiMaggio himself, hitting for 61 games in the Pacific Coast League of 1933. For Joe DiMaggio to hold two of the top three spots on that list is nearly inconceivable. Only DiMaggio, among all players ever, had the necessary mental and physical talents to collect hits day after day after day.

Amazingly, as the pressure increased, DiMaggio got even better. He did his worst hitting early in the streak. After Lou Gehrig's funeral, DiMaggio hit .439. After game 30, when he set the Yankee team record and the streak became widely known, DiMaggio hit .457. After breaking Keeler's mark in game 44, when DiMaggio entered a no-man's-land of previous performance, he hit .510.

But the streak's greatest significance was the impact it had on the Yankee team, a consequence that generally receives little mention. The streak did more than help to spur the Yankee turnaround after

Joe DiMaggio and wife, Dorothy, relax on the terrace of their penthouse on West End Avenue in New York City in the summer of 1941.   (Photograph courtesy of the Boston Globe*)*

May 15. On June 2, the Yankees lost, then were informed of Lou Gehrig's death. Distracted, they lost twice more before Gehrig was laid to rest. All the work the Yankees had done to claw back into the pennant race over the previous two weeks was in danger of coming undone. To lose a teammate is one of the most disruptive experiences in sports, particularly one with the status of Gehrig. Although it had been more than two years since Gehrig played, he remained close to many of his teammates. He was, after all, the Yankee captain, and a hero to many players, including DiMaggio. It was understandable that the Yankees might falter.

At this precise moment, DiMaggio went on a streak within the streak. If he was hot before Gehrig's death, he was on fire afterward, hitting a robust .468 from June 7 to June 20, as the Yankees went 10–2 to begin a stretch in which New York won 41 of the next 47 games. If the Yankees mourned for Gehrig, they did so in private. On the field, DiMaggio led by example. If there was anything truly heroic about the streak, it was the way DiMaggio played in the wake of Gehrig's death.

No one could have faulted DiMaggio had he suffered a letdown when the streak ended. Instead, he started another. On June 18, as the

Indians edged the Yankees 2–1 behind Bob Feller to keep Cleveland's pennant hopes alive, DiMaggio went 2 for 4, narrowly missing a home run in the eighth, and knocked in the Yankees' only run. He kept going from there, and so did the Yankees, who ripped off another nine wins in a row as DiMaggio hit in every game. On July 22 through July 24, they knocked Cleveland from the pennant race for good with a three-game sweep. During the game of July 23, DiMaggio faced Al Smith again and hit a home run. After beating Cleveland the Yankees swept Chicago three in a row, destroying their pennant hopes.

DiMaggio's new streak ran to 16 games before he went hitless in two straight games, first against John Niggeling and then Bob Harris, as the Yankees dropped both games of a doubleheader against St. Louis on August 3. The first game was also the first since May 2 that DiMaggio had failed to reach base. By that time, the American League pennant race was all but over. New York's lead was into double figures.

With the pennant race decided, attention focused on Ted Williams's pursuit of .400. DiMaggio may have felt relief as Williams now received the attention that had been his for most of the summer.

Despite DiMaggio's remarkable streak, he trailed Williams and teammate Charlie Keller for American League home-run honors, and Keller for RBI. For a while, it appeared as if DiMaggio might catch each, but on August 20 he suffered a badly sprained ankle against Detroit and was out of the lineup for most of the next three weeks.

While Joe recuperated, his Yankee teammates took stock of his performance and decided to do something. They planned an evening to honor him on August 29 at Washington's Shoreham Hotel.

In secret, pitcher Johnny Murphy and his wife got a craftsman from Tiffany's jeweler's to fashion an elegant silver humidor. On the lid was a bas-relief of DiMaggio on a raised diamond, showing his inimitable follow-through after swinging the bat. Raised letters on either side read "56 games" and "91 hits." On the front of the box it read simply, *Presented to Joe DiMaggio by his fellow players on the New York Yankees to express their admiration for his world's consecutive game hitting record—1941.* The inside of the lid was engraved with the signatures of the Yankee players.

Lefty Gomez worked a ruse to get DiMaggio to stop by Murphy's suite, and when Joe entered, he was surprised to discover the entire Yankee team. The players planned the evening and paid for the humidor themselves. Their gesture was genuine and heartfelt. DiMaggio was deeply touched, and later said that "when Gomez turned the handle of that door in the Shoreham, he paved the way for the greatest thrill I've ever had in baseball."

DiMaggio had come a long way in the eyes of his teammates. What had sometimes been interpreted as aloofness on DiMaggio's part was now correctly seen by his teammates as shyness. The pressures of the streak had graphically illustrated DiMaggio's role on the club and his importance to baseball. The humidor remains his most treasured possession.

The Yankees rolled through the remainder of the season, clinching the pennant on September 4, the earliest clinching in baseball history. Later that month, Charlie Keller also sprained an ankle, and the injury cost him both the league RBI and home-run title. DiMaggio finished with a batting average of .357, third best in the AL behind Williams and Washington's Cecil Travis, with 30 home runs and 125 RBI in 139 games. Keller finished with 122 RBI and 33 home runs, second to Ted Williams's 37. Williams won the batting title with a .406 average. The Yankees ended the season 101–53, seventeen games ahead of second-

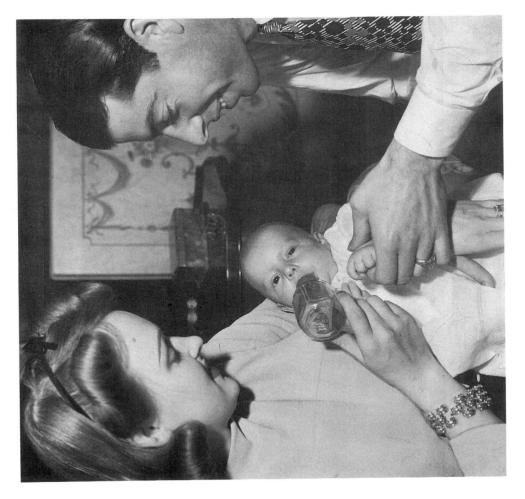

Mr. and Mrs. Joe DiMaggio feed Joe Jr. a bottle on Joe senior's twenty-seventh birthday on November 25, 1941. (Photograph courtesy of the Boston Herald*)*

place Boston, the only team in the entire league to finish closer to first place than last.

In the National League, the Brooklyn Dodgers fought a different kind of pennant race, edging St. Louis in the final week to finish 100–54 and win their first pennant since 1920, creating the first all-New York World Series since 1937.

The Dodgers were a powerful club, paced by hard-hitting first baseman Dolf Camilli, who led the NL in home runs and RBI, and an outfield of Joe Medwick, Dixie Walker, and Pete Reiser, all of whom hit over .300, with Reiser's .343 best in the NL. Their pitching was paced by Kirby Higbe and Whitlow Wyatt, each of whom won 22 games.

Still, the Yankees were 2-to-1 favorites, a betting line that seemed appropriate when New York beat Brooklyn 3–2 before a record crowd of 68,540 fans at Yankee Stadium on October 1 in game one. DiMaggio went hitless, but was robbed by Joe Medwick of a home run in the fourth, as Medwick leaned far over the left-field fence to catch DiMaggio's drive. Joe Gordon was the Yankee hitting star with a home run and two RBI, and Red Ruffing pitched a complete game.

Brooklyn evened the series the next day, winning 3–2 behind Whit Wyatt. DiMaggio again went hitless. He seemed to be embarking on another streak, one somewhat less impressive.

Game three in Brooklyn was scoreless through seven innings. DiMaggio finally came through in the second with a single but was left stranded. Both the Yankees' Marius Russo and the Dodgers' Freddie Fitzsimmons pitched magnificently.

In the Yankee seventh, Russo drove Fitzsimmons from the game with a line drive off the pitcher's left leg that was caught by Pee Wee Reese for the third out. Hugh Casey took over for Brooklyn in the eighth.

Johnny Sturm flied out to center before Red Rolfe singled to right. Henrich then reached on an infield hit when Casey neglected to cover the bag. DiMaggio stepped up with two on.

Casey's gaff proved costly. DiMaggio worked the count to 3 and 2, then drove a single to center, scoring Rolfe. Keller singled home Henrich and the Yankees led 2–0. Brooklyn managed to score once in the bottom of the inning, but Russo held on to put the Yankees up two games to one.

Game four is one of the most talked-about contests in Series history. DiMaggio's performance played a key role in that perception.

Brooklyn's Hugh Casey entered the game in the fifth with the bases loaded and the Yankees up 3–2. Casey got Joe Gordon to fly out. In the bottom of the inning, Pete Reiser cracked a two-run home run to give the Dodgers a 4–3 lead, which Casey made stand, giving up only a hit to Johnny Sturm in the sixth and one of DiMaggio's patented World Series infield hits in the seventh. Entering the ninth inning, Brooklyn was three outs away from tying the Series.

Johnny Sturm grounded to second for the first out, then Red Rolfe bounced back to Casey for out number two. With the partisan crowd roaring approval, Henrich worked the count to 3 and 2.

Casey's next pitch fooled Henrich completely. He swung wildly at a ball on the inside corner, for strike three. But Dodger catcher Mickey Owen was equally fooled. The pitch glanced off his glove and rolled behind the plate.

Much of the Yankee team had already headed for the clubhouse when they saw the ball squirt away. They scrambled back as Henrich tore for first. Half of Brooklyn's police force had left the Dodger dugout and swarmed onto the field. Owen recovered the ball but was unable to throw through the borough's finest, and Henrich reached first safely.

The Yankees still had a chance, albeit a slim one. DiMaggio stepped up and lined a single to left. Then Charlie Keller whaled a line drive off the right-field screen. Henrich scored easily to tie the score and DiMaggio again demonstrated his baserunning ability, tearing around third and sliding home, just beating the relay, to put the Yankees ahead 5–4. Bill Dickey walked and Gordon doubled two more home before Casey was able to get out of the inning. The Dodgers now trailed 7–4.

The stunned Bums went out quietly in the ninth, unable to believe their fate. After the game, some tried to blame the police, but Owen would have none of it, saying simply, "I shoulda caught the ball . . . it was a sharp curve, inside and low, and I just didn't get it." Since that time, many have speculated that what Owen described as a curve was, in fact, a spitball, a notoriously hard pitch to catch. Sadly, the career of Mickey Owen, who was one of the best defensive catchers, is forever colored by the mishap.

The Dodgers were unable to recover in game five. Joe Gordon led the Yankee attack and New York led 2–1 entering the fifth. Brooklyn pitcher Whitlow Wyatt had pitched well, even striking out DiMaggio twice.

But Henrich homered in the fifth to give New York a 3–1 lead. DiMaggio then stepped up, and this at bat provided a rare insight into his on-field attitude.

Earlier in the year, Wyatt had created a controversy when he told a reporter that the best way to stop DiMaggio was to put him on his back. Now he tried to make good on his promise. After Henrich's home run, he greeted DiMaggio with two pitches under his chin. Di-Maggio then flied out to Reiser in deep center.

As DiMaggio trotted past the mound, he yelled at Wyatt, "The Series isn't over yet." Wyatt responded profanely that if DiMaggio couldn't take it, he should get out of the game.

DiMaggio stopped in his tracks and started walking toward the mound. Both benches emptied and the incident passed without contact between the two men. If Wyatt hoped to intimidate DiMaggio and goad him into a fight, he failed.

The Yankee lead held as Ernie Bonham went the distance, giving New York the Series in five games. Joe Gordon was the acknowledged star, hitting .500 and driving in five runs. DiMaggio hit only .263, scoring only once and knocking in a single run, yet his contribution was significant. Joe's hit after Casey's failure to cover the bag in game three plated the Yanks' first run in the 2–1 win, and it was DiMaggio who first took advantage of Owen's error in game four. It was a typical DiMaggio World Series performance, with typical results. The Yankees won.

After such a remarkable year, the off-season provided DiMaggio more good fortune. On October 23, Dorothy gave birth to a son, Joe Jr. Three weeks later, DiMaggio learned that for the second time he had been selected by the Base Ball Writers of America as the American League's Most Valuable Player.

DiMaggio was named on all twenty-four ballots and outpolled Boston's Ted Williams, collecting fifteen first-place votes and 291 points to eight first-place votes for Williams and 254 points. In retrospect, some have questioned the wisdom of the balloting, as Williams's .406 batting average has increased in stature, making DiMaggio's hitting streak seem a little less amazing. But hitting .400 was not quite the rarity in 1941 that it is today. Although Williams was the first man to bat over .400 since Bill Terry in 1930, eleven league leaders had hit .360 or better in the ensuing ten seasons. Three, including DiMaggio, had bettered .380. DiMaggio's contributions to the Yankee pennant were far more significant in the voters' minds than Williams's individual achievement for a team that finished only 84–70.

When the 1941 season began, it appeared as if Joe DiMaggio had done just about everything there was to do in the game of baseball. Somehow, he managed to do even more.

The Streak of Streaks

Stephen Jay Gould

My father was a court stenographer. At his less than princely salary, we watched Yankee games from the bleachers or high in the third deck. But one of the judges had season tickets, so we occasionally sat in the lower boxes when hizzoner couldn't attend. One afternoon, while DiMaggio was going 0 for 4 against, of all people, the lowly St. Louis Browns, the great man fouled one in our direction. "Catch it, Dad," I screamed. "You never get them," he replied, but stuck up his hand like the Statue of Liberty—and the ball fell right in. I mailed it to DiMaggio, and, bless him, he actually sent the ball back, signed and in a box marked "insured."

Insured, that is, to make me the envy of the neighborhood, and DiMaggio the model and hero of my life.

I met DiMaggio a few years ago on a small playing field at the Presidio of San Francisco. My son, wearing DiMaggio's old number 5 on his Little League jersey, accompanied me, exactly one generation after my father caught that ball. DiMaggio gave him a pointer or two on batting and then signed a baseball for him. One generation passeth away, and another generation cometh: But the earth abideth forever.

My son, uncoached by Dad, and given the chance that comes but once in a lifetime, asked DiMaggio as his only

query about life and career: "Suppose you had walked every time up during one game of your 56-game hitting streak?

DiMaggio savors his new record in front of his Yankee Stadium locker. (Lloyd E. Klos photograph)

"Would the streak have been over?" DiMaggio replied that, under 1941 rules, the streak would have ended, but that this unfair statute has since been revised, and such a game would not count today.

My son's choice for a single question tells us something vital about the nature of legend. A man may labor for a professional lifetime, especially in sport or in battle, but posterity needs a single transcendant event to fix him in permanent memory. Every hero must be a Wellington on the right side of his personal Waterloo; general-ity of excellence is too diffuse. The unambiguous factuality of a single achievement is adaman-tine. Detractors can argue for-ever about the general tenor of your life and works, but they can never erase a great event.

In 1941, as I gestated in my mother's womb, Joe DiMaggio got at least one hit in each of 56 successive games. Most records are only incrementally superior to runners-up; Roger Maris hit 61 homers in 1961, but Babe Ruth hit 60 in 1927 and 59 in 1921, while Hank Greenberg (1938) and Jimmie Foxx (1932) both hit 58. But DiMaggio's 56-game hitting streak is ridiculously, almost unreachably far from all challengers (Wee Willie Keeler and Pete Rose, both with 44, come second). Among sabermetricians (a happy neologism based on an acronym for members of the Society for

American Baseball Research, and referring to the statistical mavens of the sport)—a contentious lot not known for agree-ment about anything—we find virtual consensus that DiMag-gio's 56-game hitting streak is the greatest accomplishment in the history of baseball, if not all modern sport.

The reasons for this respect are not far to seek. Single mo-ments of unexpected suprem-acy—Johnny Vander Meer's back-to-back no-hitters in 1938, Don Larsen's perfect game in the 1956 World Series—can occur at any time to almost any-body, and have an irreducibly capricious character. Achieve-ments of a full season—such as Maris's 61 homers in 1961 and Ted Williams's batting average of .406, also posted in 1941 and not equaled since—have a cer-tain overall majesty, but they don't demand unfailing consis-tency every single day; you can slump for a while, so long as your average holds. But a streak must be absolutely exception-less; you are not allowed a sin-gle day of subpar play, or even bad luck. You bat only four or five times in an average game. Sometimes two or three of these efforts yield walks, and you get only one or two shots at a hit. Moreover, as tension mounts and notice increases, your life becomes unbearable. Reporters dog your every step; fans are even more intrusive than usual (one stole DiMaggio's favorite

bat right in the middle of his streak). You cannot make a sin-gle mistake.

Thus Joe DiMaggio's 56-game hitting streak is both the greatest factual achievement in the history of baseball and a principal icon of American my-thology. What shall we do with such a central item of our cul-tural history?

Statistics and mythology may strike us as the most unlikely of bedfellows. How can we quan-tify Caruso or measure *Middle-march*? But if God could mete out heaven with the span (Isaiah 40:12), perhaps we can say something useful about hitting streaks. The statistics of "runs," defined as continuous series of good or bad results (including baseball's streaks and slumps), is a well-developed branch of the profession, and can yield clear—but wildly counterintu-itive—results. (The fact that we find these conclusions so sur-prising is the key to appreciating DiMaggio's achievement, the gateway to an important insight about the human mind.)

Start with a phenomenon that nearly everyone both ac-cepts and considers well under-stood—"hot hands" in basketball. Now and then, someone just gets hot, and can't be stopped. Basket after basket falls in—or out as with "cold hands," when a man can't buy a bucket for love or money (choose your cliché). The reason for this phenomenon is clear enough: It lies embodied in the maxim, "When you're hot, you're hot; and when you're not, you're not." You get that touch, build confidence; all nervousness fades, you find your rhythm; *swish, swish, swish.* Or you miss a few, get rattled, endure the booing, experience despair; hands start shaking and you realize that you shoulda stood in bed.

Everybody knows about hot hands. The only problem is that no such phenomenon exists. Stanford psychologist Amos Tversky studied every basket made by the Philadelphia 76ers for more than a season. He found, first of all, that the probability of making a second basket did not rise following a successful shot. Moreover, the number of "runs," or baskets in succession, was no greater than what a standard random, or coin-tossing, model would predict. (If the chance of making each basket is 0.5, for example, a reasonable value for good shooters, five hits in a row will occur, on average, once in 32 sequences—just as you can expect to toss five successive heads about once in 32 times, or 0.5^5.)

Of course Larry Bird, the great forward of the Boston Celtics, will have more se-quences of five than Joe Airball—but not because he has greater will or gets in that magic rhythm more often. Larry has longer runs because his average success rate is so much higher, and random models predict more frequent and longer sequences. If Larry shoots field goals at 0.6 probability of success, he will get five in a row about once every 13 sequences (0.6^5). If Joe, by contrast, shoots only 0.3, he will get his five straight only about once in 412 times. In other words, we need no special explanation for the apparent pattern of long runs. There is no ineffable "causality of circumstance" (to coin a phrase), no definite reason born of the particulars that make for heroic myths—courage in the clinch, strength in adversity, etc. You only have to know a person's ordinary play in order to predict his sequences. (I rather suspect that we are convinced of the contrary not only because we need myths so badly, but also because we remember the successes and simply allow the failures to fade from memory. More on this later.) But how does this revisionist pessimism work for baseball?

My colleague Ed Purcell, Nobel laureate in physics but, for purposes of this subject, just another baseball fan, has done a comprehensive study of all baseball streak and slump records. His firm conclusion is easily and swiftly summarized. Nothing ever happened in baseball above and beyond the frequency predicted by coin-tossing models. The longest runs of wins or losses are as long as they should be, and occur about as often as they ought to. Even the hapless Orioles, at 0 and 21 to start the 1988 season, only fell victim to the laws of probability (and not to the vengeful God of racism, out to punish major league baseball's only black manager).*

But "treasure your exceptions," as the old motto goes. Purcell's rule has but one major exception, one sequence so many standard deviations above the expected distribution that it should never have occurred at all: Joe DiMaggio's 56-game hitting streak in 1941. The intuition of baseball aficionados has been vindicated. Purcell calculated that to make it likely (probability greater than 50 percent) that a run of even 50 games will occur once in the history of baseball up to now (and 56 is a lot more than 50 in this kind of league), baseball's rosters would have to include either four lifetime .400 batters or 52 lifetime .350 batters over careers of 1,000 games. In actuality, only three men have lifetime batting averages in excess of .350, and no one is anywhere

---

*When I wrote this essay, Frank Robinson, the Baltimore skipper, was the only black man at the helm of a major league team. For more on the stats of Baltimore's slump, see my article "Winning and Losing: It's All in the Game," *Rotunda*, Spring 1989.

near .400 (Ty Cobb at .367, Rogers Hornsby at .358, and Shoeless Joe Jackson at .356). DiMaggio's streak is the most extraordinary thing that ever happened in American sports. He sits on the shoulders of two bearers—mythology and science. For Joe DiMaggio accomplished what no other ballplayer

has done. He beat the hardest taskmaster of all, a woman who makes Nolan Ryan's fastball look like a cantaloupe in slow motion—Lady Luck.

A larger issue lies behind basic documentation and simple appreciation. For we don't understand the truly special quandary of our lives (*Rubaiyat of Omar Khayyám*, Edward Fitzgerald, trans.):

because we are so poorly equipped, whether by habits of culture or by our modes of cognition, to grasp the workings of random processes and patterning in nature.

Omar Khayyám, the old Persian tentmaker, understood the character of DiMaggio's record

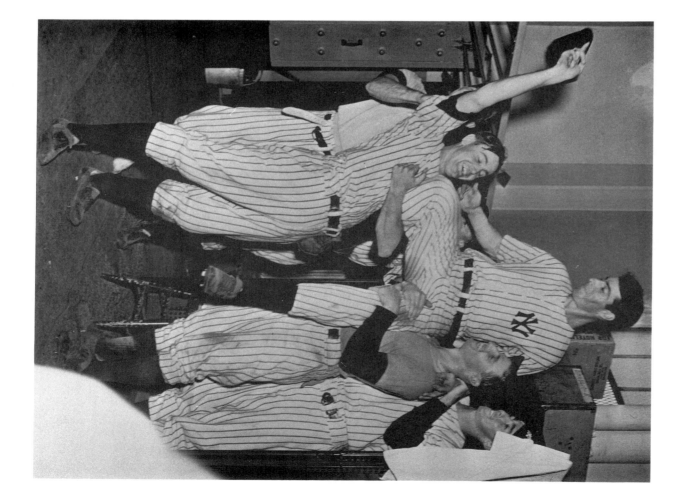

Yankee teammates Johnny Sturm (l) and Tommy Henrich lift DiMaggio on their shoulders following his record-setting 45th straight game with a hit. He would hit safely in another 11 games, establishing an untouchable record and one of baseball's most honored. (Photograph from Bettmann Archives)

Into this Universe, and
   Why not knowing,
Nor Whence, like Water
   willy-nilly flowing;
And out of it, as Wind
   along the Waste,
I know not Whither, willy-
   nilly blowing.

But we cannot bear it. We must have comforting answers. We see pattern, for pattern surely exists, even in a purely random world. (Only a highly nonran-dom universe could possibly cancel out the clumping that we perceive as pattern. We think we see constellations be-cause stars are dispersed at random in the heavens, and therefore clump in our sight. Our error lies not in the per-ception of pattern but in auto-matically imbuing pattern with meaning, especially with meaning that can bring us comfort, or dispel confusion. Again, Omar took the more honest approach:

Ah, love! could you and I
   with Fate conspire
To grasp this sorry Scheme
   of Things entire,
Would not we shatter it to
   bits—and then
Re-mould it nearer to the
   Heart's Desire!

We, instead, have tried to im-pose that "heart's desire" upon the actual earth and its largely random patterns (Alexander

Pope, *Essay on Man*, end of Epistle 1):

All Nature is but Art,
   unknown to thee;
All Chance, Direction,
   which thou canst not
   see;
All Discord, Harmony not
   understood:
All partial Evil, universal
   Good.

Sorry to wax so poetic and ten-dentious about something that leads back to DiMaggio's hitting streak, but this broader setting forms the source of our misin-terpretation. We believe in "hot hands" because we must impart meaning to a pattern—and we like meanings that tell stories about heroism, valor, and excel-lence. We believe that long streaks and slumps must have direct causes internal to the se-quence itself, and we have no feel for the frequency and length of sequences in random data. Thus, while we under-stand that DiMaggio's hitting streak was the longest ever, we don't appreciate its truly special character because we view all the others as equally patterned by cause, only a little shorter. We distinguish DiMaggio's feat merely by quantity along a con-tinuum of courage; we should, instead, view his 56-game hit-ting streak as a unique assault upon the otherwise unblemish-ed record of Dame Probability. Amos Tversky, who studied

"hot hands," has performed, with Daniel Kahneman, a series of elegant psychological experi-ments. These long-term studies have provided our finest insight into "natural reasoning" and its curious departure from logical truth. To cite an example, they construct a fictional description of a young woman: "Linda is 31 years old, single, outspoken, and very bright. She majored in philosophy. As a student, she was deeply concerned with is-sues of discrimination and social justice, and also participated in anti-nuclear demonstrations." Subjects are then given a list of hypothetical statements about Linda: They must rank these in order of presumed likelihood, most to least probable. Tversky and Kahneman list eight state-ments, but five are a blind, and only three make up the true ex-periment:

Linda is active in the
   feminist movement;
Linda is a bank teller;
Linda is a bank teller and is
   active in the feminist
   movement.

Now it simply must be true that the third statement is least likely, since any conjunc-tion has to be less probable than either of its parts considered separately. Everybody can understand this when the principle is explained explicitly and patiently. But all groups of subjects, sophisticated students who have pondered logic and probability as well as folks off the street corner, rank the last statement as more probable than the second. (I am particularly fond of this example because I know that the third statement is least probable, yet a little homunculus in my head continues to jump up and down, shouting at me—"but she can't just be a bank teller; read the description.")

Why do we so consistently make this simple logical error? Tversky and Kahneman argue, correctly I think, that our minds are not built (for whatever reason) to work by the rules of probability, though these rules clearly govern our universe. We do something else that usually serves us well, but fails in crucial instances: We "match to type." We abstract what we consider the "essence" of an entity, and then arrange our judgments by their degree of similarity to this assumed type. Since we are given a "type" for Linda that implies feminism, but definitely not a bank job, we rank any statement matching the type as more probable than another that only contains material contrary to the type. This propensity may help us to understand an entire range of human preferences, from Plato's theory of form to modern stereotyping of race or gender.

We might also understand the world better, and free our-

selves of unseemly prejudice, if we properly grasped the workings of probability and its inexorable hold, through laws of logic, upon much of nature's pattern. "Matching to type" is one common error; failure to understand random patterning in streaks and slumps is another—hence Tversky's study of both the fictional Linda and the 76ers' baskets. Our failure to appreciate the uniqueness of DiMaggio's streak derives from the same unnatural and uncomfortable relationship that we maintain with probability. (If we knew Lady Luck better, Las Vegas might still be a roadstop in the desert.)

My favorite illustration of this basic misunderstanding, as applied to DiMaggio's hitting streak, appeared in a recent article by baseball writer John Holway, "A Little Help from His Friends," and subtitled "Hits or Hype in '41" (*Sports Heritage*, 1987). Holway points out that five of DiMaggio's successes were narrow escapes and lucky breaks. He received two benefits-of-the-doubt from official scorers on plays that might have been judged as errors. In each of two games, his only hit was a cheapie. In game 16, a ball dropped untouched in the outfield and had to be called a hit, even though the ball had been misjudged and could have been caught; in game 54, DiMaggio dribbled one down the third-

base line, easily beating the throw because the third baseman, expecting the usual, was playing far back. The fifth incident is an oft-told tale, perhaps the most interesting story of the streak. In game 38, DiMaggio was 0 for 3 going into the last inning. Scheduled to bat fourth, he might have been denied a chance to hit at all, Johnny Sturm popped up to begin the inning, but Red Rolfe then walked. Slugger Tommy Henrich, up next, was suddenly swept with a premonitory fear: Suppose I ground into a double play and end the inning? An elegant solution immediately occurred to him: Why not bunt (an odd strategy for a power hitter). Henrich laid down a beauty; DiMaggio, up next, promptly drilled a double to left.

I enjoyed Holway's account, but his premise is entirely, almost preciously, wrong. First of all, none of the five incidents represents an egregious miscall. The two hits were less than elegant, but undoubtedly legitimate; the two boosts from official scorers were close calls on judgment plays, not gifts. As for Henrich, I can only repeat manager Joe McCarthy's comment when Tommy asked him for permission to bunt: "Yeah, that's a good idea." Not a terrible strategy either—to put a man into scoring position for an insurance run when you're up 3–1.

But these details do not

touch the main point: Holway's premise is false because he accepts the conventional mythology about long sequences. He believes that streaks are unbroken runs of causal courage—so that any prolongation by hook-or-crook becomes an outrage against the deep meaning of the phenomenon. But extended sequences are not pure exercises in valor. Long streaks always are, and must be, a matter of extraordinary luck imposed upon great skill. Please don't make the vulgar mistake of thinking that Purcell or Tversky or I or anyone else would attribute a long streak to ''just luck''—as though everyone's chances are exactly the same, and streaks represent nothing more than the lucky atom that kept moving in one direction. Long hitting streaks happen to the greatest players—Sisler, Keeler, DiMaggio, Rose—because their general chance of getting a hit is so much higher than average. Just as Joe Airball cannot match Larry Bird for runs of baskets, Joe's cousin Bill Ofer, with a lifetime batting average of .184, will never have a streak to match DiMaggio's with

a lifetime average of .325. The statistics show something else, and something fascinating: There is no ''causality of circumstance,'' no ''extra'' that the great can draw from the soul of their valor to extend a streak beyond the ordinary expectation of coin-tossing models for a series of unconnected events, each occurring with a characteristic probability for that particular player. Good players have higher characteristic probabilities, hence longer streaks.

Of course DiMaggio had a little luck during his streak. That's what streaks are all about. No long sequence has ever been entirely sustained in any other way (the Orioles almost won several of those 21 games). DiMaggio's remarkable achievement—its uniqueness, in the unvarnished literal sense of that word—lies in whatever he did to extend his success well beyond the reasonable expectations of random models that have governed every other streak or slump in the history of baseball.

Probability does pervade the universe—and in this sense, the old chestnut about baseball imi-

tating life really has validity. The statistics of streaks and slumps, properly understood, do teach an important lesson about epistemology, and life in general. The history of a species, or any natural phenomenon that requires unbroken continuity in a world of trouble, works like a batting streak. All are games of a gambler playing with a limited stake against a house with infinite resources. The gambler must eventually go bust. His aim can only be to stick around as long as possible, to have some fun while he's at it, and, if he happens to be a moral agent as well, to worry about staying the course with honor. The best of us will try to live by a few simple rules: Do justly, love mercy, walk humbly with thy God, and never draw to an inside straight.

DiMaggio's hitting streak is the finest of legitimate legends because it embodies the essence of the battle that truly defines our lives. DiMaggio activated the greatest and most unattainable dream of all humanity, the hope and chimera of all sages and shamans: He cheated death, at least for a while.

The War at Home:
1942–45

O n December 7, 1941, Joe DiMaggio was at the Polo Grounds watching a football game when the Japanese bombed Pearl Harbor. The onset of war changed almost everything and everyone in America, and not even the great Joe DiMaggio was immune.

In the aftermath of Pearl Harbor, baseball worried over the war's impact on the 1942 season. On January 15, President Roosevelt responded to a query from Baseball Commissioner Landis by saying, "I honestly feel it would be best for the country to keep baseball going."

Because of war with Japan, normal activities on the West Coast were highly restricted. North Beach and Fisherman's Wharf were declared a restricted strategic zone, meaning that "no enemy alien will be permitted to live in a forbidden zone, to work there, or even visit there." While the restrictions were aimed primarily at the Japanese, they covered any aliens whose country of birth was that of a country at war with the United States. On January 31, 1942, the War Department issued evacuation orders, effective February 24, to remove all such aliens from the restricted zones.

Giuseppe DiMaggio was one of those aliens. He barely spoke English and had never bothered to become a citizen. Now, barely six months after his son Joe had been heralded as an American hero, this country wanted to move DiMaggio's father to an internment camp.

Fortunately for the DiMaggios, in mid-February at hearings held in Washington, it was decided that it was possible to establish the loyalty of German and Italian aliens. In one of the saddest decisions in American history, Japanese-Americans, even those with U.S. citizenship, were sent to camps. European aliens like Giuseppe DiMaggio could remain in their homes, but he would not be allowed on Fisherman's Wharf.

It is not overstating the case to say that Joe DiMaggio played a role in the eventual suspension of the order in regard to Italians. German-Americans were well-established in American society, yet Italians were more recent immigrants, and were still looked down upon by many Americans. When Joe DiMaggio became one of the most famous men in America, his celebrity status helped inspire the acceptance of Italians into American society. His stature in the wake of the 56-game hitting streak may well have helped prevent thousands of Italian immigrants from being placed in internment camps.

There were other, more significant reasons why Italians were not included in the order. Italians were Caucasian, and Italian immigrants formed a large constituency in urban politics, particularly in the Democratic party, and Roosevelt, a Democrat, was in the White House. To intern Italians would have caused serious political repercussions, whereas Japanese-Americans had no significant political clout.

The onset of war also played a role in DiMaggio's contract talks with the Yankees. He knew that his performance in 1941 had set the

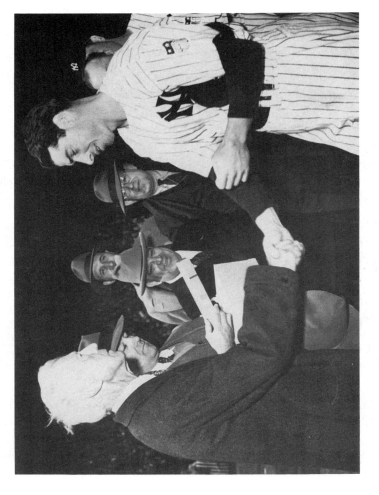

DiMaggio receives bis 1941 American League MVP Award from Baseball Commissioner Kenesaw Mountain Landis. (Photograph from Bettmann Archives)

(l–r) Ted Williams, Dom DiMaggio, Joe DiMaggio, and Tommy Henrich are shown prior to a game at Fenway Park in 1942. (Photograph from the Maxwell Collection)

turnstiles spinning, and he felt he was due a substantial raise. He asked for $45,000, but the Yankees countered with an offer identical to that of 1941, claiming that the war made it impossible for them to give anyone a raise, and that DiMaggio should feel honored his salary wasn't being cut.

DiMaggio didn't accept the Yankees' reasoning. After a winter of posturing, in mid-March Joe finally signed a contract for $42,000.

DiMaggio was at his peak, and despite the distraction over his father's alien status, he sounded confident as he spoke to reporters after arriving in Florida. Like most of his Yankee teammates, DiMaggio's marital status gave him a 3-A draft classification, still safe from the draft. His greatest concern was going head-to-head for the batting title against the player who some now thought his offensive equal, Ted Williams.

"Don't misunderstand me about Ted," he told the writers. "He's the greatest hitter I ever saw. . . . You never see Ted go for a bad ball. And you have never seen anybody like him with two strikes against him. But with all that, he can be caught." By the end of the season, Ted Williams's batting average would be the least of DiMaggio's concerns.

DiMaggio's right arm was sore when he arrived at spring training, but he wasn't unduly concerned, quipping, "I'm getting to be an old man." Joe didn't hit well during his brief period of training, but when the season began on April 14, no one was concerned.

The Yankees won their first four and eight of their first ten to move into first place. DiMaggio started slowly but appeared to break out against Philadelphia at Yankee Stadium April 22, walloping his 200th career home run and two triples, one to the 461 sign in dead center and another to the 457 mark in left center. In his other at bat in the 11–5 win, he flied out to deep center field. Al Laney in the *Herald Tribune* did the math and concluded that "if his day's work with the bat had been stretched out, it would have measured more than 1,500 feet. This was an unusual day's work, even for DiMaggio, but no more than one expects frequently from the great man." In any other ballpark, he would have had four home runs. After 1941, the extraordinary was expected.

In the early months of the season, Joe was inconsistent at the plate. On May 5, after the Yankees fell behind Chicago 4–0, DiMaggio won the game by himself, 5–4, with two home runs and a tenth-inning triple. But the occasional extraordinary game was usually followed by a stretch of mostly ordinary performances. It didn't help that Charlie Keller, batting fifth behind DiMaggio, was also in a slump.

In June, Joe slumped badly. With the Yankees already way ahead of the rest of the American League, New York went on a road trip in mid-month and lost six of eight to Cleveland and Detroit, cutting their lead to seven games. DiMaggio hit a paltry .172 during the slide, dropping his average to .253. When the Yankees returned home, Joe started hearing about it from the crowd.

The jeers were motivated by more than DiMaggio's slump. Some fans, whose brothers and cousins were already spilling blood all over the globe, resented the fact that most baseball players were as yet unaffected by the war. Stars like DiMaggio received the brunt of their wrath. It did not help that DiMaggio was Italian, and the United States was at war with Italy.

Fortunately for New York, other players picked up the slack. Yankee pitching had never been better, and second baseman Joe Gordon provided just enough punch. The Yankees reached the All-Star break with a record of 50–26. DiMaggio was again named to the starting lineup, but for the first time his presence was due more to his reputation than his performance.

Two All-Star games were played in 1942, although only one was considered "official," as baseball tried to do its part raising money for the war effort. In the official contest, played at the Polo Grounds on July 6, the American League defeated the Nationals, 3–1. The next day in Cleveland, the winning club faced the Service All-Stars, whose ranks already included Bob Feller, the Yankees' Johnny Sturm, and the Senators' Cecil Travis. DiMaggio played center field for the AL in both games, knocking in the clubs' first run against the Service club with a first-inning single.

The Yankees still won the pennant with ease, clinching on September 14 with an 8–3 win over Cleveland as Ernie Bonham notched his 20th win. New York finished 103–51, a better record than 1941. But DiMaggio's numbers were down in virtually every category, despite the fact that he remained healthy all year and played in all 154 games. He hit only .305, over forty points below his career average, with 21 home runs, second best on the Yankees to Keller's 26, and 114 RBI. Ted Williams, on the other hand, won the American League Triple Crown with an average of .356, 36 home runs, and 137 RBI. The torch representing the league's best hitter passed from DiMaggio to Williams. In *The DiMaggio Albums*, published in 1991, DiMaggio's record for the year is accurately titled "Mortality."

In the National League, St. Louis bettered the Yankees' record by winning 106 games, just edging Brooklyn, who won 104. Despite the Cardinals' record, the Yankees were again favored in the World Series. New York won the first game, played on September 30 in St. Louis, 7–4. DiMaggio, beginning to make up for his lackluster regular-season performance, scored New York's first run in the fourth, plated the second run with a force-out in the fifth, and started New York's three-run outburst in the eighth with a leadoff single.

DiMaggio got on track after the break and the Yankees responded with another torrid win streak, winning seventeen of their next twenty, as DiMaggio finally lifted his average above .300. Joe's preseason prognostication was still way off. He trailed Ted Williams badly in most offensive categories and was unable to catch Williams.

Yankee pitcher Red Ruffing held the Cardinals hitless into the eighth, but with two out in the bottom of the ninth the Cardinals erupted for four runs to put a scare into New York. St. Louis, whose lineup, on average, was the youngest to play in a World Series, gained confidence from the comeback.

They proved so the next day. Led by pitcher Johnny Beazley, St. Louis led 3–0 entering the eighth. With two out and a man on, DiMaggio singled to score one, and Keller followed with a home run to tie the game. In other years, against other teams, similar Yankee comebacks had led to crushing defeats for opponents. But St. Louis was different. They won the game in the bottom of the inning when Stan Musial singled home Enos Slaughter to tie the Series at a game apiece.

Yankee fans were shocked when St. Louis defeated New York 2–0 at the Stadium on Ernie White's six-hit shutout in game three on October 3. DiMaggio was the only New York batter to do well, singling in the fourth and the ninth, and going out in the seventh on a deep drive to left center that Cardinal center fielder Terry Moore caught on the run. For the first time, a team with Joe DiMaggio on the roster was behind in the World Series.

St. Louis jumped out to a 6–1 lead in the fourth inning the next day, chasing Hank Borowy, who had held St. Louis hitless through three. The Yanks tied it with five runs in the sixth, three scoring on Keller's home run, but the bull pen failed to stop St. Louis and the Cardinals won, 9–6. DiMaggio went hitless in the contest.

The Yankees were grim before game five. No man on the team had ever been in such a position. As an incentive, one Yankee club official wrote on a blackboard in the clubhouse "Train for St. Louis leaves 8 pm tonight. Grand Central terminal. Bring your hand luggage." But one less train left for St. Louis that night, and a lot of New York Yankees took their hand luggage home by subway.

The Cardinals couldn't be stopped. With the score tied at one in the fourth, DiMaggio singled home Red Rolfe to put the Yankees ahead. The Cardinals tied the game in the sixth, then took the lead in the ninth as Whitey Kurowski of the Cards homered off Ruffing. St. Louis led, 4–2.

The Yankees threatened in the ninth. Joe Gordon singled and Bill Dickey reached base safely on an error. But Gordon was picked off at second by a throw from catcher Walker Cooper to shortstop Marty Marion. Gerry Priddy popped out and George Selkirk, pinch-hitting for Ruffing, grounded out to end the game. For only the second time in seven seasons, the New York Yankees were not world champions.

Although he was pleased when Italians were freed of alien restrictions in mid-October, DiMaggio played much of the season distracted. He worried about his parents, and despite the birth of his son, his marriage was beginning to fall apart. DiMaggio was accustomed to spending his free time with his cronies at Toots Shor's, and neither his marriage nor the birth of his son changed his habits. Dorothy and Joe lived in an apartment in New York during the season, but in the off-season they lived in San Francisco. Dorothy still had professional ambitions and wanted to live in Los Angeles, but Joe had little use for the city. His family and off-season business concerns were in San Francisco. Dorothy expected Joe to be a full-time husband and father,

Among the major leaguers called to duty in the Pacific theater were (standing l–r) Sgt. Walter Judnich (St. Louis Browns), Cpl. Mike McCormick (Cincinnati Reds), and Staff Sgt. Joe DiMaggio (Yankees). Front (l–r): Sgt. Dario Lodigiani (Chicago White Sox), and Pfc. Gerald Priddy (Washington Senators). (Photograph courtesy of the Boston Herald)

Joe DiMaggio is shown with fellow soldiers during his first drill at the Presidio on February 18, 1943. (Photograph courtesy of the *Boston Herald*)

while Joe expected Dorothy to be content to stay home alone while he behaved like the celebrity he was. Conflict was inevitable.

On December 3, only a week after DiMaggio's twenty-eighth birthday, Dorothy took Joe Jr. and moved into the Riverside Hotel in Reno, Nevada, in order to secure a divorce.

The move caught DiMaggio by surprise. He knew she was dissatisfied, but DiMaggio was a practicing Catholic, albeit less so than in his youth. Divorce was something he had not considered.

He was also worried about being drafted. His 3-A classification wouldn't protect him forever, and wouldn't protect him at all if he divorced. Joe knew he would have to eventually enter the service, and wanted to get it over with.

In early January, still angry about Dorothy's threats of divorce, DiMaggio followed her to Reno. A few days later, he returned to San Francisco and spoke by telephone to columnist Prescott Sullivan of the *San Francisco Examiner.* In a rare slip, DiMaggio said things he later regretted.

Sullivan pressed DiMaggio for a comment on the status of his marriage, and DiMaggio snapped, "It's none of your business." Sullivan moved on to baseball matters. Due to travel restrictions, the Yankees planned to hold spring training in New Jersey. He asked if DiMaggio thought that would affect his preparation for the upcoming season.

"Spring training won't concern me this year," replied DiMaggio cryptically. Sullivan asked DiMaggio if that meant he planned to enlist, and DiMaggio groused, "I'm not saying. You can draw your own conclusions." Sullivan did, and the next day every paper in the country carried a story that said DiMaggio planned to enlist in the service, a decision that was a surprise to both the Yankees and DiMaggio's writer friends in New York, who were upset Joe hadn't given them the scoop.

In reality, DiMaggio didn't know what he was going to do. Everything was coming apart.

He made one last attempt to save his marriage. He went back to Reno and spent hours talking with Dorothy at the hotel, trying to decide on the fate of his marriage and the fate of his baseball career.

In the end, the marriage was saved at the expense of his career in baseball. He and Dorothy appeared arm-in-arm before the press in Reno on January 13 and announced that they had patched things up. Furthermore, DiMaggio said, "I'm going to try to get into the Armed Forces in the near future, as soon as I can get a few things straightened out." Dorothy concurred with his decision. She expected that

DiMaggio poses with (l–r) Vice Admiral Robert L. Ghormley, Brooklyn Dodger shortstop Harold "Pee Wee" Reese, and Brigadier General William J. Flood prior to a Central Pacific Champion-ship Service Game in which the Aeia Heights Naval Hos-pital defeated DiMaggio's 7th Army Air Force team by a score of 5–4. (Associated Press photograph)

the service was likely to use DiMaggio for public relations, playing ball to entertain the troops. It was unlikely he would be stationed overseas. She could be near him, and he would be away from his life on the road with the Yankees or with the boys at Shor's. For Joe DiMaggio, life in the service during wartime appeared to be less disruptive than life as a civilian.

DiMaggio enlisted in the Army on February 17, trading his pinstripes and $43,750-a-year salary for khakis and $50 a month. Dorothy moved with Joe Jr. to Los Angeles.

Dorothy was right in her estimation of the Army's use of her husband. While DiMaggio requested no special treatment, he spent most of his duty stateside playing baseball for three years. Most other notable major leaguers did the same, although some saw real combat. Only two major league veterans, Harry O'Neill and Joe Gedeon, who had played a total of six games between them, died in the war. A few more suffered serious injury, such as the Senators' fine third baseman Cecil Travis, whose feet froze during the Battle of the Bulge, an injury that caused a premature end to his career.

But most major-league ballplayers served on the baseball diamond, acting as physical training instructors when not playing ball. Military service teams played for the entertainment of regular troops and for the public. While it was better than being in combat, such service was no picnic. The players were still subject to the usual military discipline. Their commanders usually cared little if players were fatigued, and a number of major league pitchers threw their arms out in service ball.

DiMaggio's reputation later suffered when his service history was compared to that of some other stars. The Indians' Bob Feller, for example, requested combat duty and served with distinction in the South Pacific. But DiMaggio's experience was more the norm than the exception for a major-league ballplayer. While it is true that he didn't request combat duty, few ballplayers did. They took the military's position that they were performing a useful service at face value.

DiMaggio was assigned to Special Services and stationed at the Santa Ana Air Base in California, where he reached the rank of sergeant in August of 1943. Joe was the only major leaguer on his team, and they played against nearby college teams and semipro clubs, as well as against PCL teams in a few exhibitions. DiMaggio put up with the duty without complaint. His wife and son were nearby and he was able to visit often.

Despite his proximity to his family, the marriage faltered. On October 11 in Los Angeles, Dorothy filed for divorce a second time, on the catch-all grounds of cruelty. Her timing couldn't have been worse. On the same day, the DiMaggio-less Yankees defeated the St. Louis Cardinals 2–0 to win the 1943 World Series in five games.

The divorce was granted early in 1944. Dorothy received $500 per month in alimony, plus $150 in child support and custody of Joe Jr.

In the spring of 1944, an Army survey indicated that most professional players had not seen duty overseas. Sensitive to charges of special treatment, the Army transferred DiMaggio and a host of major leaguers to Hawaii in the summer of 1944. The Navy, aware the Army was creating a powerhouse, followed suit.

Military commanders took the game seriously and behaved like

Joe DiMaggio is shown in the Yankee clubhouse with his wife, Dorothy, and son, Joe Jr., following his release from the U.S. Army. (Photograph courtesy of the Boston Globe)

After two years of army food, Staff Sergeant Joe DiMaggio is ready to chow down with Toots Shor at the latter's New York restaurant. Shor and DiMaggio were long-time friends, and DiMaggio spent many an evening in Shor's restaurant, a place where he was left to himself and his coterie of friends. (Photograph courtesy of the Boston Herald)

baseball magnates, transferring the best talent in the Armed Forces to Hawaii. DiMaggio's teammates included Red Ruffing, Johnny Beazley, and Joe Gordon. The Navy countered with a club featuring Phil Rizzuto, Pee Wee Reese, Johnny Mize, and Dominic DiMaggio, who like his brother had enlisted in 1943. In midsummer, the two clubs played a ten-game series. The Navy won eight times, but Joe was side-lined by stomach trouble the entire series.

The players were then split into several clubs. DiMaggio joined the Seventh Army Air Force team. The club played nearly a full schedule in 1944, and was easily the class of the Far East. DiMaggio reportedly hit .401 in ninety games before he was sidelined again with a stomach ailment.

He was diagnosed with ulcers, and the remainder of his tenure in the military was spent going back and forth from Army hospitals. Service life and the breakup of his marriage grated on DiMaggio, and without major league baseball, he floundered. Army ball, at any level, wasn't the same.

In October of 1944, Joe was sent back to San Francisco and he spent three weeks in the hospital. There was speculation he'd be mustered out, but the Army didn't want anyone to think Joe DiMaggio was receiving special treatment. When he left the hospital he received a twenty-one-day furlough.

DiMaggio went to New York and took a room at the Chatham Hotel, not far from where Dorothy was staying with Joe Jr. While in New York, DiMaggio arranged a luncheon with writers at Toots Shor's.

The press reported that DiMaggio looked healthy, if a little thin. DiMaggio appeared in excellent spirits, but refused to say if he was trying to get back with Dorothy. He said little of import but appeared pleased to be back among friends at Shor's.

DiMaggio was assigned to duty with the Special Services in Atlantic City, where he played more ball before his ulcers flared up again. There was no lasting reconciliation with his ex-wife. In August of 1945, as the war in Europe was ending, he was sent to an Army Hospital in St. Petersburg, Florida, for more treatment of his ulcers.

The New York press downplayed DiMaggio's illness and speculated

Following their divorce, Dorothy Arnold still remained friendly with Joe DiMaggio. Here they are shown on Christmas 1945 enjoying their son, Joe Jr., and pursuing a reconciliation that didn't work.   (Photograph courtesy of the Boston Herald)

he'd be discharged in time to join the Yankees for the end of the 1945 pennant race, but the Army moved at its own speed and DiMaggio wasn't let go until September 14. By then, the Yankees were virtually out of the race. DiMaggio offered to suit up, but Yankee president Larry MacPhail told him to rest for the 1946 season. DiMaggio spent a few days in New York after his discharge, even attending a double-header between the Browns and the Yankees on September 16, then returned home to San Francisco.

DiMaggio saw no combat and emerged from the war better off than millions of others, but he was not unscathed by the experience. No one was. The incident with his father reinforced his awareness of ethnic bias. His marriage was over, and he saw little of his son. While he played baseball during the war, service play had been poor preparation for the rigors of major-league competition and had not provided the same reinforcement to his self-esteem.

At age thirty-one, three years older than when he joined the service, DiMaggio was no longer in his prime years as an athlete. He expected to resume his career at his same prewar level of performance, but there were no guarantees. Many of his old Yankee teammates—Red Rolfe, George Selkirk, Bill Dickey, Frank Crosetti, and Lefty Gomez—had either retired or seen their skills erode. Joe DiMaggio himself was in poor health, troubled by ulcers and ten or fifteen pounds under his ideal playing weight.

In the winter of 1945, Joe DiMaggio had many questions and few answers.

CHAPTER SIX

The Agony of Achilles:
1946–49

The Yankee ballclub Joe DiMaggio rejoined in the spring of 1946 was very different from the one he left in 1942. Larry MacPhail, a flamboyant promoter who had already reinvigorated two franchises—the Cincinnati Reds and the Brooklyn Dodgers—rightly sensed that major league baseball was destined to boom in the postwar years. In 1945, he put together a syndicate with moneymen Dan Topping and Del Webb and purchased the Yankees for 2.8 million dollars from the Ruppert estate. Ed Barrow was pushed into the background and MacPhail became the dominant figure in the front office.

MacPhail cared little for tradition, and had pioneered night baseball in Cincinnati a decade before. The Yankee players, while constantly fighting with Ruppert and Barrow over contracts, nonetheless had flourished on the field under their patrician style. MacPhail was different.

They learned just how different in 1945, as MacPhail publicly blasted players, and summarily waived and then sold Hank Borowy, New York's best pitcher, to the Cubs. The move probably cost New York the pennant. Manager Joe McCarthy hated MacPhail, and took a three-week hiatus from the club under the gloss of gallbladder trouble; in reality his problems had more to do with alcohol. McCarthy

*Following the seventh game
of the 1947 World Series,
Yankee general manager
Larry MacPhail embraces
Joe DiMaggio within min-
utes of the final out. (Photograph by Bob Olen)*

tried to resign, but MacPhail held him to his contract. Despite the
return of the heart and soul of the Yankee ballclub in 1946, McCarthy
wasn't looking forward to the upcoming season.

MacPhail initiated more changes late in the winter of 1946. In mid-
February, he ordered the Yankees to Balboa, Panama, for extended
workouts in advance of formal spring training in Florida. MacPhail
saw spring training as something more than a physical exercise. It
was an opportunity to make money.

DiMaggio went to Panama with the rest of the Yankees, eager to
get in shape for the season. But the Yankees spent little time in actual
training. MacPhail initiated the exhibition season almost immediately.
MacPhail had guessed right about baseball's postwar popularity.
When the team broke camp from Florida in late March, they went on
an extended barnstorming trip, playing minor league clubs all over

the South and Midwest. The *Herald Tribune*'s Red Smith referred to it as MacPhail's "weird Chautauqua tours." The Yankees appeared ready to resume their familiar spot atop the American League, winning handily against subpar competition. DiMaggio led the way, knocking in 52 runs in 42 games, cracking 19 home runs, and hitting nearly .370. In an exhibition against Brooklyn at Ebbets Field on April 13, Smith observed after a DiMaggio home run, "You'd have thought the joint was full of Yankee fans to hear the cheering . . . But it wasn't Joe they were cheering. It was the return of big league baseball."

By the time the season opened on April 16, the Yankees had played nearly fifty exhibitions before more than a quarter of a million fans.

DiMaggio didn't know it yet, but the nature of his career had undergone a distinct change. Before the war, he was the best player on a veteran team of stars. His personal performance contributed to the success of the team, but except for a few instances, it was not absolutely critical. New York was by far the best team in baseball. Six of DiMaggio's prewar teammates eventually were elected to the Baseball Hall of Fame. The Yankees usually jumped into first place early, stretched their lead through the summer, clinched in early September, and got ready for the World Series.

After the war, it was different. Other teams, particularly Boston and Cleveland, challenged Yankee dominance. A New York pennant was no longer a foregone conclusion. In comparison to the rest of the league, DiMaggio's surrounding cast was less talented. The postwar Yankees were a team, except for DiMaggio, of solid performers and role players. DiMaggio was far more critical to the club's success. Before the war, his achievements were sometimes lost among those of his teammates. After the war, everyone looked to Joe DiMaggio.

Still, New York opened the 1946 season playing like the old Yankees, beating Philadelphia 5–0 on Spud Chandler's shutout. DiMaggio announced his return with a long two-run homer in the sixth.

By the time the Yankees faced Boston for a three-game series beginning on May 10, their record was a stellar 16–8. There was only one problem. The team from the Bronx wasn't the only club playing like the old Yankees. So were the Red Sox, and the team from Boston was better at it than the New Yorkers.

Red Sox owner Tom Yawkey's millions were finally paying off. For once, Boston had enough pitching to back up their vaunted offense. The Red Sox had won fourteen in a row on their way to a record of 20–3, $4\frac{1}{2}$ games ahead of the Yankees by the time they met in May.

More than 64,000 fans packed Yankee Stadium for the first game of the series. MacPhail used the occasion to mount one of his first promotions, holding a special "Ladies' Day." He passed out more than 125,000 free passes (only 6,000 were used), gave away 500 pairs of nylons, and held a pregame fashion show in which models were driven around the field in pastel-colored jeeps. As the *Herald Tribune* reported, "Yesterday's show had just about everything in it but a New York victory." The Yankee players couldn't believe it.

Boston won 5–4, for their fifteenth consecutive victory. DiMaggio accounted for all of New York's scoring with a fifth-inning grand slam, the only one of his career 13 career grand slams that came in a losing effort. While the Yankees snapped the Red Sox streak the next day with a 2–0 win, the Sox took the third game and pushed their lead over New York to 5¹/₂ games. The Yankees did not get close the rest of the season.

On May 21, Yankee manager Joe McCarthy reached the breaking point. As the Yankees flew from Cleveland to Detroit—air travel was another of MacPhail's innovations—McCarthy lost control. Drinking heavily, he berated Yankee pitcher Joe Page over Page's own indiscretions, then went on to castigate everyone else he could think of, including MacPhail. By the time the plane landed in Detroit, McCarthy's days were numbered.

Dom DiMaggio is shown with his sister Marie and an unidentified youngster in 1946. (Photograph courtesy of the Boston Herald)

He left the club to dry out, and resigned by telegram three days later, citing health reasons, just as the Yankees began another do-or-die series with Boston. The real reason for his resignation was Mac-Phail. MacPhail named Bill Dickey manager, and the Yankees died in Boston, dropping two of three.

McCarthy, who had served as Yankee manager since 1931, left an enviable record of eight pennants and seven world championships in just over fourteen seasons. He was popular with his players. The Yankees considered themselves professionals and so did McCarthy, who treated them as such.

Joe DiMaggio was not alone when he said, "I consider Joe McCarthy the best manager I ever played for," adding, "he was like a father to us." To describe someone in familial terms was DiMaggio's highest compliment.

As the Yankees dropped farther behind Boston, DiMaggio, after cracking 20 home runs in New York's first forty-one games, went into a slump. He took some of the blame, and plenty of boos, for the Yankees' performance. Just before the All-Star break, in the first game of a doubleheader in Philadelphia, DiMaggio slid into second, caught his spikes, and twisted his left leg. Joe had to be helped from the field, having suffered torn cartilage in the left knee and a sprained ankle. For the first time, he missed the All-Star Game.

At the time of the injury, the Red Sox lead was approaching double figures. DiMaggio was hitting only .266. While he was still considered one of the best players in the game, if not the very best, his disappointing first half chipped away at that image. Ted Williams, hitting .345, was clearly his superior as a hitter. While there were still days when DiMaggio's skills made him stand out among all others, there were too many days when fans left the ballpark talking about the ballplayer DiMaggio used to be.

Dominic DiMaggio started in Joe's place at the All-Star Game. Joe was out of the Yankee lineup until August. When he returned, he started to hit, though without his usual power. He favored the leg, which made his left heel hurt. On the basepaths and in the field, DiMaggio sometimes coasted, saving full effort for moments that mattered.

Bill Dickey feuded with MacPhail and resigned in September. Coach Johnny Neun finished out the season. The Yankees tumbled to third place, 87–67, seventeen games behind the Red Sox. DiMaggio finished with his worst batting average to date, .290, with 25 home runs and 95 RBI. In his last 92 games, he hit only five home runs.

Few recognized it at the time, but DiMaggio's career was at a crossroads. Except for the first six weeks of the season, he had not been the same player he was before the war. Coupled with his disappointing performance in 1942, it appeared as if DiMaggio was a player of diminishing impact.

MacPhail felt precisely that, and in the off-season offered DiMaggio straight up to the Washington Senators for 1946 batting champ Mickey Vernon, a first baseman three years younger than DiMaggio but without his myriad skills. To the Yankees' later relief, the Senators turned down the deal.

That didn't stop MacPhail. Other changes were afoot. On October 19 he traded Joe Gordon, who hit only .210 in 1946 and openly feuded with MacPhail, to Cleveland. On DiMaggio's recommendation, the Yankees received pitcher Allie Reynolds. Two days later, pitcher Ernie Bonham was traded to Pittsburgh for hurler Cookie Cuccurullo. Two weeks later, after denying rumors that he tried to hire the Dodgers' Leo Durocher and the Cardinals' Frankie Frisch, MacPhail hired veteran manager Bucky Harris, and then signed Brooklyn's Charlie Dressen as coach. Ed Barrow, age seventy-eight and very much out of the loop in the Yankees' front office, resigned two weeks later. In a final move, after the Senators rebuffed the trade for Vernon, MacPhail

The infamous heel spur that plagued DiMaggio is shown in this X-ray image from 1947, prior to the surgical removal of the spur. (Photograph from The Sporting News)

signed George McQuinn, the A's' slick-fielding but aging first baseman, as a free agent. If nothing else, MacPhail stayed busy.

Amid all the off-season activity, it was easy to overlook the fact that on January 7, Joe DiMaggio underwent surgery at Beth David Hospital in New York to remove a spur on his left heel. The injury was first diagnosed by X ray in September, and was likely a by-product of the knee injury. Surgeon Jules Gordon told the Yankees DiMaggio would be ready for spring training, scheduled to begin in Puerto Rico in mid-February.

DiMaggio traveled to Puerto Rico with the team, but his heel looked as if the surgery had just taken place. The wound failed to heal over, and after waiting two weeks in San Juan for some improvement, Yankee doctors sent DiMaggio to Johns Hopkins Hospital in Baltimore to have the wound assessed.

A week later, after DiMaggio failed to respond to penicillin treatment, doctors decided to do a skin graft. On March 11, a piece of skin 2 inches long and 1 1/2 inches wide was removed from DiMaggio's right thigh and grafted over the open wound.

On March 26, DiMaggio returned to spring training walking on crutches. Harris and MacPhail were already bickering, and MacPhail was in trouble with the commissioner's office due to a long-running dispute with Leo Durocher and Branch Rickey. The Yankees wanted DiMaggio to travel with the team on their barnstorming tour, but Joe thought his recovery would be better served if he stayed in Florida. DiMaggio won the argument.

He started working out a few days later, and within a week was able to run. Joe joined the Yankees for opening day on April 15, but as usual, wasn't well enough to play in the Yanks' 6–1 win. Johnny Lindell played center field.

DiMaggio nearly never made another appearance for the Yankees at all. In early April, Yankee owner Dan Topping and Red Sox owner Tom Yawkey reportedly spent an evening drinking, at the conclusion of which they agreed to trade Joe DiMaggio for Ted Williams. With DiMaggio still injured, the trade was lopsided in New York's favor, but Boston owner Tom Yawkey, who collected ballplayers like others collected knickknacks, wanted DiMaggio. When the alcoholic haze lifted the following morning, both parties apparently reconsidered the greatest trade never made.

The 1947 Yankees were much changed. McQuinn played first, Snuffy Stirnweiss replaced Gordon at second, and Billy Johnson took over at third. Rookies Larry Berra (not yet known as Yogi) and infielder Bobby Brown played key backup roles, while Allie Reynolds and Spec Shea joined Joe Page, Spud Chandler, and Bill Bevens on the pitching staff. Members of the team were still feeling each other out, and it showed on the field, even after DiMaggio returned to the lineup.

He pinch-hit on April 20, then started in the first game of a double-header against Philadelphia the next day, belting a three-run home run in his second at bat.

The Yankees couldn't get going, even losing to Washington, 1–0, on April 27 as 58,339 fans turned out at the Stadium on Babe Ruth Day. Fortunately for New York, the heavily favored Red Sox weren't playing any better; Boo Ferriss, Tex Hughson, and Mickey Harris all had arm woes. Detroit, Cleveland, and Chicago battled for the top spot early as the Yankees and Red Sox struggled to play .500.

The Yankees came together as a team on one subject: MacPhail. As the club prepared to play the Red Sox in a key four-game series on May 23, MacPhail slapped fines of $25 to $100 on six Yankee players, including DiMaggio. Charlie Keller, catcher Aaron Robinson, and Di-Maggio were fined after refusing to appear in a special newsreel shoot set up by MacPhail for the Army Signal Corps. Johnny Lindell, Don Johnson, and an unidentified Yankee rookie were fined when Johnson and the rookie took Lindell's advice and failed to make a promotional appearance.

DiMaggio's $100 fine was the largest and the first of his career. The Yankees were further angered when MacPhail, who wanted the team to travel by air, told the players that those who refused to fly were responsible for their own transportation.

DiMaggio and the other Yankee players were incensed. They grated against MacPhail's incessant promotions, which they felt belit-tled them as individuals and made a mockery of the Yankee tradition. Red Smith captured the club's feeling when he wrote that "a seal that can play Beethoven's Fifth on an oboe is more beautiful to L. S. Mac-Phail than a twenty-game pitcher."

Faced with intense criticism over the fines, MacPhail returned the money to the players. DiMaggio refused to accept McPhail's offer and impressed his teammates when he snapped back, "Give mine to the Damon Runyon Cancer Fund."

The incident brought the club together, and DiMaggio proved he was still the team leader. Although he denied the incident had anything to do with his surge, in his next sixteen games he hit .493. New York crushed Boston in four straight. In the first two games, the

Joe DiMaggio Jr. and Sr. pose for photographers at Yankee Stadium in 1947.   (Photograph from Transcendental Graphics, Mark Rucker)

Red Sox failed to score as the Yankees won 9–0 and 5–0. In the series' final two games, Yankee bats did the damage. DiMaggio lifted his average above .300 with four hits in the third game to key a 17–2 win, then hit a three-run homer in New York's 9–3 victory to sweep the series. DiMaggio was 9 for 16 in the series, while Ted Williams was silent. Any doubts about DiMaggio or of his importance to the Yankee club were erased. The Red Sox were dead and the Yankees on a roll.

The Yankees beat Detroit three of four in early June to close to within a game of the Tigers. Writing in the *World-Telegram*, Joe Williams commented, "There used to be a saying 'As Ruth goes so go the Yankees.' It was more than a saying. It was a lively fact. You can say that about DiMaggio these days . . . As a matter of record, DiMaggio has been the answer since the first year he joined the Yankees." While the Yanks lost Charlie Keller, leading the league in home runs and RBI, to a back injury, nothing could stop DiMaggio's Yankees.

The Yankees pushed into first place in mid-June and stayed there. DiMaggio played his best baseball since 1941, at one point hitting in 25 of 27 games for a blistering .468 average. Only DiMaggio and a few teammates knew he was playing with a sore right elbow. He was good for only one strong throw a game, and in fact threw out only two base runners all year, but his judicious use of that single throw kept other teams from catching on.

By the All-Star break DiMaggio had pushed his average over .340. The Yankees had won eight in a row and their lead over Boston and Detroit approached double figures. In the All-Star Game, DiMaggio resumed his customary position in center field for the AL and contributed a single to the league's 2–1 win.

The Yankees suffered a potential setback after the All-Star break when Spec Shea and Spud Chandler were injured, but the Yankees claimed veteran Bobo Newsom on waivers from Washington and called up twenty-eight-year-old Vic Raschi from Portland. New York stretched the winning streak to nineteen games with a doubleheader sweep of Cleveland on July 17, tying the league record set by the 1906 White Sox. The winning pitchers were Newsom, the 200th win of his career, and Raschi.

Although the streak ended the next day when New York was shut out by Detroit pitcher Fred Hutchinson, the pennant race was over. Neither Boston nor Detroit could keep pace.

DiMaggio gave the Yankees a scare in late July. First his neck and shoulder started giving him trouble, then his heel acted up, and he missed eight games. After playing in the Yankees' 10–6 win over Boston July 31, the tendons in his left leg swelled, sidelining him again. DiMaggio was disconsolate, admitting to Dan Daniel, "I wonder if I ever will play again. It seems as if a jinx has set out to ruin me." But Joe rested and recovered in a few weeks.

But by then, DiMaggio's absence made no difference. The Yankees clinched on September 15 and finished 97–57, twelve games ahead of Detroit and fourteen better than the Red Sox. Although DiMaggio tailed off in September, the season represented a significant comeback. His final average of .315, with 20 home runs and 97 RBI in 139 games, modest totals for DiMaggio, belied his true worth. He reclaimed his place as one of the best players in the game.

MacPhail's old team, the Dodgers, won the National League pennant by five games over St. Louis. Keyed by the play of rookie Jackie

Robinson, the first African-American to play major league baseball in the twentieth century, and rookie pitcher Ralph Branca's 21 wins, the underdog Dodgers were a scrappy team not easily intimidated. The seven-game series was one of the best ever.

The biggest World Series crowd in history, 73,365, packed Yankee Stadium for game one on September 30. In the first inning, Brooklyn scored when Jackie Robinson walked, stole second, then got caught in a rundown between second and third on Pete Reiser's tap back to the box. Robinson's baserunning allowed Reiser to move to second, and Dixie Walker, the man the Yankees sold to make room for DiMaggio in 1936, singled him home.

For four innings, Branca held the Yankees hitless. DiMaggio led off the fifth with a ground ball to deep short and beat Pee Wee Reese's throw for the first Yankee hit. Yankee fans knew what to expect next. Branca came undone, walking McQuinn and hitting Johnson before Lindell doubled, scoring two. By the time Brooklyn got out of the inning, Branca was gone and the Yankees had scored three more to go ahead 5–1. The lead held, and New York won, 5–3.

The New York press ballyhooed DiMaggio after game two, although he had only one meaningless hit in the 10–3 Yankee rout. But DiMaggio shined in the field, while his counterpart on the Dodgers, Pete Reiser, battled the sun and shadows all day and lost, misplaying several fly balls into base hits. By doing what he did normally, DiMaggio was a star.

After the game, Bob Cooke of the *Herald Tribune* wrote: "It is difficult to suggest to DiMaggio that he played a great game. After a while it becomes redundant because it is a DiMaggio habit." Cooke asked DiMaggio if the outfield conditions were tough, and if they bothered him as much as they did Reiser. DiMaggio sagely replied, "It's always like that in the fall. It gets a lot darker around home plate and a haze settles in the background. It's no cinch to see a fly ball coming out of the shadows. [But] don't worry about the old boy. I've been playing in this park a long while."

The Series moved to Brooklyn's Ebbets Field for game three on October 2. The Yankees started Bobo Newsom against his old teammates, but Newsom didn't make it into the third inning as the Dodgers routed him with six runs. DiMaggio singled home a run in the third, then cracked a two-run homer in the fifth off Joe Hatten, but the Yankees failed to catch the Dodgers, who won 9–8 as Hugh Casey shut New York down in the last three innings.

Game four was one of the most memorable in World Series history.

The Yankees scored in the first when DiMaggio walked with the bases loaded and no out, but Brooklyn manager Burt Shotton pulled starter Harry Taylor and relief pitcher Hal Gregg got out of the inning. The Yankees scored again in the fourth when Billy Johnson tripled and Lindell doubled.

Brooklyn came back to score a run in the fifth without a base hit. Yankee pitcher Bill Bevens walked Spider Jorgensen and Hal Gregg to start the inning. Eddie Stanky sacrificed and Jorgensen scored on a fielder's choice. Most fans then became aware that Bevens, who was wild all day, was throwing a no-hitter.

The Yankee lead held, as Bevens wiggled out of trouble inning after inning. In the sixth, Walker led off with a walk but was stranded. In the seventh, according to Red Smith, DiMaggio caught Spider Jorgensen's "monstrous drive like a well fed banquet guest picking his teeth," to preserve the no-hitter. In the eighth, Tommy Henrich robbed Gene Hermanski, leaping up against the wall in right for the third out.

The Yankees led into the ninth. A weary Bill Bevens took the mound needing only three outs to make Series history.

Brooklyn catcher Bruce Edwards led off. He hit a fly ball to deep left and Johnny Lindell drifted back and caught it at the base of the fence for the first out. Then Carl Furillo stepped to the plate.

Bevens worked Furillo carefully. After struggling with control all day, Bevens was wild in the ninth as well. Furillo walked and Al Gionfriddo came in to pinch-run.

Spider Jorgensen, up next, fouled out to McQuinn. Bevens was one out away from a no-hitter, and the Dodgers were one out away from falling behind three games to one.

But the Dodgers didn't give up. Brooklyn manager Burt Shotton, knowing Yankee catcher Larry Berra was in the game for his bat, not his defense, called for a steal and Gionfriddo made second as Berra's throw wasn't close. The tying run was 180 feet from home.

Now Bucky Harris made his move. Bevens walked Pete Reiser intentionally, his tenth walk of the game. Shotton responded by sending Eddie Miksis in to run for Reiser, who was playing with a bad leg, and batting Cookie Lavagetto for Hugh Casey.

Bevens got a strike on Lavagetto, then threw his next pitch over the plate. Lavagetto reached out and slapped at the ball.

It sailed to right field with Tommy Henrich in quick pursuit. Henrich tried for the catch. With two outs, both runners were moving. He reached for the ball at the base of the wall, but it tailed away and bounded off the fence.

Brooklyn Dodger reserve out-fielder Al Gionfriddo makes one of the greatest catches in World Series history as he saves game six for the Dodgers by robbing Joe DiMaggio of a game-tying home run.   (Photograph from Bettmann Archives)

First Gionfriddo, then Miksis rounded third and scored. The no-hitter was gone, and the Dodgers won, 3–2. The Dodger players, and several hundred fans, mobbed Lavagetto. He was half-carried, half-pushed into a celebration in the Dodger clubhouse.

Other teams might have collapsed after such a defeat. The loss was bitter and the disappointment real. But the Yankees didn't collapse. DiMaggio did not allow it.

The next game, Spec Shea shut down Brooklyn with a four-hitter. Dodger pitchers couldn't find the plate, as starter Rex Barney walked nine in 4⅔ innings for Brooklyn. But like Bevens the day before, Barney was wild enough to keep the Yankees off balance.

Shea helped his cause by knocking a run in the fourth. In the fifth, with one out and the bases empty, DiMaggio settled the game with a home run into the left-field stands. Brooklyn touched Shea for a single run in the sixth, but the Yankees won, 2–1.

Another record crowd greeted the clubs when the Series returned to the Bronx for game six on October 5. Brooklyn scored two in the first and two in the third to take a 4–0 lead. New York responded in the bottom of the third with four runs, knotting the score.

Entering the sixth, New York led 5–4 after scoring a run in the fourth. This time the Dodgers exploded for four runs to lead 8–5.

Up three runs, Burt Shotton played defense. He pulled Ralph Branca, installed Cookie Lavagetto at third in place of Jorgensen, and replaced Eddie Miksis in left with Al Gionfriddo.

With one out in the Yankee sixth, Snuffy Stirnweiss walked and Henrich fouled out. Then Berra singled to left, Stirnweiss stopping at second.

DiMaggio came to bat in the kind of situation he excelled at. Time and time again, DiMaggio got the big hit in similar situations. The Yankees needed him once more.

DiMaggio hit the ball on a line to left. Gionfriddo, inexplicably playing shallow, raced to his right and twisted around as he and the ball reached the low left-field fence at the same time.

Gionfriddo reached with his glove hand as he turned in front of the wall. DiMaggio's drive stuck in his glove, cutting off the cheers of nearly 75,000 fans. By the narrowest of margins, the catch prevented a three-run home run.

The Yankee threat was over. DiMaggio, watching the play, pulled up near second as he saw Gionfriddo make the catch. He took a halfskip then registered his disappointment by kicking the ground. DiMaggio rarely expressed emotion on the field, and his gesture did not pass unnoticed. The Yankees went on to lose, 8–6. Gionfriddo's catch was the difference.

After the game, the press crowded around the two outfielders. Gionfriddo was effusive. "I figure I must have run about eighty-five feet," said the beaming outfielder. "I started back for the ball and then turned around. It was still way over my head. So I turned again and had to twist around to make the catch. The ball landed in the webbing of my glove. It would have been a home run, for sure."

DiMaggio didn't have much to say. Privately, he said Gionfriddo was out of position and made what should have been an easy catch look difficult, but Joe was still disappointed the ball had been caught.

After the histrionics of the first six games, game seven was anticlimactic. Brooklyn scored twice in the second to take a 2–0 lead, but the Yankees pecked away, scoring a single run in the second, two in the fourth, and one more in the sixth and seventh. Yankee relief pitcher Joe Page stifled Brooklyn on only one hit over the final five innings. New York won, 5–2, taking the Series.

As the Yankees celebrated, Larry MacPhail shocked everyone by announcing his retirement. Later, at the team victory party, he tried to renege, blasted everyone, got into a fistfight with at least one other reveler and tried to fire assistant George Weiss. In the end, MacPhail was fired and Weiss became the Yankees' new general manager. The players bade MacPhail farewell and good riddance. His leaving made victory twice as sweet.

Although DiMaggio went hitless in the finale, the win was satisfying. It had been six long years since he had last played, and won, a World Series. While he hit only .231, he played a crucial role in several Yankee wins. He did hit two home runs, and missed a third by inches.

His contributions did not go unnoticed. After the series, Branch Rickey of the Dodgers was philosophical. "We were beaten by a darn good ball club," he said. "Any team with Henrich and DiMaggio is a darn good team. Better put DiMaggio's name down first, incidentally."

Rickey wasn't the only person who felt that way. In 1947, DiMaggio proved that while he might no longer have been the best hitter in the game, he was still the best player. His team had won again.

Those impressions were confirmed in late November. While Joe was recovering from surgery to remove bone chips in his right elbow, the Base Ball Writers of America selected DiMaggio as the American League's Most Valuable Player for the third time.

The award was not without debate. Boston's Ted Williams won the

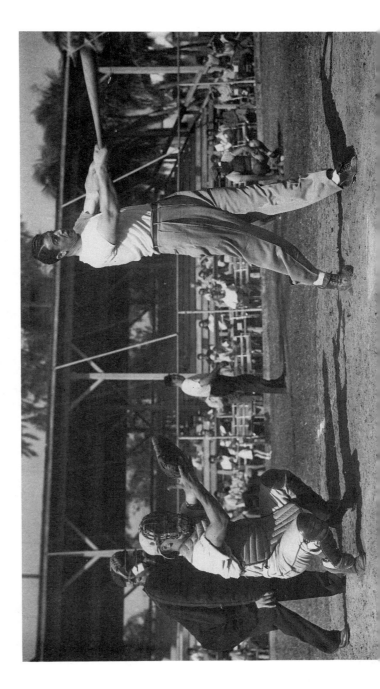

Joe DiMaggio takes a cut in a charity game between the sportscasters and Miami Beach All-Stars at Flamingo Park on February 23, 1948.   (Photograph courtesy of the Boston Globe*)*

Joe DiMaggio singles to left in his first appearance of the 1949 season on June 28 at Fenway Park. (Photograph from Transcendental Graphics, Mark Rucker)

triple crown with a .343 average, 32 home runs, and 114 RBI, yet Di-Maggio defeated Williams for the award by one point, 202 to 201. Williams felt he was robbed. He later blamed Mel Webb, a Boston sportswriter, for his loss of the award. Ted received a vote on only 23 of the 24 ballots. Williams claimed Webb maliciously left Williams's name off his MVP ballot, not even selecting him as one of the ten most valuable players in the league.

For years, baseball historians took Williams's claims at face value. But while researching the topic for a 1991 biography of Williams, this writer uncovered information that disproved Williams's claims. In that book, and in a follow-up story published in *The Sporting News* on December 20, 1993, this author documented what actually happened during the MVP balloting.

While it was true that Williams was left off a ballot, the guilty party wasn't Mel Webb. Boston sportswriter Harold Kaese's private papers reveal that Webb didn't even have a vote in 1947. Williams's three first-place votes, the only he received, came from three Boston writers: Joe Cashman, Burt Whitman, and Jack Malaney. Kaese claimed the guilty party was a writer in a Midwest city.

But even that didn't cost Williams the award. For several seasons, the pattern of MVP voting, done by writers covering each league, had been highly suspicious. That was true again in 1947. DiMaggio, who received eight first-place votes, was left off the ballot by not just one, but *three* writers. Yet Yogi Berra, who played in only 85 games and finished 15th in the balloting, received two second-place votes, and Eddie Joost, who hit only .206, received two first-place votes.

Two years later in *The Sporting News*, Dan Daniel broke a story that revealed what may have happened. After the announcement of the 1949 award, he learned that some writers were betting substantial amounts of money on the outcome of the vote. What the bookies didn't know was that the writers knew the results a week in advance of the public announcement. Armed with inside information, they bet accordingly. Daniel estimated that in 1949, in New York alone, as much as $500,000 changed hands. As a result of Daniel's story, Baseball Commissioner Happy Chandler forced the BBWA to change their voting procedure.

The inequities of the 1947 vote were likely the result of an attempt by some writers to skew the outcome in their favor. Sadly, this unfortunate incident cast doubt on whether or not DiMaggio was a worthy recipient of the award. Although his season-ending numbers pale next to Williams's, his performance when the pennant was at stake proved his value. DiMaggio was as worthy of the award as any winner in other years.

The accolades continued in the off-season. Although DiMaggio's statistics were down, observers now gave his contributions more weight. He wasn't a kid anymore. The New York writers were glad to have him back and glad to have the Yankees in first place again. As DiMaggio approached baseball middle age, the writers were increasingly sympathetic. They found it easier to identify with this postwar, physically challenged DiMaggio than with the prewar, perfect player. His occasional loss due to injury only made him appear better when he did play.

The respect the writers felt toward DiMaggio was perilously close to outright awe. He was not only a hero to the fans, he was a hero to the writers. Joe Williams of the *World-Telegram* was effusive in his praise, and his comments mirrored those of other writers. Before the 1948 season, Williams wrote that DiMaggio "has grown into one of our most impressive institutions. . . . There is nothing DiMaggio can't do on a baseball field. Literally nothing. Name a better right-handed hitter. Or a better thrower when his arm is right. A better fielder or a better baserunner . . . Watch him when he hits the dirt. Watch him slide in and hook the bag with his toe. Perfect, absolutely perfect. . . He's an artist in the exact sense of the word, a Cezanne with a finger mitt, a Van Gogh with a Louisville slugger."

The Yankees thought so too. On January 5, 1948, DiMaggio signed a contract worth $65,000, his first raise since 1942. Only Bob Feller and Ted Williams were better paid.

In spring training, DiMaggio appeared fully recovered from the heel spur and sore elbow, running easily and making throws with accustomed accuracy. If anything, the Yankees appeared even stronger than the previous year, as veteran pitcher Eddie Lopat joined the Yankees' rotation.

The Yankees opened the 1948 season in Washington on April 19. On the 21st, while the Yankees fell to the Senators 6–3, DiMaggio answered any lingering doubt about his physical condition by hitting one of the longest home runs in Griffith Stadium history and cutting down Mickey Vernon at third base with a great throw.

The Yankees opened at the Stadium against Boston two days later in a gala celebration of the ballpark's silver anniversary. DiMaggio collected his MVP award before the game, but the Yankees lost to Boston, 4–0, to drop their record to 1–3.

New York quickly righted itself, winning five in a row to bring their record to 6–3. But the Cleveland Indians went undefeated in April, and the Yanks played catch-up all season.

As the Yankees struggled to catch Cleveland, DiMaggio displayed the full range of his talents. Although his average hovered at about .280, on May 20 against Chicago, DiMaggio led the Yankees to a 13–2 win with his best game of the year, cracking two home runs while hitting for the cycle and driving in six. Two days later, as the Yankees split a doubleheader with the Indians to remain two games out of first, DiMaggio hit three home runs in the first game, two against Bob Feller, and drove in all six Yankee runs in New York's 6–5 win. But Joe went hitless in game two, and New York lost a chance to move into a first-place tie.

He continued his hot hitting, literally carrying the Yankees in their

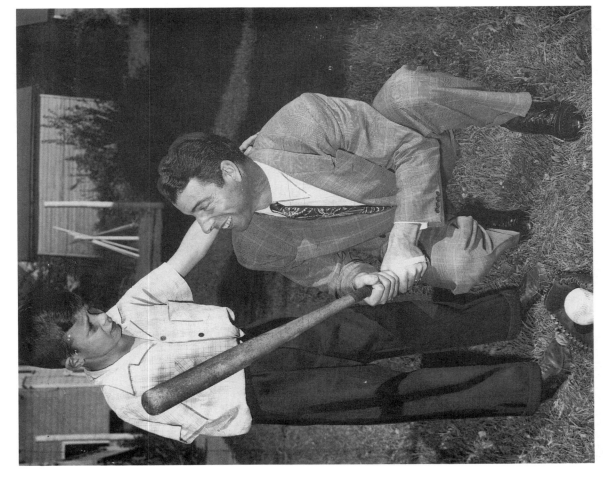

Eleven-year-old Bill Provance of Joliet, Illinois, received an unexpected visitor when Joe DiMaggio came to share batting tips and baseball talk for over two hours in September 1948. Provance had lost his right arm in a merry-go-round accident the previous summer.
(Photograph courtesy of the Boston Herald)

pursuit of the Indians, hitting three homers in a doubleheader sweep of St. Louis on June 20. Facing Cleveland in the first game of a four-game set two days later, DiMaggio's 15th home run of the year sparked a Yankee rally and the club charged to a 13–2 win. New York took three of four to pull to within a game and a half of first.

It wasn't enough. The Indians, paced by player-manager Lou Boudreau and a pitching rotation that supplemented Feller with Bob Lemon and Gene Bearden, refused to falter.

In late June, DiMaggio started breaking down. This time the problem was his right heel. He had been playing hurt, but his agony increased with each game. Finally, on July 11, DiMaggio sat out against Washington, missing his first game of the year. In the All-Star Game two days later, DiMaggio pulled himself from the starting lineup and made only a pinch-hitting appearance in the eighth, knocking in a run with a sacrifice fly in the AL's 5–2 victory.

While the Yankees chased Cleveland, the Red Sox, under new manager Joe McCarthy, made their move. The Sox went 24–9 in July and surged past New York and Cleveland. Entering the final two months of the season, only a few games separated the Indians, Red Sox, Yankees, and the surprising Philadelphia Athletics.

DiMaggio kept the Yankees close, single-handedly winning games with his bat, but they couldn't catch Cleveland. Over the last two months of the season, as his physical woes mounted, DiMaggio played under increasing pain. But like the boxers he admired, DiMaggio fought like a champion against a younger, more talented foe. His legs were gone and his head said stop, but his heart wouldn't let him. He just kept punching as his opponents, and the men in his own corner, marveled at his tenacity.

In early August, the Yankees appeared out of the race, losing three of four in Cleveland, dropping two to Boston in the Stadium, and splitting a four-game series with the A's to drop to fourth place. Then, on August 16, Babe Ruth died.

The Bambino's death pushed the pennant race to the back pages, although the Yankees kept their diminishing hopes alive with two wins over the Senators. On the morning of August 19, as the Yankees prepared to play in Washington, 75,000 people stood in a drenching rain on Fifth Avenue as another 6,000 crowded into St. Patrick's Cathedral for Ruth's funeral. Despite the pennant race, DiMaggio left his Yankee teammates and served as an honorary pallbearer as America laid Ruth to rest.

After the funeral, DiMaggio had to catch a plane back to Washington, but the crowds made it next to impossible to grab a cab. Toots Shor saw Bill Paley, the president of CBS, roll past in a limousine. Shor chased down Paley's car, explained DiMaggio's predicament, and Paley climbed out, waving DiMaggio inside, and told his driver to take DiMaggio to LaGuardia airport.

DiMaggio arrived at Griffith Stadium in the third inning and replaced Cliff Mapes in the Yankee outfield. Washington led, 1–0.

But now the Yankees had DiMaggio. He opened the fourth with a single off Early Wynn and the Yankees exploded for six runs, eventually winning, 8–1. Just as DiMaggio led the Yankees on a winning streak following Gehrig's death a decade before, he did so again. The Yankees won twenty out of twenty-three following Ruth's death. DiMaggio hit seven home runs and averaged nearly an RBI a game during the win skein.

In October 1948 Joe DiMaggio spent one of only three World Series–less Octobers in his entire career. He instead came to Boston, where he waited in his hotel room for the Red Sox and brother Dominic to face the Indians in a pennant play-off game at Fenway Park. (Photograph courtesy of the Boston Globe)

But the Red Sox matched the surge, winning twenty-two of twenty-six. In the season's final month, the two clubs played each other eight times. The Yankees came into Boston on September 9 for a three-game series still 1½ games behind the Red Sox.

The first game typified their battles, as each club went for the knockout, then struggled to hang on. The Yankees battered Boston's starting pitcher Joe Dobson for four runs in the top of the first. DiMaggio contributed a run-scoring single.

The Red Sox came back before their home crowd in the bottom of the inning with five runs off Spec Shea. The game was tied at six when the Red Sox scored four in the seventh to win, 10–6. The next day, the Red Sox did it again. After the Yankees took a 3–0 lead, the Sox used a six-run outburst in the fifth to win going away, 9–4. The Yankees dropped three and a half games back.

The game of September 10 was a must-win for New York. With the score tied at 6, the game entered extra innings. In the tenth, Red Sox reliever Earl Caldwell walked two and hit a batter. He also struck out Charlie Keller and Hank Bauer. DiMaggio came up with two out and the bases loaded.

Red Smith provided the quintessential description of the matchup. After DiMaggio fouled the first pitch back over the grandstand, "Caldwell threw another . . . Joe hit. The crowd made a noise like a fat man punched in the stomach. But the screaming liner went a few feet foul before it rocketed into the wire catch-all surmounting the left field wall." After two balls "Caldwell threw another within reach. Joe's brother Dom in center field whirled and started running. Then he stopped . . . The ball went a bit to the right of the flagpole, six, eight, maybe ten rows up in the bleachers. There had been five pitches. Three were within reach. All three went out of the ballpark. One was a fair ball. That is the end of the story." The Yankees won, 11–6, and stayed alive.

Despite winning five of their next six, the Yankees failed to head off Boston. Each day DiMaggio made the supreme effort and each day he broke down a little more. On September 16, a writer wrote that DiMaggio needed heel surgery and planned to hold out for $125,000 in 1949. DiMaggio exploded. The salary demands were a fiction, and while his heel pained him, he didn't like the idea of a writer letting everybody know it. DiMaggio had played hurt much of the year, but tried to disguise the extent of his injury, even convincing Jimmy Cannon not to print that he had to take stairs one at a time. He constantly quizzed his own teammates, asking, "How do I look, do I look okay?" lest he give away the extent of his injuries to the opposition.

"As for having the operation on my heel, I don't know," he snapped, "I'm playing. I feel like a mummy. To hold the bandage on my left thigh where the charley horse is, I have to have a bandage around my middle; I have a patch on my hip where I have a strawberry, and I have another bandage on my left hand." Then DiMaggio went out and cracked his 300th career home run as the Yankees split with Detroit.

The Red Sox finally stumbled, and Cleveland clawed back into the race. On September 24, all three clubs were within a game of each other as the league made plans for every possible play-off scenario. The Yankees played host to Boston for three games.

New York scored two in the first off Ellis Kinder as DiMaggio contributed a sacrifice fly, but Ted Williams's two-run double in the third gave Boston a 3–2 lead. DiMaggio counterpunched in the bottom of the inning, as his single scored Bobby Brown to tie the score.

Boston came back with one in the fourth before Bucky Harris pulled Vic Raschi in favor of Joe Page. Page gave up one run, walking Ted Williams with the bases loaded, but got out of the inning. The Yankees exploded for four runs in the fifth and two more in the sixth as Page shut down the Red Sox. The Yankees won, 9–6. Cleveland, Boston, and New York all shared first place.

The next day, Boston came back behind Jack Kramer's seven-hitter to win, 7–3, despite DiMaggio's two hits. Cleveland also won and the Yankees fell to second place. The next day, New York pitcher Tommy Byrne silenced Boston on five hits and the Yankees, keyed by Henrich's first-inning home run, won 6–2 to pull even with Boston again. Cleveland remained in the lead with a win.

While the Yankees won two of three against Philadelphia, Cleveland matched their mark, and the Red Sox won three in a row. One last showdown remained.

The Yanks came to Boston for the final two games of the season, trailing the Red Sox and Indians by one. With a sweep, New York could conceivably win the pennant. With a loss, they were finished.

In the first game, for once, Ted Williams outperformed DiMaggio, but Williams had help. DiMaggio was just about the entire Yankee attack. Ted hit a two-run homer in the first to put the Red Sox up. In the third, with Johnny Pesky on first, Williams hit one to the gap in right, but DiMaggio glided over and cut the ball off, holding Pesky at third. But other hits went in other directions and the Red Sox scored two more.

The Yankees trailed 5–0 when DiMaggio came up in the seventh.

An exterior view of DiMaggio's Famous Restaurant at Fisherman's Wharf in San Francisco, c. 1949. For many years the restaurant was managed by Tom DiMaggio, Joe's older brother.   (Photograph from The Sporting News)

He crashed a double off the left field wall. Then, despite dragging his left leg behind him—as one writer described, "like a wounded animal"—he took third on a ground ball and scored on a sacrifice fly to make the score 5–1.

No one left Fenway Park until DiMaggio batted to lead off the ninth. He grounded out. The Red Sox clinched a tie for the pennant. New York's pennant race was over.

There was no reason in the world for DiMaggio to play in the season finale the next day, except for the fact that he was Joe DiMaggio. He was hurt, and New York's season was over. But the Red Sox were still battling Cleveland for first place. DiMaggio had only missed one game all season, and felt it wouldn't be fair if he sat this one out.

New York lost to Boston 10–5, but the Tigers defeated the Indians, forcing a play-off for the pennant the next day. Even in defeat, DiMaggio was magnificent. He went 4 for 5, giving the Yankees a 1–0 lead in the first, knocking in Henrich with a double, smacking another double as New York pulled to within one of the Red Sox in the fifth, then knocking a single in the seventh as the Yankees threatened. But it wasn't enough.

In the ninth, DiMaggio singled again for his fourth hit of the game. Yankee manager Bucky Harris sent Steve Souchock in to pinch-run.

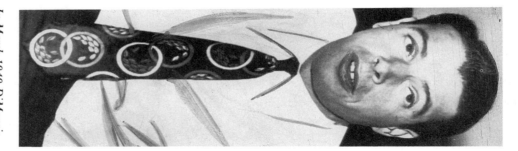

In March 1949 DiMaggio visited the office of Dr. G. E. Bennett to have his aching heel checked. (Photograph courtesy of the Washington Post)

The Fenway Park crowd cheered DiMaggio as he gingerly ran from the field, his season finally over. His performance over the last month had single-handedly kept New York in the race and nearly kept Boston out of it. The Red Sox fans appreciated his effort. DiMaggio tipped his cap and disappeared into the dugout.

DiMaggio's performance impressed everyone. After the game, Red Smith wrote of the Red Sox win, "It wasn't easy. The Yankees have a guy named Joe DiMaggio. Sometimes a fellow gets a little tired of writing about DiMaggio; a fellow thinks 'There must be another ball-player in the world worth mentioning.' But there isn't really, not worth mentioning in the same breath as Joe DiMaggio."

Boston fans might have withheld their applause for DiMaggio had they known what would happen in Fenway Park the next day in the play-off against Cleveland. Manager Joe McCarthy surprised everyone by choosing veteran Denny Galehouse to pitch. Galehouse was shelled, and Cleveland won 8–3, winning the right to play the World Series against the Boston Braves. Boston fans still talk about what happened.

Although the Yankees were in New York, DiMaggio played a role in the Cleveland win. In the regular-season finale, DiMaggio's performance forced Joe McCarthy to use three pitchers: Joe Dobson, Earl Johnson, and Boo Ferriss. Each was unavailable to pitch against Cleveland the next day. While both Ellis Kinder and Mel Parnell were rested and available, for reasons known only to McCarthy he chose not to start either in the play-off. Instead, he pitched journeyman Denny Galehouse.

In a 1988 interview with this author, his first ever about the play-off, Galehouse revealed that in the season finale against New York, as DiMaggio kept the game close, Joe McCarthy kept him warming up for six full innings. McCarthy knew better than anyone what DiMaggio was capable of. He wasn't taking chances. He wanted a right-handed pitcher ready at all times.

McCarthy sent catcher Birdie Tebbetts to talk with each pitcher after the win over New York. Based upon what each said to Tebbetts, McCarthy told Galehouse he would pitch the next day. To this day, Tebbetts refuses to reveal what was said. In 1988, he told this author that he committed his story to an audiotape that will be released only after his death.

For reasons known only to himself, and, perhaps a bottle of scotch, McCarthy inexplicably chose Galehouse to pitch the play-off game. The move made no sense then and makes no sense now. Kinder and

Parnell were both available. McCarthy knew full well that Galehouse spent most of the previous day warming up. Any chance Galehouse had to win had been left in the bull pen, all because DiMaggio refused to give up.

DiMaggio finished the year with a .320 batting average, 39 home runs, and 155 RBI, both league highs and his best numbers since 1937. Moreover, he played in 153 games and set a career high with 441 putouts.

Joe paid a dear price for his effort. He had played hurt all year, each injury adding to the last, and he was never the same player again. Had he taken time off to heal in 1948, he might have avoided the chronic injuries that marked his final seasons. But the Yankees were fighting for a pennant and they needed him.

Lou Boudreau outpaced both DiMaggio and Williams for the American League MVP Award, but DiMaggio was more concerned with his health. On November 12, he entered Johns Hopkins Hospital for surgery on his right heel.

The injury was a duplicate of the one to his left heel two years before, and the nature of the impairment added to DiMaggio's luster in the eyes of the writers. DiMaggio's previous injuries—bone chips, pulled muscles, strained ligaments, and sprains—were subtle. While DiMaggio was obviously hurt, the manifest signs of these injuries were athletic tape. The bone spurs were different. On each occasion, photo X rays of DiMaggio's injured heel were made available to the press. The X rays showed a spur, not unlike that attached to fighting cocks, curving down from the heel bone straight into the flesh of the heel. The photographs provided visceral evidence of DiMaggio's pain. A muscle pull or ligament strain seemed like a minor annoyance in comparison to the violent stab of the spur. Yet DiMaggio played anyway.

The Yankees were similarly impressed with DiMaggio's perseverance, and apparently unconcerned about the lasting effects of the surgery. On February 7, DiMaggio met with Dan Topping and George Weiss for forty-five minutes in the Yankees' Fifth Avenue offices.

He emerged with the largest contract in baseball history, $100,000: more than the $80,000 Babe Ruth earned in 1930, the previous Yankee high, and more than the reported $82,000 the Indians paid Bob Feller in 1948. Red Smith observed that unlike Ruth, DiMaggio earned his raise, "for professional performances alone." Ruth's gate appeal and personality were as important to the Yankees as his on-field performance. Compared to the Babe, DiMaggio was colorless. As Smith noted, "His drawing power stems from his ability to make the team win . . . he never struts or clowns or consciously plays up to the crowd; he is not a physical freak or a zany character. He is simply a superb craftsman. In this, he is the most highly paid ballplayer of all time . . . nobody else ever got so much money just for playing baseball well."

After the end of the 1948 season, the Yankees released manager Bucky Harris. Despite Harris's popularity with fans and players, George Weiss felt Harris was too easygoing, and blamed the Yankees' third-place finish on his lax attitude. Weiss surprised everyone by naming Casey Stengel the new Yankee manager.

Stengel's selection puzzled most observers. He had already failed at the major-league level in stints as manager of the Boston Braves and the Brooklyn Dodgers, finishing above .500 only once in nine years. While Stengel was successful as a minor-league manager for the Yankees at Kansas City in 1945, and most recently surprised the PCL by leading the Oakland Oaks to a pennant with a veteran club coast writers referred to as "the nine old men," he enjoyed a well-deserved reputation as a baseball clown. Many thought Stengel was a poor fit with the tradition-bound Yankees. There was open speculation Weiss planned to rebuild the club, and that Stengel was simply a fun-loving caretaker chosen to provide entertainment during the construction

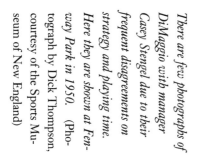

There are few photographs of DiMaggio with manager Casey Stengel due to their frequent disagreements on strategy and playing time. Here they are shown at Fenway Park in 1950. (Photograph by Dick Thompson, courtesy of the Sports Museum of New England)

DiMaggio arrives in Boston in June 1949 for a series with the Red Sox. (Photograph courtesy of the *Boston Herald*)

process. Finishing second or third would be more fun with Casey around. Boston sportswriter Harold Kaese concurred, writing that when Casey was with the Braves, "it was alot more fun losing with Stengel than winning with someone else."

But Stengel, despite his eccentricities and practiced fracturing of the English language, knew baseball. He'd learned as a player from the master himself, the New York Giants' John McGraw. He was confident, a fine judge of talent, and his ego was a match for any player. Stengel had little to lose as Yankee skipper and wasn't afraid to make changes or take chances. In one of his first moves, he brought in former Yankee catcher Bill Dickey as Yogi Berra's personal tutor.

After signing his contract, DiMaggio went to Mexico to relax with several weeks of deep-sea fishing. When the Yankees opened spring training in St. Petersburg on March 1, DiMaggio worked out on the first day like every other player, and was even reported to be taking the role of instructor with younger members of the Yankee outfield.

Stengel's task became much more difficult the next day. After only one day in spikes, DiMaggio could hardly walk. His right heel flared up. This time, the Yankees took no chances. On March 2, they sent Joe back to Johns Hopkins to have the heel evaluated.

Doctors were mystified. This time, the wound had healed as expected, yet DiMaggio was still in pain. The heel was swollen and warm to the touch. Doctors speculated that during the first day of training, DiMaggio broke loose adhesions. They didn't consider the setback serious, and expected DiMaggio to be able to play in a short time.

DiMaggio rejoined the club several weeks later and took part in light training. The heel was still sore, but Joe was told to expect some pain. He felt he could play through the injury.

He played cautiously, careful not to exacerbate the injury. On April 9, in an exhibition game in Beaumont, Texas, DiMaggio's baseball instincts took over. DiMaggio singled, and when the next Yankee batter followed with a hit, DiMaggio took off. He rounded second at full speed and raced to third, playing the way he always had.

As he pulled into third base, the pain in the heel was back. Joe tried to play the next two days in exhibitions in Greenville, Texas, and Dallas, but each time the painful heel forced him to leave the game after only two and a half innings.

That was enough. He wasn't getting any better. On April 11, for the second time in two weeks, DiMaggio was shipped back to Johns Hopkins.

DiMaggio was disconsolate. At the Dallas airport he talked to reporters, angry at suggestions that he was considering retirement. "I am not going to retire from baseball. There's a lot of folks who would like to see me retire. Sadistic people, you know . . ." With that statement, DiMaggio refused to answer any more questions.

This time the doctors decided the pain was due to "immature calcium deposits in tissues adjacent to the heel bone." Whatever the explanation, DiMaggio was in pain and the doctors couldn't offer any timetable for his recovery.

When the Yankees opened the season in New York on April 19, Joe DiMaggio was on the bench for the eighth time in eleven seasons. As the Yankees unveiled a monument to Babe Ruth in the outfield and Cliff Mapes played center in the Yankees' 3–2 win, Joe sat in the dugout wrapped in an overcoat.

DiMaggio's loss lowered expectations for Stengel's team. Boston was a heavy favorite to win the pennant, with Cleveland picked to finish second and the Yankees expected to battle Detroit for third. Stengel downplayed expectations even further, quipping, "Third ain't so bad. I never finished third before. That's pretty high up." Yet DiMaggio's injury actually worked to Stengel's benefit. With his best player out, and expectations low, Stengel was free to do what he wanted with the Yankee lineup.

Early on, Stengel characterized his approach as "new and baffling." It was precisely that. The Yankees were top-heavy with outfielders but

The poise, balance, and grace of a ballplayer who made his craft into art. DiMaggio at bat. (Photograph from Transcendental Graphics, Mark Rucker)

needed a first baseman to replace George McQuinn, who'd been let go. Stengel plugged in veteran outfielder Tommy Henrich at first. He needed a second baseman, so he switched rookie Jerry Coleman, a shortstop, to second. With DiMaggio out, he figured the Yanks would need every hit they could get, so he platooned Billy Johnson and Bobby Brown at third. Stengel followed a similar strategy among the remaining four Yankee outfielders, often deciding who would play on the basis of who was pitching for the opposition.

Although the players griped about Stengel's constant tinkering with the lineup, the strategy worked. The Yankees opened the season with four straight wins and finished April 10–2, taking four of five against the Red Sox. They weren't scoring a lot of runs, but Tommy Henrich made up for DiMaggio's loss with timely hitting, and the pitching was spectacular.

DiMaggio simply waited to get better. On May 3, his misery was aggravated by the death of his father. He went to San Francisco for the funeral, then returned to New York, where he sat in his hotel room, depressed, watching the Yankees on television and worrying about his heel while his ulcers flared up. He was further distracted by an increasingly bizarre series of notes from a woman he didn't know who threatened to kill herself unless DiMaggio promised her his affections. DiMaggio lived as a hermit, retreating deeper into private exile. Thus far, 1949 was a nightmare.

By June, the Yankees were 25–12, 5^1/$_2$ games ahead of the second-place A's. Stengel was in his glory. DiMaggio was an afterthought. The Yankees were winning without him, and Stengel, who played the press at least as well as DiMaggio, was an instant genius.

In late May, DiMaggio quietly began working out. For a while, the workouts followed an alarming pattern. DiMaggio took batting practice and shagged flies, and the next day the heel would flare up, forcing him to stop. A few days later, he'd try again, only to be disappointed once more.

Finally, after one such workout in mid-June, DiMaggio rose from his bed at the Edison Hotel pain-free. As Joe described it, the heel now felt "cool." His workouts began in earnest.

DiMaggio still wasn't fully confident of his recovery. The baseball shoe on his right foot didn't have spikes on the heel, and a special doughnut, designed by former Boston Bruin George Owen, was inserted to cushion the heel. The pain stayed away.

Joe was out of shape, but decided to give himself a test on June 27, when the Yankees hosted the Giants in the annual benefit for New

York City sandlot baseball, the Mayor's Trophy Game. A crowd of 37,537 enthusiastic fans turned out to see what he could do. DiMaggio played nine innings, but his timing was off. He hit a home run in a pregame batting contest, but in the game he popped up to the infield four times and walked once in five appearances. The Yankees won the exhibition contest, 5–3.

New York left for Boston after the game for an important three-game series with the Red Sox. Boston was in third place and trailed New York by five games. They looked to the series as an opportunity to make up ground before it was too late.

DiMaggio timed his return perfectly. He always hit well in Boston, and before the first game told Stengel he wanted to play. Stengel agreed and DiMaggio celebrated his return in his inimitable fashion.

Fenway Park was jammed with over 36,000 fans, a record for a night game in Boston. Joe DiMaggio was of secondary importance. Sox fans were concerned with the pennant race, and with the performance of Dominic DiMaggio, who had hit in 32 consecutive games.

After a scoreless first inning, Joe led off the second against Boston

Tom DiMaggio, older brother of Joe and Dom DiMaggio, chats with Joe in the Yankee clubhouse after the Yankees-Athletics game was postponed by rain on September 30, 1949. Tom was in New York for Joe DiMaggio Day, scheduled for October 1 when the Red Sox played the Yankees in a crucial pennant-deciding series. (Associated Press photograph courtesy of the Boston Herald)

The DiMaggio clan gathers for Joe DiMaggio Day at Yankee Stadium on October 1, 1949. From left are Dom DiMaggio, Rosalie DiMaggio, Tom DiMaggio, Joe Jr., and Joe Sr. (Photograph courtesy of the Boston Globe)

pitcher Mickey McDermott. He singled to left. After two Yankee strikeouts, Johnny Lindell walked and Hank Bauer homered to give New York a 3–0 lead.

In the third, Phil Rizzuto singled. McDermott struck out Jerry Coleman and Henrich, got two strikes on DiMaggio, and then DiMaggio hit the third pitch over the screen atop the left-field wall, putting New York up 5–0.

Boston got two runs back in the fifth, but now DiMaggio was playing with confidence. In the eighth he took out Red Sox shortstop Junior Stephens at second on a force-out, a play that drew boos from the Boston crowd but smiles from his Yankee teammates. The Sox scored one in the eighth and another in the ninth before Ted Williams, with the tying run on third, lifted a fly to DiMaggio to end the game. The Yankees won and DiMaggio was back.

The next day, he was better. The Red Sox led 7–1 after four innings before DiMaggio took over the game. In the top of the fifth, with two out, pitcher Ellis Kinder walked Rizzuto and Henrich. DiMaggio made Kinder pay as he knocked the next pitch into the screen to make the score 7–4.

The Yankees scored three in the seventh on Gene Woodling's bases-clearing double, and tied the score. In the eighth, with Earl Johnson pitching for Boston, DiMaggio came up again. This time, Joe's drive cleared the screen. New York led 8–7 and went on to win 9–7. Nothing went right for Boston. Even Dominic DiMaggio's streak ended at 34 games.

Before the final game of the series, a plane flew above Fenway Park trailing a banner that read "THE GREAT DIMAGGIO." As one observer quipped, while there were two DiMaggios present, one was only very good, so the banner must have been in reference to Joe. If it was not, it was by the time the game ended.

With two on and New York up 3–2 in the seventh, DiMaggio punished the wall one more time, hitting yet another home run over the screen to give New York a 6–2 lead in the eventual 6–3 win. The crowd at Fenway Park had seen enough. While they had politely applauded DiMaggio's earlier homers, now they booed as he trotted around the bases. Boston fans were hungry for a pennant and DiMaggio's hero act in Fenway Park had grown tiresome. Boston tumbled to fifth place, eight games out.

Over the next two weeks DiMaggio continued his timely hitting. New York kept winning, and DiMaggio's return became ever more important, as Yogi Berra, Phil Rizzuto, and Tommy Henrich

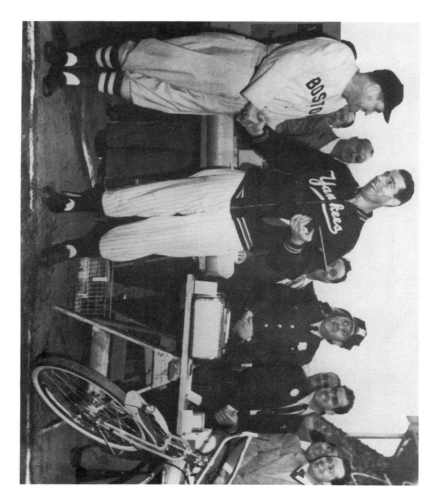

were bothered by injuries. A doubleheader sweep of the Red Sox in New York on July 4 seemingly finished Boston. The losses were Boston's seventh and eighth in a row, beginning with DiMaggio's first game back, and the Red Sox fell below .500 at 35–36, 12 games out.

At the All-Star break on July 11, New York was in first place with a 50–27 record, 5½ games ahead of Cleveland. DiMaggio was hitting .360. American League manager Lou Boudreau ignored the All-Star ballots and named Joe DiMaggio his center fielder. Dominic, the people's choice in Joe's absence, played right field.

In a sloppy game at Ebbets Field, marred by walks and errors, DiMaggio played mistake-free baseball in the best All-Star outing of his career. In the first inning, after Warren Spahn struck out Ted Williams for the second out, DiMaggio singled in George Kell from second for the AL's first run and sparked a four-run rally. In the sixth, Joe's double to deep left field off Howie Pollet plated two more and provided the winning run in the AL's 11–7 win.

After the All-Star break, the Yankees seemed poised to duplicate one of their patented prewar pennants, leading the entire year and clinching in September. But the Red Sox weren't finished.

In early August Boston returned to the pennant race by beating

New York two out of three in Fenway Park, as Ted Williams stole DiMaggio's thunder, lashing out seven hits in the series. While the Yankees continued to play well despite injuries to key players, the Red Sox played better. In August, Boston went 24–8 to draw within two games of New York.

The final month of the season was a virtual replay of 1948, except this time the Yankees and Red Sox had the stage to themselves.

On September 7 and 9, the clubs split in New York around a rainout, as the Yankees maintained a 1½ game lead. On September 18, New York beat Cleveland 7–3 and led Boston by 2½ games with only thirteen left to play.

But the rest of the season was played by an entirely different set of rules. Joe DiMaggio sat out the win over Cleveland with a temperature of 102. DiMaggio's illness, which deteriorated into pneumonia, was disastrous for the Yankees. The patchwork lineup of the past several weeks came apart. The Yankees lost two of three before heading to Boston on September 24. The Sox trailed by only two games.

It wasn't close. Kinder shut out New York in the first game, 3–0, to get the Red Sox within one. The next day, Mel Parnell won his 25th as the Yankees again failed to hit and Boston pulled into a tie, winning 4–1.

Joe DiMaggio drives a pitch in this photograph from 1949.   (Photograph from Transcendental Graphics, Mark Rucker)

Joe DiMaggio Jr. sits waiting with eager anticipation as the Yankees and Red Sox play a crucial weekend series that will decide the outcome of the 1949 season. On this day Joe DiMaggio Sr. would be honored with a special day and receive over $50,000 worth of gifts from fans, teammates, and management. (Photograph courtesy of the Boston Herald)

After the game Red Smith summed up the feeling in New York, writing of Boston that "this is a city with a large Irish-American population, plenty of Poles, Czechs and Russians, and not enough Italians. If there had been one more Roman named DiMaggio in town today, the Yankees might be coming home with an interlocking grip on the American League championship."

The teams traveled to the Stadium to make up the rainout earlier in the month. DiMaggio was still sick. In a dozen similar situations over the course of his career he had always proved to be the difference. He was again.

He didn't play and the Yankees lost, 7–6. With only five games to play, the Red Sox now led by one and Joe DiMaggio was still on his back in the hospital.

The Red Sox lead held as each club won two of the next three. DiMaggio pulled himself out of his hospital bed and worked out before the Yankees lost to Philadelphia, 4–1, on September 30. DiMaggio looked ill but wanted to play in the final games of the season. Stengel agreed, but admitted, "How far he'll be able to go, I don't know." In another case of luck by the schedule-makers, the Red Sox traveled to New York one last time, needing only one victory in the season's last two games to win the pennant.

The Yankees pulled out all the stops and designated October 1, the day of the first game of the two-game set, "Joe DiMaggio Day." Before the game, DiMaggio, who hadn't played in two weeks, stood on the field and listened to speeches as nearly 70,000 fans in Yankee Stadium cheered themselves hoarse. DiMaggio was exhausted, physically and emotionally, and broke down in tears during the ceremony, crying for only the second time in his adult life. The first had been during Lou Gehrig's farewell address.

DiMaggio received gifts of every kind, worth over $50,000, including two cars, one boat, three watches, taxi service for three hundred, 300 quarts of ice cream, a college scholarship for his son, 500 Joe DiMaggio T-shirts, and a case of lima beans. His mother and brother Tom came from San Francisco and joined him on the field, as did Dominic.

In the top of the first, Dominic led his own celebration with a single for Boston, lest anyone forget there were two DiMaggio brothers still playing the game. Pesky forced him at second, but Williams singled and Pesky eventually scored on a sacrifice fly by Junior Stephens. The Sox scored three more in the third to take a 4–0 lead.

Joe DiMaggio looked sick and struck out in his first at bat against

DiMaggio is greeted at home plate following his fourth-inning solo home run in the fifth and decisive game of the 1949 World Series at Ebbets Field. The Yankees would win the game by a score of 10–6. (Photograph from the National Baseball Library & Archive, Cooperstown, N.Y.)

"I'd like to thank the Good Lord for making me a Yankee." —Joe DiMaggio, as quoted from his speech at Yankee Stadium on Joe DiMaggio Day, October 1, 1949. (Photograph from the Maxwell Collection)

Mel Parnell. In the fourth, DiMaggio fought off a pitch and bounced it into the stands in right for a ground-rule double. One out later, he scored from second on Hank Bauer's single. Bauer later scored to make the score 4–2.

New York got two more runs in the fifth. On consecutive pitches, Rizzuto, Henrich, and Berra singled, Rizzuto scoring on Berra's hit. With DiMaggio coming up, McCarthy pulled Parnell in favor of right-handed Joe Dobson.

DiMaggio hit the ball on a line back through the box. Dobson deflected the ball with his glove, but everyone was safe. Billy Johnson then hit into a double play, scoring Henrich to tie the game.

The Yankees' Johnny Lindell hit his first home run in two months in the eighth inning, giving New York a 5–4 win. With only one game left to play, the Yankees and Red Sox were tied.

For the season finale, McCarthy chose Ellis Kinder, already the winner of 23. Stengel countered with his own 20-game winner, Vic Raschi.

After the Red Sox went down in the first, Phil Rizzuto tripled past Pesky at third. Tommy Henrich, hitting the opposite way, drove Rizzuto home with a ground ball to second. New York led, 1–0.

Then Raschi and Kinder took over. Inning after inning each set

Rosalie DiMaggio kisses her son upon departing New York following the 1949 World Series. (Photograph courtesy of the Boston Herald)

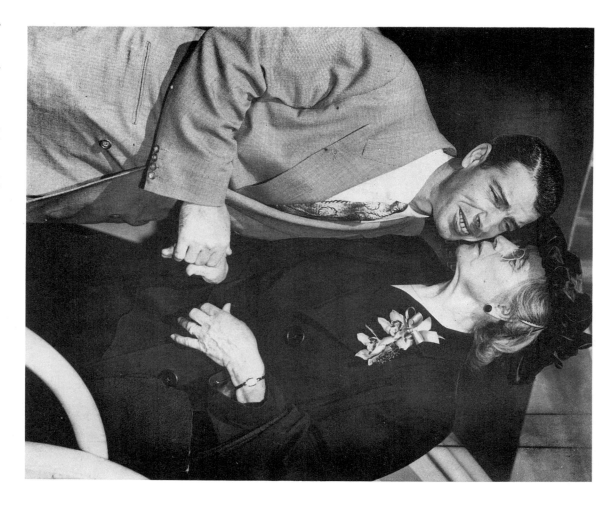

down the opposition without a threat. Both teams stood toe-to-toe, waiting for the other to blink. At the last possible minute, Red Sox manager Joe McCarthy blinked.

With one out in the eighth, McCarthy pinch-hit outfielder Tom Wright for Kinder. Sox fans groaned at his decision, for the Red Sox bull pen had been weak all year. Wright walked, but Dom DiMaggio hit into a double play to end the inning. A tired Mel Parnell came on to pitch for Boston in the top of the ninth.

The Yankees didn't waste time. Henrich led off with a home run. Yogi Berra singled and McCarthy pulled Parnell in favor of Tex Hughson. He didn't want DiMaggio to face a left-hander.

It didn't matter. DiMaggio was spent. He was still sick, and even his own teammates questioned whether he should keep playing. DiMaggio hit into a double play, but it didn't matter. His presence was inspiration enough.

Johnny Lindell followed with a single, as did Billy Johnson. In left field, Ted Williams bobbled the ball, and Hank Bauer, running for Lindell, took third. Cliff Mapes was walked intentionally so Hughson could face Jerry Coleman.

The rookie took a defensive swing at a high fastball and popped a soft fly ball off the end of his bat to shallow right field. Right fielder Al Zarilla raced in and second baseman Bobby Doerr raced back as the soft fly curved toward the foul line.

Zarilla dove. He missed the ball by two inches. Three runs scored and Coleman scurried all the way to third. The Yankees led, 5–1.

The Red Sox had spent most of the season coming back. They did so one more time. With one out, Raschi pitched carefully and walked Ted Williams. Junior Stephens singled, and Bobby Doerr drove the ball to deep center field.

DiMaggio turned and ran after the ball, but his legs refused to obey the message his mind was sending. He stumbled, and a ball he would normally have caught fell over his head. Both runners scored and Doerr pulled into third with a triple.

DiMaggio was done. He waved to Stengel to bring in a replacement. He was too sick to chase down Doerr's ball and wouldn't risk it happening again. Cliff Mapes moved over from right field and DiMaggio jogged off to a standing ovation. Whatever happened, his regular season was over.

Zarilla popped out to Mapes, then Goodman singled to score Doerr, making the score 5–4. Raschi was almost finished, but Stengel left him in. With the tying run at first, he induced Birdie Tebbetts to pop out to first baseman Tommy Henrich.

For the Yankees, the realization of all that had just happened came in a rush. The season was done. The game was over. The Yankees had won the pennant.

Then they exploded from the dugout, clapping each other on the back and fairly dancing on their way to the Yankee clubhouse. Inside, the celebration continued, but at some point each Yankee player made his way over to DiMaggio, who sat quietly in front of his locker, gaunt and pale, utterly exhausted, his uniform soaked with sweat. To a man, they shook his hand. In his own way, he had come through for them once more.

In the National League, the Brooklyn Dodgers fought a gut-wrenching battle with the Cardinals, sweeping past St. Louis in the final week to capture the pennant with a 97–75 record, identical to the Yankees. Still, oddsmakers made New York 2-to-1 favorites.

Despite identical records, the two clubs were drastically different. New York had won on pitching and Stengel's adept use of the platoon. No Yankee regular hit over 25 home runs or knocked in a hundred runs. Only DiMaggio, who hit .346 in 76 games, bettered the .300 mark.

The Dodgers, on the other hand, featured a powerful lineup. Gil Hodges, Jackie Robinson, and Carl Furillo all knocked in more than 100 runs, and six players hit 16 or more home runs. Robinson capped an MVP year with an NL-best .342 average. The Dodger pitching staff was considered relatively weak.

That wasn't the case in game one, played in Yankee Stadium on October 5. Dodger starter Don Newcombe and Allie Reynolds matched each other for two hours and twenty minutes, neither giving up a run and striking out 20 between them. Tommy Henrich, the first Yankee batter in the ninth, knocked Newcombe's final pitch into the right-field stands to give the Yankees a 1–0 win. DiMaggio, who had lost fifteen pounds while sick, went hitless.

Dodger pitching held again in game two. In the second, Jackie Robinson scored on Gil Hodges's single off Vic Raschi to give Brooklyn a 1–0 lead. Pitcher Preacher Roe scattered five hits over eight innings and held New York scoreless.

DiMaggio led off the ninth for New York. He singled for the Yankees' sixth hit. But that was all. Roe held on and won 1–0, the first shutout against the Yankees in Yankee Stadium since the first game of the 1948 season.

Pitching ruled again in game three in Brooklyn. In the third, New York pushed across a run against Ralph Branca as Cliff Mapes singled, went to third on Tommy Byrne's hit-and-run single, and scored on Rizzuto's sacrifice fly.

Brooklyn countered with a single run in the fourth on Pee Wee Reese's home run. The homer rattled Byrne, who loaded the bases on a hit and two walks before Stengel pulled him for Joe Page. Page and Branca held the other team scoreless into the ninth. Henrich opened for New York by grounding out, then Berra walked. DiMaggio failed this time, popping up for the second out.

No matter. Bobby Brown singled, then Gene Woodling walked. Stengel pinch-hit Johnny Mize for Cliff Mapes and Mize singled to score two. Coleman's hit knocked in one more and the Yankees led 4–1.

Brooklyn didn't quit. With one out, Luis Olmo hit only his second home run of the season to make the score 4–2. Page buckled down and struck out Duke Snider, then Roy Campanella duplicated Olmo's feat with another home run.

For the past three seasons pitcher Joe Page had been the best relief pitcher in baseball. He was again, as he struck out pinch hitter Bruce Edwards to end the game and give the Yankees a 4–3 win. New York led the series, 2–1.

The Yankees went up 3–1 the next day, knocking out Don Newcombe in the third with three runs and scoring three more in the fourth. Meanwhile Yankee pitcher Ed Lopat, with help from Allie Reynolds, pitched just well enough to win and give the Yankees a 6–4 victory.

The Yankees didn't waste time in the Series finale. Rizzuto walked to open the game against Rex Barney and moved to third on a walk to Henrich and a botched pickoff. DiMaggio knocked home New York's first run with a fly ball Snider caught against the fence in dead center, for the first of two runs.

The Yankees increased their lead to 5–0 in the third, and still led 5–1 when DiMaggio came up in the fourth. He had struggled all series, but now he greeted pitcher Jack Banta with a home run just fair down the line in left to put New York up 6–1. Yankee fans in the bleachers let DiMaggio know how they felt when he took center field in the Brooklyn half of the inning. They stood and cheered his effort.

One run in the fifth and three more in the sixth made the score 10–2 before Raschi faltered. Once again, Joe Page came on to shut down the Dodgers. The Yankees won, 10–6, taking the Series in five games.

DiMaggio had played the Series on guts alone, collecting only two hits and a sacrifice fly in 18 at bats. Yet even those meager contributions came at critical times. His team won again, and that was what really mattered. DiMaggio's insistence on playing in the last two games against Boston and in the Series, despite his illness, impressed his teammates and made them better. Both Berra and Henrich were injured, but if DiMaggio could play, so could they. On paper, Brooklyn was probably the better team. On paper, even the Red Sox were probably a better team. On paper, DiMaggio shouldn't have even played. On the field, where the game is played, the Yankees and Joe DiMaggio were still the best.

After the game, Joe Jr. joined his father in the Yankee clubhouse and complained he'd lost a baseball his father had given him. "That's all right," responded the father with a tired smile. Then, thinking of his home run, he said, "I lost one myself today."

God of Our Fathers

Luke Salisbury

A conflict between perfection and death underlies sports, particularly baseball. Death is easy to see: the life of each at bat, the continuation of an inning, the loss and win of the game, death in the pennant race, the quick and dead after the World Series. Perfection is more difficult. When our fathers say Joe DiMaggio was better than Willie Mays, the last word is "You had to see him," and the argument may as well be about the Holy Ghost. DiMaggio played baseball in a state of grace those who saw him never saw again. For them he was the center of what the game could be. He is in its most profound place. He had the ultimate style of the ultimate performer: perfection.

A reputation is as interesting as a career. Who becomes an icon, and what do icons tell us about ourselves? Player reputations are not frozen like a plaque in Cooperstown. Reputations fluctuate like the stock market. Ted Williams, Joe DiMaggio, and Mickey Mantle go up. Hank Aaron, Willie Mays, and Sandy Koufax remain in limbo below them. Stan Musial and Bob Feller's are lower than when they played. Perhaps only Williams and DiMaggio, and especially DiMaggio, are close enough to perfect to deliver us from the cycle of winning and losing, which is a cycle of living and dying. Perfection stands outside time. In 1969, major league baseball's self-declared centennial, Joe DiMaggio was

named greatest living ballplayer. A quarter century later, he remains so.

An icon satisfies our deepest needs, most powerful fantasies, strongest desires. Who was Joe DiMaggio? What was Joe DiMaggio? Why do we miss him? First and last, he was a winner. If America has a national religion, it's winning. Losers can be celebrities, not icons. In DiMaggio's thirteen years, the Yankees won ten pennants—not TV-rigged divisions, but pennants: 154 game matches, no excuses, no second-place qualifiers, no bullshit: pennants. The Yankees won nine of those ten World Series. "If personality is an unbroken series of successful gestures," as Fitzgerald says, then nine out of ten World Se-

Joe DiMaggio drives a pitch in this 1939 game against the Red Sox at Fenway Park. (Photograph courtesy of the Brearley Collection)

ries is untarnishable reputation. Ruth won seven of ten, including three as a pitcher. Mantle won seven of twelve, Berra nine of fourteen. In the Series, Joe's clubs were almost perfect.

But there's more to DiMaggio than winning. Player after player said he was the best they ever saw. Managers from Joe McCarthy, who adored him, to Casey Stengel, who didn't, said he was the most complete player. Teammate Charlie Keller said, "There was one thing about Joe that nobody every came close to. That was the kind of competitor he was, how he took responsibility for winning or losing, how he got the big hits in the big spots." Joe was the best center fielder, the best base runner, the best clutch hitter. He played hurt, never letting down, saying one person in the stands might not have seen Joe DiMaggio and he wasn't going to disappoint that person—Joe DiMaggio understood what it meant to be Joe DiMaggio. He quit at thirty-seven, not hanging around like Mantle or Mays, whose careers died on the field. DiMaggio insisted on being DiMaggio, and when he couldn't, he left. Bob Feller summed it up: "I guess he just never had a weakness."

Joe played with a confidence unimaginable now. A telling detail is Hank Greenberg's remark that when pitchers threw at him, which they did before he was an immortal, DiMaggio merely moved his head, not his body. Joe didn't show anger or fear. Pitchers and pressure didn't get to him. Today batters charge the mound even when they haven't been hit. A pitch too close is an unbearable insult to their masculinity, their "respect." This detail is important because DiMaggio wasn't caught on film. Photographs show the tremendous power in that open stance and the fine balance of his hard swing, but we don't have a watershed video like that of Mays in the '54 Series, or Pete Rose recapturing a dropped foul pop in '80. We have the Streak, which is Joe's piece of immortality, because in baseball numbers speak loud—but we don't have a visual record. We have the awe of men who played with and against him, and of our fathers. They say DiMaggio was a model for how a man ought to carry himself.

The Torah says no man does not cast a shadow, and icons also cast shadows. There is DiMaggio *noire*, and like everything else in his remarkable life, it fits. If Joe were only perfect, if the persona were unbreakable, if he were only an emblem of a lost America—an America where baseball was king and New York was the center of Saturday night, and the Clipper always came through—then Joltin' Joe would not just be gone, he would be boring. If Joe DiMaggio only played golf and tended his image, then he might fade as Musial and Hornsby have faded. But there was Marilyn Monroe.

When I first heard Joe DiMaggio had been married to Marilyn Monroe, I didn't believe it. I thought it was the sort

of cultural bravado that attributes anatomical irregularities to John Dillinger, and coupled Jack Kennedy with Miss Monroe. It was simply too good to be true. Wouldn't it be wonderful if a baseball hero, the model for all you could desire at twelve, then turned out to be a pathfinder in the promised land of sexuality? It was too good to be true. The marriage lasted 274 days. "He struck out." Marilyn was on the way up, Joe was tending a legend. It would be nice to think they talked about the loneliness of celebrity, the hunger that makes success, the hardness of a world that demands and eats celebri-

ties. After she died, Joe could love something as perfect and unreal as his own mystique. He had a public reason to be private. His mystery was wedded to Another. The legends blend: the winner and loser; the man who needed no one and the woman who needed everyone; Perfection and its shadow.

The final word should not be his myth, no matter how attractive. The final word must be baseball. Joe DiMaggio did the hardest thing in sports. With all respect to Ted Williams, the hardest thing is not hitting a baseball. The hardest thing is winning.

Joe DiMaggio signs autographs at Old-Timers' Day on July 25, 1964. (Photograph by Bob Olen)

C H A P T E R   S E V E N

The Clipper in Twilight: 1950–51

The agonies of the past four seasons took a toll on DiMaggio. Baseball, the game he played with such grace and expertise, became more and more a chore as his body betrayed him. After the 1949 World Series, DiMaggio began to think of retirement.

There were reasons, apart from his physical maladies, to stop playing. Joe Jr. was getting older and needed more of his father's time. His ex-wife Dorothy had remarried, and now it appeared that marriage was breaking up. DiMaggio worried about its impact on his young son. In the weeks following the 1949 season, he reportedly told Yankee owner Dan Topping he intended to retire, but Topping talked him out of it.

DiMaggio spent the winter playing golf, a newly acquired passion, and hunting. Walking up to twenty miles a day, he was encouraged by his physical recovery. He gained back the weight he lost with pneumonia, and told a reporter, "My legs feel better than they have for years." Although DiMaggio knew he was in the twilight of his career, he was optimistic. In late January, DiMaggio signed for $100,000.

To his teammates, DiMaggio was still the most important member of the team. In an off-season survey of all players on the Yankee roster, more than half the Yankees selected DiMaggio as one player in baseball history they most admired.

However, DiMaggio was preparing for the day he no longer was able to play. He signed with CBS to do a weekly radio show, saying, "My friends tell me I can earn a living in radio after I'm too old for baseball."

In spring training before the 1950 season DiMaggio worked out at his own pace, trying to get in shape and trying to stay healthy. Stengel was amenable and let the veteran player tell him when he was ready to play.

Stengel and the Yankees still needed DiMaggio. Despite their victory in 1949, most thought the Red Sox were the team to beat. The Yankees had changed dramatically since the war; only DiMaggio, Rizzuto, and Tommy Henrich remained from the 1942 American League champions. While Stengel's platoon system got the most from his lineup, none of the younger Yankees appeared able to take over DiMaggio's role on the club. Even as his skills diminished, he was still the player expected to provide power and leadership.

When he played, DiMaggio played well in spring training, hitting nearly .400. But the Yankees struggled, and finished the exhibition season below .500. They began 1950 with more questions than answers.

DiMaggio provided one answer in New York's 6–4 win over Brooklyn in the final exhibition game, at Yankee Stadium on April 15. In the fifth inning, Roy Campanella hit the ball to deep left center and Joe brought the crowd to its feet as he made a sensational one-handed grab in front of the monuments. In the bottom of the inning, he hit a long home run to left to start the winning rally. All appeared right with the Yankees.

New York resumed its regular-season war with Boston on opening day on April 18 at Fenway Park. The result of the 1949 season was duplicated in nine short innings.

After five innings, the Red Sox led 9–0. Mel Parnell was virtually unhittable, the Red Sox battered starter Allie Reynolds, and Ted Williams even robbed Tommy Henrich of extra bases with a spectacular catch in left center.

If the Red Sox were sending a message, the Yankees didn't get it. They answered in the eighth. Fourteen Yankee batters went to the plate. Nine scored, five Red Sox pitchers were skewered in the process, and the Yankees went on to win, 15–10. DiMaggio collected a single, a double, and a triple for the day. If it were possible for a team to bury an opponent in the first game of the season, the Yankees did so to the Red Sox. While Boston stayed in the pennant race all year, they never led the Yankees or held first place.

The Tigers started fast and led in early May, but the Yankees went 20–6 for the month and took the top spot on May 16. DiMaggio, while leading the Yankees in home runs and RBI, struggled with a batting average below .250.

That was fine as long as the Yankees maintained their lead over Detroit. After three weeks in first, the Yankees fell behind the Tigers in mid-June.

DiMaggio was distracted. For the first time in his baseball career, he found it difficult to keep his mind on the game. He never said so, but a number of teammates later said that in the first half of 1950, DiMaggio was concerned about his son and pining for his ex-wife. Joe wanted to get back together and be a family again. Dorothy, recently freed from her second marriage, wanted to resume her acting career. While Dorothy put him off, Joe stewed.

Stengel remained patient—for a while. Late in the month, DiMaggio showed signs of shaking his slump. On June 20, the Yankees beat Cleveland 8–2 as Detroit lost, and the Bombers were within one. DiMaggio smacked out two hits and drove in three runs in the win. Moreover, he collected the 1,999th and 2,000th hits of his career. After cracking his second hit to center field in the seventh, Indian outfielder Larry Doby threw the ball in to pitcher Marino Pieretti. The pitcher tossed the ball in to DiMaggio, who flipped it to first-base coach Bill Dickey for safekeeping.

DiMaggio was only the eighty-eighth man in baseball history to collect 2,000 hits. Of all active players, only Luke Appling and Wally Moses had more hits than DiMaggio. Despite his struggles in recent years, his career average was still .331. But if DiMaggio had ever dreamed of 3,000 hits, he had to know that number was out of reach.

The Yankees followed the win by losing two before heading to Detroit for a key series. In the first game, DiMaggio cracked a home run, his 15th, to help the Yankees to a 6–0 lead. But Detroit stormed back to win 10–9. The Yankees hit six home runs for the game, the Tigers five, and the 11 combined home runs set a major league record.

Detroit took three of four to increase their lead to three games. Stengel's patience was wearing thin.

Much would later be written about the relationship between Stengel and DiMaggio, although neither man ever made a public statement criticizing the other. Beginning in July of 1950, Stengel's attitude toward DiMaggio changed. Until now, he had deferred to the Yankee star and DiMaggio had responded as he always had, by playing the best baseball in the American League. DiMaggio had never been included in Stengel's platoon system. Now, with DiMaggio's average hovering eighty points below his career average, Stengel changed his approach.

Before the Yankees played Boston on July 2, Stengel asked owner Dan Topping to relay a request to DiMaggio. Casey wanted DiMaggio to play first base. Stengel was no fool. He knew if the request came from Topping, DiMaggio was in no position to argue. Topping signed the checks, and DiMaggio respected authority.

Topping told DiMaggio Stengel's request was for the good of the team, and suggested the move just might enable DiMaggio to prolong his career. DiMaggio was put off that Stengel hadn't had the guts to make the request himself, but told Topping he would do whatever they felt was best for the team. Before the game, DiMaggio worked out at first base. When the game began, he returned to center field and hit his 17th home run in New York's 15–9 win over Boston. The experiment would begin in Washington the next day.

Stengel had several reasons for the change. He had used Tommy Henrich, Johnny Mize, and Joe Collins at first, but all three were left-handed hitters, leaving the Yankees vulnerable to left-handed pitching. Mize and Henrich were both bothered by injuries, and Collins didn't provide the power Stengel wanted from the position. The Yankees were top-heavy with outfielders, and Stengel wanted to get the most from his lineup. From his perspective, shifting an outfielder to first base made sense.

Why Stengel decided DiMaggio was that outfielder is another story. While it did allow Stengel to put another right-handed bat in the lineup, as Jackie Jensen moved into left and Cliff Mapes took over in center, it would have made just as much sense to move Jensen or Bauer to first base. Stengel may have recognized that DiMaggio was the best athlete, and reasoned that playing first base might relieve DiMaggio of the physical demands of playing center field. Or he might have been trying to light a fire under DiMaggio and assert his own authority, showing that no single player was more important than the team, not even Joe DiMaggio. Given the events of the remainder of the season, the latter explanation seems closest to the truth.

The Yankees arrived in Washington on July 3 and DiMaggio worked out at first base before the game. Press photographers crowded around the bag, jostling each other for position, but DiMaggio was

In a noble but doomed experiment, DiMaggio tried his hand as a first baseman in Washington on July 2, 1950. Although he handled the position like an infield regular, he quickly switched back to the outfield. (Photograph courtesy of the Boston Herald)

uncooperative. While he'd agreed with the experiment, he didn't like it, although publicly he said the right things, announcing before the game that "now if somebody will show me where first base is, I'm ready."

In pregame stories, the press made much of the fact that DiMaggio had not played the position since his sandlot days. They were almost correct. In the spring of 1933, DiMaggio's manager with the San Francisco Seals, Ike Caveney, had correctly concluded DiMaggio was no shortstop and tried him at first base.

Stengel's experiment lasted as long as Caveney's. In the 7–2 Yankee loss, DiMaggio handled thirteen chances without an error. He fielded two ground balls, one a difficult chance to his left behind first base. He made no errors, did make one difficult catch off the bag and tagged the runner, but failed to catch Coleman's wide throw after Rizzuto stabbed Sam Dente's line drive and threw to Coleman for a double play. Had DiMaggio come up with the catch, the Yankees would have had a triple play.

The experiment ended in the seventh inning when Hank Bauer sprained his ankle sliding into second base. That left the Yankees short of outfielders, and DiMaggio moved back into center field the next day. DiMaggio celebrated his return with a bases-loaded triple to center field in the ninth inning of the Yankees' 16–9 win.

While DiMaggio had agreed to Stengel's move for the good of the team, in private he felt belittled and believed Stengel needlessly embarrassed him. The relationship between the two men cooled from businesslike to something less.

At the All-Star break the Yankees trailed Detroit by 3 1/2 games. DiMaggio was named to the team, but didn't start as Cleveland's Larry Doby played center field. DiMaggio didn't play until the ninth inning, when he relieved Hoot Evers in right field. The National League tied the game at 3–3 on Ralph Kiner's home run, and DiMaggio played the final five innings of the NL's 4–3 win, going hitless and grounding into a double play in the fourteenth inning to end the game.

For the next month, the Yankees tried to catch Detroit but failed to gain ground. On August 10, New York lost to the A's 5–3 and fell three games back. DiMaggio went hitless for the second game in a row, and had only four hits in his last 38 times at bat. Stengel had even dropped him to fifth in the batting order.

The next day, Stengel made a decision. For the first time in his career, DiMaggio was benched.

Stengel said, "I hope to be able to rest Joe six or seven days if I can.

He's having trouble with his knees and his shoulder, and I'm sure a few days off will do him good." DiMaggio was ailing but felt able to play. He did not appreciate Stengel's form of compassion, and feared once he left the lineup there was no guarantee he'd return as a regular.

It was a gutsy move on Stengel's part, and one fraught with peril since he risked alienating DiMaggio. But it looked brilliant on August 11, as DiMaggio's replacement, Cliff Mapes, beat the A's 7–6 with a seventh-inning home run. Yet the change had no effect on the pennant race. New York played .500 ball with DiMaggio out of the lineup.

Once again, it was an injury to Bauer that brought DiMaggio back to center field. On August 17, while on base in the third inning of a 2–1 loss to the Senators, Bauer was struck by a throw to third and carried from the field. Cliff Mapes took his place, but when Stengel sent in a pinch-hitter for Jackie Jensen in the eighth, he was out of outfielders. DiMaggio entered the game as a defensive replacement. If DiMaggio was healthy enough to play the outfield, Stengel could no longer claim DiMaggio was hurt. After the game, Casey announced DiMaggio would start in center field the next day.

If Stengel made his decision to bench DiMaggio based upon how the Clipper played when he returned to the Yankee lineup, Stengel made the right choice. When DiMaggio regained his starting spot, he wasn't the struggling, aging star, but the spectacular all-around performer of his youth. Joe responded with six weeks of play equal to any of his career.

The Yankees played a night game in Philadelphia on August 18. DiMaggio started in center field and hit in his accustomed cleanup spot. Just over 6,000 fans turned out to see the ever-struggling A's. Most were more interested in DiMaggio. Entering the ninth, the score was tied 2–2. Leading off was DiMaggio, who so far was hitless.

Pitcher Lou Brissie pitched carefully, but DiMaggio slammed a pitch high and deep to left. It landed in the upper deck, his 22nd home run of the year and first since July 30. As DiMaggio circled the bases, several dozen fans leapt from the stands and accompanied him on his tour of the bases, slapping his back and celebrating his return. DiMaggio actually had to fight through a crowd to find home plate. The Yankees won, 3–2, and trailed Detroit by four games.

Over the next eleven games, DiMaggio hit .400 and the Yankees won ten as New York pulled into a virtual dead heat with the Tigers. Then DiMaggio broke down. His knees ached and he could barely run. It didn't matter. New York was on its way. DiMaggio sat on the

DiMaggio was one of the only ballplayers who looked graceful even hitting into a double play. He is shown here being caught in just such a twin killing after tapping a soft grounder to Senator third baseman Eddie Yost.   (Associated Press photograph)

Joe DiMaggio and Yankee pitcher Tommy Byrne outside the Yankee clubhouse at the 1950 World Series.   (Photograph courtesy of the Boston Herald)

bench as the Yankees swept Cleveland at the end of August, finishing the Indians.

He returned to the lineup in September and continued his torrid hitting. For the first two weeks of the month, New York and Detroit went back and forth, neither able to extend a lead beyond two games.

Then the Yankees stumbled, losing three straight, including two to Boston, who pulled to within two games of the leaders. DiMaggio, though he collected a hit in every game, cooled, and some writers speculated that Stengel was again prepared to drop DiMaggio from the lineup. On September 10 in Washington, DiMaggio responded to the reports with one of the biggest games of his career.

Washington's Griffith Stadium was one of the largest parks in major-league baseball. In left field, it measured an imposing 405 feet down the line.

DiMaggio came to bat five times. Three times he drove the ball long and deep to left, and three times the ball landed over the distant fence for a home run. No other player had ever hit three home runs in one game at Griffith Stadium. In his other two at bats, DiMaggio walked and doubled. For the day he knocked in four runs to put him over the 100 mark on the season. New York won, 8–1, pulling the Yankees to within half a game of the Tigers.

The Yankees traveled to Detroit on September 14, still trailing the Tigers by half a game. DiMaggio homered and the Yanks won the opener, 7–5, New York edged into first place.

After losing game two, despite three home runs by Johnny Mize, New York regained the lead on September 16. Rookie Whitey Ford went the distance for his seventh consecutive win and DiMaggio cracked his 30th home run, as the Yankees broke a 1–1 tie with seven ninth-inning runs, winning 8–1.

The Tigers tailed off, but the Yankees couldn't shake Boston, splitting four games before hosting the Red Sox on September 23 and 24. The Sox trailed by only two games and needed a sweep.

DiMaggio didn't let it happen. If he was a great player against other teams, against the Red Sox he was Babe Ruth, Ty Cobb, and Frank Merriwell all wrapped together. As Ed Lopat shut down the Red Sox on five hits, DiMaggio cracked a two-run home run off Mel Parnell in the first to give New York the only runs needed in the 8–0 win. Despite two home runs by Ted Williams the next day, the Yankees won again, 9–5, as eventual AL MVP Phil Rizzuto and Yogi Berra keyed the Yankee attack. With eight games left to play, New York led the Tigers by 2 1/2 and the Red Sox by 4.

The Yankees traveled to Washington on September 25 and rendered the rest of the season immaterial, spanking the Senators in a doubleheader, 8–3 and 7–4. DiMaggio banged out three singles in the first game, then smacked a bases-loaded double in the third inning of game two, turning a 2–0 deficit into a 3–2 Yankee lead.

New York clinched the pennant during a rainout in Boston on September 29, as Cleveland beat the Tigers. After DiMaggio returned to the lineup on August 18, he had hit .376 for the rest of the season, including 9 home runs and 30 RBI in the month of September, and the Yankees went 31–11. The surge pushed his average above .300, and he finished the year at .301, with 32 home runs, 122 RBI, and an AL-best slugging percentage of .585. The Yankees finished three games ahead of Detroit at 98–56, champions once again.

The youthful Philadelphia Phillies, dubbed the "Whiz Kids" by the press, surprised everyone by edging the Dodgers by two games for the National League pennant. The Phillies were led by their pitching staff, which included 20-game winner Robin Roberts and junkball re-

DiMaggio races to make a running catch of a towering drive by Del Ennis of the Phillies in the sixth inning of the second game of the 1950 World Series. The Yankees would win the game 2–1 thanks to a tenth-inning home run by DiMaggio. (Associated Press photograph)

lief pitcher Jim Konstanty, who capped an MVP season with 16 wins, 22 saves, and a major-league-record 74 appearances.

The Series opened in Philadelphia on October 4. No one gave the Phillies a chance against the vaunted Yankees.

Stengel's staff was well-rested, and he chose Vic Raschi as his starter in game one. Philadelphia manager Eddie Sawyer gambled and gave Jim Konstanty his first start of the year.

His strategy nearly worked. Konstanty kept the Yankees off balance with a repertoire of off-speed pitches. In the fourth, the Yankees' Bobby Brown doubled off the wall down the left-field line, moved to third on a fly ball by Hank Bauer, and scored on another fly off the bat of Jerry Coleman, giving the Yankees a 1–0 lead.

That was all New York needed. Vic Raschi gave up only two fifth-inning singles and shut out the Phillies. The Yankees won, 1–0.

Pitching ruled game two, as the Yankees' Allie Reynolds and the Phillies' young star Robin Roberts matched each other inning by inning. New York pushed across a run in the third when Coleman singled, went to third on Reynolds's base hit, and scored on Gene Woodling's slow roller to short. But Philadelphia tied the game on Richie Ashburn's sacrifice fly in the fifth, which scored second baseman Mike Goliat.

In the sixth, DiMaggio kept the Yankees out of trouble when he caught Del Ennis's deep drive to center with a fine over-the-shoulder catch, the equal of any in his career. Philadelphia threatened in the ninth. With one out, shortstop Granny Hamner hit a line drive to right center. DiMaggio moved over, but the ball fell in the gap and started to skip by. If it got past DiMaggio, Hamner had a triple. If Joe botched the play, the hit was good for a home run.

The play typified DiMaggio's subtle contributions to the team, those so easy to overlook. DiMaggio glided to his left, and as the ball hit the ground, he stretched out and stabbed the ball like a second baseman, then spun and fired the ball back in. A surprised Hamner stopped rounding second, and the Phillies failed to bring him around. At the end of nine, the score was tied 1–1.

Joe DiMaggio led off the tenth inning. Philadelphia pitcher Robin Roberts was confident. In four previous at bats, he had fed DiMaggio nothing but fastballs. DiMaggio hadn't gotten around on the ball and had popped up all four times to the infield. Roberts later said, "I really wasn't concerned about him. . . . I never threw harder than I did that year."

After throwing one ball and one strike, Roberts missed with the next pitch to fall behind. He didn't think of throwing a curve. He didn't want to give DiMaggio a pitch he could get around on. His previous success made him cocky. He threw another fastball.

Joe DiMaggio attends to business with a hotel cashier in Boston in October 1950. His Yankees had just won their eighth world championship in his tenure with the team. (Photograph courtesy of the *Boston Herald*)

As soon as it left his hand, Roberts knew he had underestimated DiMaggio. The pitch was low, but not as low as Roberts hoped. DiMaggio timed it perfectly and sent the ball soaring on a line to left center field. It kept rising and landed in the upper deck for a home run. The hit was DiMaggio's first of the Series, and when the Phillies went in order in the bottom of the inning, the Yankees had won, 1–0.

After the game, Roberts insisted the pitch was a fastball, while DiMaggio said it was a slider. Years later, DiMaggio and Roberts met at an old-timers' game, and DiMaggio told Roberts, "You know, Robin, I can still see that pitch up over the plate. I could just see it, it seemed to tail away when I swung at it." No matter. It ended up in the stands.

The series moved to New York with the Yankees up two games to none. In game three, as Rud Rennie of the *Herald Tribune* wrote, "The Philadelphia Whiz Kids . . . started showing off yesterday. . . . They were out in front when the Yankees, the big champions, got tired of them and slapped them into a corner for the third day in succession."

The Phillies led 2–1 entering the eighth. Phillie pitcher Ken Heintzelman seemed in control. But with two out, he lost the plate. Coleman walked, as did Berra, bringing up Joe DiMaggio.

Now Heintzelman could ill afford to throw a strike. He pitched carefully and walked DiMaggio, loading the bases.

Konstanty came in to pitch, and Stengel pinch-hit Brown for Bauer. Brown bounced the ball to short, but Hamner bobbled it and Coleman scored to tie the game.

For the second day in a row, the Yankees won the game in their last at bat. With two outs in the ninth, Woodling, Rizzuto, and Coleman singled. Woodling scored on Coleman's hit and the Yankees won, 3–2.

The Phillies were dead. They'd stopped the Yankees for three games yet New York still managed to win. In game four, the Yankees put Philadelphia out of their pain early.

In the first, Woodling reached base on an error and Rizzuto moved him to second on a groundout. Berra singled Woodling home and went to third on a wild pitch. DiMaggio followed with a double to right and New York led, 2–0.

The Yankees scored three more in the sixth to put the game out of reach. Berra homered, and after DiMaggio was hit by a pitch, Brown tripled him home and scored himself on a sacrifice fly. Pitcher Whitey Ford tired in the ninth and gave up two runs, but Allie Reynolds came on in relief and struck out Stan Lopata to end the game. The Yankees had won their seventh consecutive Series game and their second straight championship. It was getting to be old hat again.

DiMaggio's numbers in the Series again belied his value. Without his bat and his glove, the Yankees wouldn't have won game two, and in game four DiMaggio helped bury the Phillies early, squelching any visions of a comeback. Over the last two months, he had answered the critics who wondered if he could still play.

After the season, DiMaggio joined his old manager Lefty O'Doul and the two men traveled to Korea and the Far East to boost the morale of American troops.

The trip was no vacation junket. O'Doul and DiMaggio kept a grueling schedule in Korea, traveling within twelve miles of the front. In seventeen days they visited eighteen hospitals, and DiMaggio dropped nearly ten pounds. After leaving Korea, they went to Japan and took in the first two games of the 1950 Japanese World Series. DiMaggio and O'Doul proved so popular they even opened the Series with a ceremonial first pitch; O'Doul threw a pitch to DiMaggio, who purposefully whiffed. The trip boosted DiMaggio's public image.

But all was not well with DiMaggio. While he had proven he still was one of the most productive hitters in baseball, his shoulders bothered him for much of the year. His left shoulder started "popping out," even in the off-season when he was playing golf and relaxing. His mother, Rosalie, was sick with cancer, and Joe spent much of the off-season at her side, in the house he bought for his parents and now shared with his sister Marie. During the off-season, he hinted that 1951 might be his last season.

He signed his third straight $100,000 contract and arrived at the Yankees' new spring training headquarters in Phoenix, Arizona, on March 1. Joe announced he was in good shape and told a reporter, "I'm out to surprise those who believe I am finishing up my career." While the statement did not directly refute the retirement rumors, it hardly prepared anyone for the bombshell that was about to drop.

On the evening of March 2, DiMaggio, speaking informally to a group of reporters, said, "This year might be my last." He added he hoped to have a good season and wanted to end his career before he was too far past his peak as a player. The reporters ran with the story, and news of DiMaggio's impending retirement filled New York papers the next morning.

DiMaggio tried to soft-pedal the announcement the next day, but didn't back down from his earlier statement. The Yankees were reportedly flabbergasted, and not pleased that DiMaggio had spoken with reporters before speaking with the front office. Stengel was quoted as saying, "You can't stop a man from doing what he wants. What am I supposed to do, get a gun and make him play? I don't own him."

DiMaggio's announcement stunned the beat writers covering the Yankees. Their brethren back in New York were miffed that DiMaggio had given out a scoop without letting them know, too. But they didn't miss a beat. If the king was dead, it was time to find another candidate for the throne. On the heels of DiMaggio's announcement, they turned their attention to a nineteen-year-old rookie with only two years of minor league experience named Mickey Mantle.

In Mantle, they saw the same kind of player they'd seen when Di-Maggio showed up at his first training camp in 1936, a player of immense physical talent and promise who appeared to be the natural successor to other Yankee stars, a list that now included DiMaggio's name after those of Ruth and Gehrig. Stengel told the writers he thought Mantle could make the jump from Class C to the major leagues. Mantle was the Yankees' first genuine phenom since Di-Maggio.

Just as DiMaggio had dominated the stories from spring training in 1936, now stories about Mantle led off every report out of Arizona. Like DiMaggio, Mantle responded with a spectacular exhibition season, leading the Yankees in home runs and runs batted in.

Mantle was not unlike the young DiMaggio. Apart from his physical assets, the nineteen-year-old was introverted and shy, at least around writers. On the field, his bat did the talking. Off the field, he said little. Just as the writers had taken bare details of DiMaggio's upbringing and created a myth worthy of the player they wanted him to be, they did the same with Mantle. Whereas DiMaggio's story became the im-

Joe DiMaggio signs his final playing contract with the Yankees at spring training in Phoenix in March 1951. He is flanked by (l–r) Yogi Berra, Del Webb, Dan Topping, and Billy Johnson. (Photograph from Transcendental Graphics, Mark Rucker)

Joseph Paul DiMaggio, Jr., gets some father'ly advice and baseball tips from his famous dad. DiMaggio Sr. was visiting his son at Black-Foxe Military Academy near Los Angeles prior to the start of his final season with the Yankees in 1951. (Photograph courtesy of the Boston Herald)

migrant's tale, Mantle's biography became a parable of the Depression.

Meanwhile, DiMaggio's spring training was virtually ignored as all eyes looked to Mantle. He received more attention for the presence of his ex-wife in Arizona than for anything he did on the field. DiMaggio was making a last-ditch attempt to renew the relationship, and so far Dorothy Arnold seemed agreeable.

DiMaggio got off to a slow start in spring training. At the end of March, he was hitting only .215. As the Yankees embarked on their annual barnstorming trip, some speculated that Mantle was now more important to the Yankees than DiMaggio.

DiMaggio responded to the whispers in the only way he knew, with his bat and with his glove. As the Yankees worked their way north, Joe woke up against the minor-league competition, and by April 9 had raised his average to .378.

Apart from DiMaggio, only Phil Rizzuto remained from the Yankee ballclub DiMaggio rejoined after the war. Two rookies, Mantle and third baseman Gil McDougald, joined the starting lineup, and another, outfielder Jackie Jensen, platooned in the outfield. DiMaggio was older than all but one man on the club, first baseman Johnny Mize.

The younger Yankees were in awe of DiMaggio. They could hardly believe they were on the same club. Their reverence usually translated into a sort of stunned silence in DiMaggio's presence.

Just as Lefty Gomez, and later Joe Page, provided DiMaggio with an entertaining companion in his earlier years, brash rookie Billy Martin, intimidated by no one, now served the same role. But apart from Martin and Phil Rizzuto, DiMaggio was aloof from his teammates. He was in a different world.

The Yankee season opener in Washington on April 16 was rained out. When the Yankees returned home the next day to host Boston, DiMaggio still played center field and still hit fourth in the lineup. Ahead of him, hitting third and playing right field, was Mickey Mantle.

New York again proved their dominance over Boston, winning 5–0. DiMaggio made a fine catch of a Billy Goodman drive in the first and saved a run, doubling brother Dom off base. Both DiMaggio and Mantle contributed a base hit and knocked in a run.

Soon after the season started, he was troubled by a series of nagging injuries. His shoulder and neck started acting up in late April and he took himself out of the lineup. He returned in mid-May, then pulled a muscle on June 8 and left the lineup again.

Joe DiMaggio welcomes Yankee prospect Bob Cerv to New York in August 1951. At the time Cerv was touted as a potential successor to DiMaggio, who was playing in his last season. A rookie named Mantle would later take that role. (Photograph courtesy of the *Boston Herald*)

Ten days later, his mother went into a coma. Joe DiMaggio left the club and rushed to San Francisco, as did Dominic, but their mother passed away without waking. Meanwhile, DiMaggio's reconciliation with Dorothy Arnold fizzled.

So far, the 1951 season was playing out as a cruel repeat of 1949. This time, there was no spectacular return. The Yankees edged into first place in late June, then stumbled just before the All-Star break, dropping five of six, including three in a row to Boston, to drop into second place.

In the first of the three Boston losses, on July 6, Stengel shocked everyone when he pulled DiMaggio in the middle of the game. After misplaying a hit in the first, DiMaggio went back out to center field to start the second. Out came right fielder Jackie Jensen, with Johnny Hopp behind him. Jensen told DiMaggio he was moving into center field and that DiMaggio was being replaced. A stunned DiMaggio ran off the field, embarrassed and angry to be pulled in mid-inning. Stengel tried to downplay the incident. He claimed he thought DiMaggio was hurt and had not intended to embarrass him. He said he tried to make the change between innings, but DiMaggio had already taken the field. DiMaggio would have none of it. The relationship between the two, while never warm, turned icy.

The incident incited the press. The subject of DiMaggio's diminishing ability was now fair game for the writers. DiMaggio's old friends, like Jimmy Cannon, defended him. Cannon wrote, "There has only been one truly great baseball player in this generation. Someone should remind Casey Stengel the man's name is Joe DiMaggio." But younger writers, who were not part of DiMaggio's entourage, used the incident as an excuse to take potshots at the veteran player, whom they criticized for being moody and self-centered.

A week later, DiMaggio was named to the All-Star team for the thirteenth time, but it was courtesy on Stengel's part. By then, DiMaggio had torn a muscle in his leg and couldn't play anyway.

If DiMaggio had hoped to go out at the top of his game, he did not. When he was hurt, the Yankees didn't seem to miss him. When he did play, he rarely provided the expected spark. His average wallowed around .250, and he wasn't hitting with his accustomed power. When he did hit, it was often to right field. DiMaggio was not trying to hit the other way, he just couldn't pull a good fastball anymore. The hero was only human.

The Yankees were stumbling. While the White Sox fell back, the Indians surged past New York. On July 20, Stengel shook up his lineup, benching Jerry Coleman and moving McDougald to second and Bobby Brown to third. After the shake-up, some of the press openly wondered why it had not included DiMaggio. For the first time in his career, DiMaggio seemed irrelevant to the pennant race.

The Yankees responded to Stengel's shake-up by winning ten of their next eleven. Even DiMaggio, at long last, finally began to show signs of life.

In a doubleheader sweep of Chicago on July 29, Joe backed Vic Raschi's winning effort in game one by hitting two home runs and knocking in five. In the second game, with the Yankees leading 1–0, DiMaggio led off the fourth with a single. After Yogi Berra flied out, Johnny Mize singled to short right. DiMaggio surprised the White Sox by taking two bases, sliding into third just ahead of the throw. Stengel called for a delayed squeeze, and as McDougald squared around and bunted the ball toward first, DiMaggio broke for home. White Sox first baseman Eddie Robinson charged the ball and threw home, but Joe slid around the tag. The Yankees won, 2–0.

The next day against Detroit, DiMaggio nearly undid the good of the day before. With one out and the Yankees ahead 3–2 in the eighth, Gerry Priddy and George Kell doubled. Steve Souchock followed with a fly to deep center field.

DiMaggio went back for the ball, made the routine catch, then, thinking the inning was over, put his head down and started to jog in. Kell tagged up at second, went to third, then headed home. By the time DiMaggio realized what was happening, Detroit led, 4–3.

The Yankees managed to tie the score in the eighth, and in the bottom of the ninth, with two out, Joe Collins doubled and Bobby Brown walked. Up came DiMaggio.

Veteran Detroit pitcher Virgil Trucks blew a fastball by DiMaggio for a strike. His next pitch was wide, and DiMaggio tried to check his swing. Instead, he connected, blooping the ball down the right-field line and scoring Collins with the winning run. It wasn't pretty, but DiMaggio had done it. The performance kept him in the lineup.

The Yankees chased Cleveland through August and into September. On the 16th, the Indians came to New York for two games, leading the Yankees by one. New York had lost four of five and was reeling. With less than two weeks left in the season, the Yankees needed to win both games.

Bob Feller started for Cleveland against Allie Reynolds as 70,040 fans packed Yankee Stadium. Feller led the major leagues with 22 wins, while Reynolds, the ex-Indian, had already beaten Cleveland four times in 1951.

Before the game, Stengel shook up the lineup, as Rud Rennie described it, "as thoroughly as an electric fan shuffles papers." Mantle led off, Rizzuto hit eighth, McDougald batted third. For the first time all year, DiMaggio was moved out of the cleanup spot. He hit fifth, behind Berra.

The strategy worked, as the Yankees jumped ahead 3–0, scoring one run in the first on Berra's triple and adding two in the second. Cleveland scored a single run in the fifth to make it 3–1.

In the Yankees' half, Mickey Mantle led off with a drag-bunt base hit. Joe Collins sacrificed him to second, then McDougald drove one deep to left. Cleveland left fielder Sam Chapman went back, leapt up, balanced on the rail, and came down with the ball.

Berra stepped to the plate. Feller thought for a moment, then walked Yogi intentionally to get to DiMaggio. While DiMaggio had always given him trouble in the past, that Joe DiMaggio no longer existed. This Joe DiMaggio, he could get out. The partisan Yankee crowd went crazy. Sure, like Feller, they knew DiMaggio wasn't the best player in the game anymore, and they knew from a baseball standpoint, the intentional walk made sense. But unlike Feller, in this situation they still believed Joe DiMaggio was the best player in history.

With one ball and two strikes, DiMaggio pulled Feller's next pitch into Death Valley, the huge tract of land in left-center field. Mantle and Berra both scored, and by the time the Cleveland outfield threw the ball back in, DiMaggio was standing on third with a triple. Cleveland never recovered, and the Yankees won, 5–1, to move into first place by .003.

The next day, Eddie Lopat of the Yankees and the Indians' Bob Lemon matched each other for eight gritty innings, each man giving up only one run. Cleveland went out without a score in the ninth, setting the stage for New York.

Berra, hitting cleanup again, grounded out. DiMaggio stepped up and pulled the ball viciously down the left-field line. Cleveland third baseman Al Rosen, no Ken Keltner, whirled to his right and knocked the ball down, but DiMaggio made first without a throw for a base hit. Gene Woodling then whistled a single between second and first, and DiMaggio raced to third. Lemon walked Bobby Brown, bringing up Phil Rizzuto.

As Lemon wound up, DiMaggio broke from third. Lemon, rightly sensing a squeeze play, threw the ball up and in, a difficult pitch to bunt. But Rizzuto was the best bunter in baseball. He flicked his bat up to his ear and dropped the ball toward first. DiMaggio scored standing up. The Yankees won, 2–1, and increased their lead to a full game.

The sweep finished Cleveland. On September 28, in a doubleheader against Boston at the Stadium, the Yankees had an opportunity to clinch the pennant.

No team was ever better at clinching the pennant than the Yankees. In game one, Allie Reynolds fired a no-hitter, winning 8–0, to clinch at least a tie. The game was not without drama, as Yogi Berra dropped a Ted Williams pop-up that should have ended the game, forcing Reynolds to retire Williams twice. He did. In the second game, New York broke out early with seven runs in the second inning to erase a 3–0 Boston lead.

It was still 7–3 when New York came to bat in the sixth. With two on and two out, DiMaggio faced Boston pitcher Chuck Stobbs.

Stobbs worked the count to 3 and 2. DiMaggio swung and the ball rose toward left field, then dropped over the fence for a home run, the 361st, and last, regular-season home run of DiMaggio's career. The Yankees won, 11–3, and clinched the pennant.

Stengel and the rest of the Yankees went out of their way to make sure DiMaggio was included in the clubhouse celebration. Stengel told reporters, "I couldn't have won it without him. He's saved me pitchers many times and his baserunning has been splendid all year." Casey Stengel knew that while DiMaggio had slipped as a hitter, Joe still found ways to contribute.

DiMaggio simply sat in front of his locker, quietly acknowledging the congratulations of his teammates, holding the ball hit to Gene Woodling by his brother Dom for the final out. "Gene gave it to me," DiMaggio told a reporter, "and this one I'm going to keep. With this ball the Yankees clinched the pennant, my tenth pennant." In the history of baseball, only Babe Ruth had ever been able to say the same thing.

The Yankees swept Boston in the season's final three games. With the American League pennant decided, attention turned to the National League, where the Dodgers and Giants went to the wire for the National League pennant, finishing in a tie to set up a three-game playoff for the championship. Like everyone else in New York City, the Yankees settled back to watch.

After splitting the first two games, the Giants won in the most dramatic fashion possible as Bobby Thomson cracked a three-run home run in the ninth inning to give the Giants the pennant. For the first time since 1937, the Yankees and Giants were in the World Series.

The Giants' dramatic win and the Yankees' hard-fought battle with Cleveland pushed talk about DiMaggio's retirement into the background. Joe wasn't talking either. Since spring training, he said he would make his final decision after the season, perhaps even during spring training in 1952, and not before. But there was little in his 1951 performance to indicate he was ready to change his mind.

DiMaggio sank to career lows in virtually every statistical category. In 122 games, he came to bat 415 times and collected only 109 hits, with 12 home runs and 71 RBI. He still held his own in center field, but no one was calling him the best center fielder in baseball. A young player with the Giants was beginning to make that plaudit his own.

The Giants were a powerful, scrappy, and well-balanced team. Manager Leo Durocher got the most from his club's talent, as the Giants featured good defense, just enough hitting, and the best pitching in the National League. In center field, the Giants had a phenom at least the equal of Mickey Mantle in twenty-year-old Willie Mays.

Over the last few weeks of the regular season, Brooklyn scout Andy High followed the Yankees in anticipation of a Dodger-Yankee Series. When the Dodgers lost, he gave his scouting report to the Giants. It was leaked to the press during the series, and appeared in *Life* magazine a few weeks later.

The report contained a devastating appraisal of DiMaggio, claiming Joe "could not stop quickly and throw hard," and that runners, "can take an extra base on him . . . He can't run and won't bunt . . . and his reflexes are very slow and he can't pull a good fastball at all." Any thoughts DiMaggio may have had of continuing his career may have died when the report was published, although he already knew the truth of what High wrote. Although the Yankees were narrow favorites in the Series, expectations about DiMaggio were low.

The Giants followed their dramatic win over the Dodgers with a 5–1 victory over the Yankees in Yankee Stadium the next day in the Series opener. The Giants jumped out to a 2–0 lead in the first, scored three more in the sixth on Alvin Dark's three-run home run, and pitcher Dave Koslo pitched a complete game. The Yankees managed only seven hits. DiMaggio flied out to the outfield four times.

After Eddie Lopat set down the Giants in the first inning of game two, Mickey Mantle bunted for a hit leading off the Yankee first. Rizzuto followed with a bunt of his own, and Mantle took third on a wild

DiMaggio celebrates his last game as a Yankee with team-mate Hank Bauer as the Yankees exult following their six-game World Series triumph over the New York Giants. DiMaggio was one of three Yankees on base when Bauer blasted the triple that gave the Yankees a 4–1 lead in a game they would win 4–3. (Associated Press photograph)

throw. McDougald singled him home to put the Yankees up 1–0, but DiMaggio grounded into a double play to end the rally. In the second, Joe Collins's home run put the Yankees up 2–0.

Leading off the fifth inning, Willie Mays hit a routine fly ball to right-center field. DiMaggio drifted over to his left as Mantle raced over from right.

As center fielder, DiMaggio had the right of way and called for the ball. Mantle applied the brakes but caught his spikes in the rubber cover of a drain on the field and dropped to the ground. DiMaggio threw the ball in, then crouched over Mantle.

Mantle tore apart his knee on the play, one of a series of leg injuries going back to his adolescence that eventually robbed him of much of his speed and may well have prevented him from becoming the greatest player in the history of the game. Years later, Mantle said he believed DiMaggio was late calling for the ball, and laid partial blame for the injury on DiMaggio. But Mantle never played outfield until 1951, and the play was clearly DiMaggio's. Besides, if not for the drain cover, Mantle would not have been hurt.

Hank Bauer replaced Mantle, who was through for the Series. While the Yankees' depth mollified Mantle's loss, it forced Stengel to adjust the batting order. The Yankees would miss Mantle's speed at the top of the order for the rest of the series.

Eddie Lopat hung on to win game two 3–1, to even the Series. DiMaggio went hitless again. The teams crossed the Harlem River to the Polo Grounds for game three.

For only the third time in DiMaggio's career, the Yankees fell behind in the Series. Giant pitcher Jim Hearn scattered four hits in $7^2/_3$ innings, and although he walked eight men, the Yankees didn't score until it was too late, losing 6–2. For the third game in a row, DiMaggio was hitless. In the *Herald Tribune* the next day, the only mention of DiMaggio was of an earlier Series performance; his catch to end the 1937 series. So far, he'd done nothing to write about in 1951.

With Mantle out of the lineup, the Yankees needed someone to pick up the slack. Game four was critical. The Yankees could ill afford to fall behind three games to one.

The Giants touched Allie Reynolds for a run in the first. In the Yankee half, New York went out in order, but DiMaggio drove a foul ball deep to left, then fouled off a half dozen pitches before striking out. The Yankees came back to score single runs against pitcher Sal Maglie in the second and fourth to lead 2–1. In the fifth, Rizzuto popped out before Berra singled.

Despite DiMaggio's slump, Stengel stuck with him. In the third inning, Joe had singled for his first hit in 12 Series at bats. Now, Maglie went to 3 and 1 on DiMaggio.

With the next pitch, DiMaggio did precisely what he was not supposed to be able to do anymore, pull the ball. It landed in the upper deck for a home run, putting the Yankees up 4–1.

When DiMaggio crossed the plate, Berra was waiting for him and nearly jumped into his arms, bouncing up and down with joy and smacking him on the back, then escorting him to the dugout where the Yankees, as a team, climbed the steps to greet him. They knew, even if the Giants didn't, what the home run meant. The Yankees had lost Mantle, but they had DiMaggio back. Reynolds went the distance and the Yankees won, 6–2. The series was even.

The postgame scene in the Yankee clubhouse was oddly familiar. Familiar in that it happened so often in the past, and odd because it hadn't happened recently.

The press crowded around DiMaggio. He was effusive for once, talking about the foul he hit in the first, calling it "the best ball I hit," and the home run, which came "on a low curve." He even admitted changing bats for the day, saying "I've been using a 35-ounce Babe Ruth model bat. Today I used a 34-ounce model." It was like old times.

The Series turned on DiMaggio's home run. The wave the Giants had ridden since their dramatic play-off win crested. In game five, after the Yankees fell behind 1–0, DiMaggio went to work.

With one out in the third, the Giants' Larry Jansen walked Gene Woodling and Phil Rizzuto. DiMaggio, still pulling the ball, singled to left and took second when Monte Irvin bobbled the ball. Johnny Mize walked and Gil McDougald slammed the door on the Giants with a grand slam, putting the Yankees up 5–1.

In the fourth, Phil Rizzuto smacked a two-run homer, and the Yankees collected two more in the sixth. In the seventh, the Yanks scored four more, the last two on DiMaggio's double—again to left—and the Bombers rolled to a 13–1 win.

When he stepped on the field for game six in the Stadium on October 6, Joe DiMaggio stepped into history. It was his fifty-first Series contest, bettering the record of fifty held by Frankie Frisch. At the end of the day, another record was his.

After Rizzuto made an out in the first, Coleman singled and Berra followed with a double to right. Giant pitcher Dave Koslo took no chances. DiMaggio, the guy with no reflexes who supposedly couldn't pull a good fastball, was walked intentionally to set up the force-out. Manager Leo Durocher and the Giants had seen enough.

Gil McDougald hit a sacrifice fly to give the Yankees a quick 1–0 lead. In the fifth, the Giants tied the score off Vic Raschi when Mays singled, moved to second on Berra's passed ball, then scored on two fly balls.

After Coleman struck out to start the sixth, Berra singled to right and went to second when Bobby Thomson fumbled the ball. DiMaggio came up, and for the second time, Koslo walked him intentionally. McDougald lined out, but Mize walked to load the bases. Hank Bauer tagged one to deep left, scoring three with a triple and putting the Yankees ahead 4–1.

It was still 4–1 in the eighth. Larry Jansen came in to pitch for the Giants. DiMaggio led off.

A party of Japanese actresses surround Joe DiMaggio and his Major League All-Star teammates upon their arrival in Tokyo in October 1951. (Photograph courtesy of the *Boston Herald*)

A murmur went through the crowd of 61,711. They knew DiMaggio might retire at the end of the series. If he did, this was probably the last at bat of his major-league career.

Jansen threw, and in his 199th appearance at the plate in a World Series, DiMaggio swung.

The ball rose on a line to the right of center as Giant outfielder Willie Mays, playing DiMaggio to pull, scrambled to his left. He had no chance. DiMaggio's drive bounded between Mays and Bobby Thomson to the wall.

A younger DiMaggio might have tried for third, but the older DiMaggio savored the moment and jogged into second, standing up with a double. Still playing to win, Stengel called on McDougald to bunt DiMaggio to third, but McDougald rolled the ball back to Jansen, whose quick throw nipped a sliding DiMaggio.

After the Giants rallied for two ninth-inning runs, Sal Yvars flied to right field. When the ball settled in Hank Bauer's glove, DiMaggio had set still another record, perhaps the most precious of his career: most times on the winning club in a World Series—nine.

During the celebration in the clubhouse, Stengel tried to make amends for the chill between himself and DiMaggio. He made the rounds of the clubhouse, shaking hands and thanking the players. When he reached DiMaggio, he grabbed Joe by the arms, looked him

Frank "Lefty" O'Doul and DiMaggio are shown in Japan in 1951. O'Doul, who first visited Japan in 1931 as a member of the Herb Hunter Major League All-Stars, was known as "O'Dou-San" and was instrumental in establishing baseball as a Japanese pastime. (Photograph courtesy of Dick Dobbins)

Enjoying the All-Star baseball tour of Japan, Joe DiMaggio and San Francisco Seals Manager Frank "Lefty" O'Doul are shown receiving flowers from a Japanese model at Tokyo's Korakuen Stadium prior to the opening game between the All-Stars and the Yomiuri Giants. (Photograph courtesy of the Boston Herald)

in the eye, and said, "If it wasn't for you, we wouldn't have done it." Stengel meant it.

DiMaggio's own teammates, realizing in the midst of their own joy that Joe had just played his last game, gathered around him, and one by one, like little boys, asked him to autograph bats, balls, and other paraphernalia. When they asked DiMaggio the question, he answered, "I've played my last game." Despite the disappointments of the 1951 season, he had fulfilled his promise to himself. He had, as he told the writers in Arizona the previous March, gone out at the top of his game.

After the season DiMaggio headed back to San Francisco. He made no formal announcement concerning his retirement, but gave no indication he was thinking of changing his mind. He planned to join Dominic and fourteen other players for an exhibition series in Japan.

Upon arrival in Tokyo on October 17, the players were paraded in open cars from the airport toward their hotel. One million fans

Joe and Dom DiMaggio were rarely on the same team, save for the occasional All-Star Game and the 1951 Major League exhibition tour of Japan. They are shown with Sgt. Frank Maxie Davis prior to the All-Stars' game against the Yomiuri Giants. (Photograph courtesy of the Boston Herald)

jammed the Tokyo streets, stopping traffic on the Ginza in the middle of rush hour for more than an hour. Police had to plead with the crowds to enable DiMaggio's car to pass.

Wherever the players appeared in Japan, they faced similar scenes. DiMaggio had supplanted Babe Ruth as Japan's favorite American baseball hero.

The team of Americans swept through Japan, winning every game they played. On November 10, DiMaggio announced he was leaving the tour early for business reasons.

Joe played his last game earlier that day, as the team of Americans faced Japan's Central League All-Stars at Meiji Park in Tokyo. The Japanese team led 1–0 in the eighth inning, and the crowd was roaring. No Japanese team had beaten a club that included major-league ballplayers since 1931.

DiMaggio stepped up to the plate to lead off the eighth. Right-hander Shigero Sugishita wound up and threw. DiMaggio hit the ball deep into the left-field stands for a home run, tying the game.

Like so many of his hits, DiMaggio's home run sparked a come-back. In the ninth inning, Dom DiMaggio's triple knocked in a run, then the Yankees' Billy Martin scored him. The Americans won, 3–2.

When DiMaggio returned to the United States, he faced the inevitable. He had hoped to find something in Japan to allow him to continue playing, but he knew what he had to do.

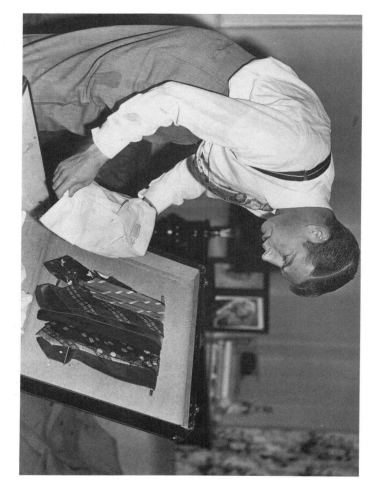

Joe DiMaggio packs his bags at the Hotel Madison in New York following the announcement of his retirement from baseball on December 11, 1951. (Photograph courtesy of the Boston Herald)

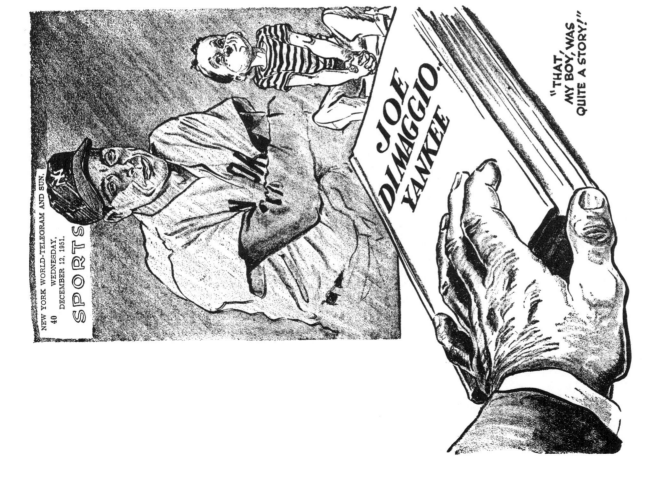

JOE DiMAGGIO. YANKEE.

"THAT, MY BOY, WAS QUITE A STORY!"

Cartoonist Willard Mullin sums up the career of Joe DiMaggio with this eloquent statement regarding the Yankee great's retirement.
(From "A Pen in Sport" by Willard Mullin)

Joe met with Yankee owners Dan Topping and Del Webb on the evening of December 10. For several hours the two men tried to convince Joe to play one more year, offering him the opportunity to pick his own spots, pinch-hit, or just play home games. They even offered him the same $100,000 he earned in 1951, but DiMaggio was adamant. He'd made his decision.

On the afternoon of December 11, the Yankees held a press conference at their offices at 745 Fifth Avenue. DiMaggio and the Yankees released a formal statement, read by the Yankees' Arthur Patterson. A few minutes later, Joe DiMaggio read the same statement himself for release over radio and on television.

It was brief and to the point. "I told you fellows last spring I thought this would be my last year. I only wish I could have had a better year. But even if I hit .350, this would have been the last year for me.

"You all know I've had more than my share of physical injuries and setbacks during my career. In recent years these have been much too frequent to laugh off. When baseball is no longer fun it's no longer a game.

"And so, I've played my last game of ball.

"Since coming to New York I've made a lot of friends and picked up a lot of advisers, but I would like to make one point clear—no one has influenced me in making this decision. It has been my problem and my decision to make.

"I feel I have reached the stage where I can no longer produce for my ballclub, my manager, my teammates, and my fans the sort of baseball their loyalty to me deserves.

"In closing, I would like to say that I have been unusually privileged to play all my major league baseball for the New York Yankees.

"But it has been an even greater privilege to play baseball at all. It has added much to my life. What I will remember most in the days to come will be the great loyalty of the fans. They have been very good to me."

DiMaggio spent the next hour answering questions and posing for pictures before a montage of photographs detailing his career, occasionally stopping to wipe a tear from his eye. He blamed night baseball for cutting at least two years from his career, said Ted Williams was the greatest hitter he'd ever seen, his brother Dominic the best outfielder, and thought his 1939 catch of the ball hit by Greenberg was his best ever. Joe said he had no interest in managing. The injuries just made it impossible to keep playing. His legs were OK, but now bone spurs in each shoulder made it difficult to throw and hit. Even bending over to pick up a ground ball was hard.

At the end of the press conference, the combination of lights for television and newsreels and radio equipment blew a fuse, throwing the Yankee office into darkness. When the lights came back on, DiMaggio was gone.

"I've played my last ball game," were the parting words from Joe DiMaggio as he retired from baseball at a press conference at the Yankees' midtown New York offices on December 11, 1951. (Photograph courtesy of the Boston Globe)

The Legend of Joe DiMaggio

Mickey Mantle with Mickey Herskowitz

When I was a boy in Oklahoma, there was nothing in sports, and not much anywhere else, that so demanded your interest as baseball's World Series. The week of the Series, teachers would let you bring portable radios to school—they were about the size of a toaster—or even excuse classes early so you could rush home and hear the broadcasts. At the movies in late October, the newsreels would

show highlights from the Series, with the announcer describing the action over the crowd noise. It seemed in every reel that Joe DiMaggio would be getting a hit and running to first.

I played in the first World Series I ever actually saw, as a rookie for the Yankees. The year was 1951 and, to this day, the memory is still strange and mixed and unreal to me. I didn't

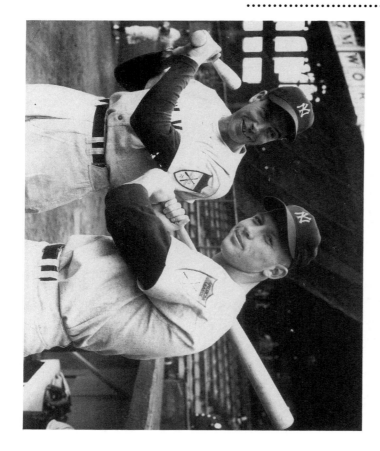

Joe DiMaggio and Mickey Mantle in 1956, the season of Mantle's Triple Crown. (Photograph from Transcendental Graphics, Mark Rucker)

really feel I belonged in the company of DiMaggio, Yogi Berra, Phil Rizzuto, and the rest. Coming out of spring training earlier in the year, the manager, Casey Stengel, had boasted about me to the press: "There's never been anyone like this kid which we got from Joplin. He has more speed than any slugger and more slug than any speedster—and nobody has ever had more of both of them together."

The buildup took on a life of its own, and the fans in New York thought they were getting a combination of Babe Ruth and Joe DiMaggio. All they really got was a scared nineteen-year-old kid from Oklahoma who didn't know anything.

That season was the last for DiMaggio. But it's no secret I wasn't comfortable around him. My locker was next to his, but I thought it would be out of line for me to speak to him first. As a result, we hardly spoke at all the entire season. I realize now I should have asked Joe to help me in some way. I think he would have liked that, but even to this day there is a time wall between us.

For me, the 1951 Series was short and ironic. My career almost ended in a play involving DiMaggio. He had been in pain most of the season from a sore Achilles tendon. I was starting in right field and Casey Stengel, the manager, told me to take anything I could reach. "The big

Dago's heel is hurting pretty bad," is the way he put it.

In the fifth inning, Willie Mays was hitting for the Giants, and he popped a fly ball into short right-center. I knew there was no way DiMaggio could get to it so I hauled ass. Just as I arrived, I heard Joe say, "I got it!" I looked over and he was *camped* under the ball. I put on the brakes and the spikes on my right shoe caught the rubber cover of a sprinkler head. There was a sound like a tire blowing out and my right knee collapsed. I fell to the ground and stayed there, motionless. A bone was sticking out the side of my leg. DiMaggio leaned over me and said, "Don't move. They're bringing a stretcher."

I guess that was about as close as Joe and I had come to a conversation. I don't know what impressed me more, the injury or the sight of an aging DiMaggio still able to make a difficult catch look easy. I celebrated my twentieth birthday in a cast after my surgery, and I wouldn't play another game the rest of my career without hurting.

DiMaggio made his retirement official after the Series, ending any doubt when he said, simply, "I'm not Joe DiMaggio anymore." Everyone knew what he meant, but it didn't lessen the sadness the fans felt in New York and across the country.

I guess it is the nature of the game that each World Series is often identified with a certain

player, a hit, a catch, a performance. In my mind, 1951 will always remind me of DiMaggio. For as little as we have known each other he cast a wide shadow over my career.

I never felt that I was competing with the record Joe left behind, and I certainly didn't compare myself to him. I do believe that near the end of my time, my teammates had a feeling for me close to what the Yankees of Joe's era had for him. I wanted my teammates to like me and I believe they did. I don't think that mattered greatly to Joe. They held him in awe and tried to give him all the space they could. He was custodian of the Yankee tradition. That was never my ambition, and I'm not sure it was Joe's, but it came naturally to him. There was never any real tension or jealousy between us—we weren't that close. But it's hard to explain how much the players on the team liked to analyze him. I never tired of hearing the stories.

It's hard to capture the qualities DiMaggio had. He was distant and austere, but a man of honor. He was unforgiving of conduct he considered crude or cheap. When Charlie Dressen joined the Yankees as a coach, he once protested an umpire's call by flinging towels and batting helmets out of the dugout. He was in the middle of making this mess when DiMaggio suddenly appeared at his side. "Go

out and pick up that stuff, now," said Joe, making it an order. Dressen started to say something and Joe cut him off. "Charlie," he said, "on this ball-club when we don't like decisions, we don't throw things. We hit home runs."

To this day, I consider DiMaggio the best all-around player in baseball history. To me, his fifty-six-game hitting streak is one of the three most impressive records that has been on the books for more than fifty years.

The two others may be even harder to break: Lou Gehrig's ironman string and Johnny Vander Meer's back-to-back no-hitters in 1939. Gehrig did not miss a game for nearly fourteen seasons, a record so astonishing that you can't imagine anyone watching so many games, much less playing in them. A pitcher may one day equal the feat of Vander Meer, but the idea of anyone beating him—that is, pitching three consecutive no-hitters—is so

unlikely, your computer would probably laugh if you asked for the odds.

Yet no record in sports has the weight and aura of DiMaggio's streak. Part of this attraction is DiMaggio himself, a man so reserved he was almost a mystery. Baseball statistics are there to be juggled with and admired. They make it possible to place legends of different generations under the same microscope. The joy is in comparing the people and the changing times. When Pete Rose hit safely in forty-four games in 1978, topping the National League mark, reporters almost had to punch him in the mouth to get him to stop talking. As an individual, Pete was as different from Joe as Muhammad Ali was from Joe Louis. The reserved DiMaggio suppressed his emotions so much that he developed ulcers. During his streak, he smoked as many as three packs of cigarettes a day, ducking into the dugout runway between innings for a drag. He would have lit one in center field if they had let him.

DiMaggio says he has always expected the streak to be broken, but is amused by the excuses that are given to explain why no one has. One of the arguments is that travel in the jet age is more hectic and more draining. Joe doesn't buy that one, and neither do I. "Train travel wasn't easy," he says. "We would leave New York after a game, ride twenty-four hours to St. Louis and sometimes go right from the station to the ballpark for a night game. The guys batting third, fourth, and fifth got a break with the berths. We would get the ones in the middle of the car. The rookies and utility players had to sleep over the wheels."

I learned a few things about fame over the years, but DiMaggio was a different kind of famous. I can't picture strangers coming up to him, as they did to me, and putting their arms around his shoulder and spilling beer in his lap. It is hard to be really honest with yourself when you try to remember how you felt forty years ago. But I admired him then and I still do. There was nothing not to like about Joe; but he wouldn't let just anybody get close to him, and after a certain time in my career I understood that.

He was beyond question one of the great players of the century. Then he became something more, when Paul Simon and Art Garfunkel wrote a song called "Mrs. Robinson" for the movie The Graduate, and it had a line that sent the country on a mass-identity crisis: "Where have you gone, Joe DiMaggio, a nation turns its lonely eyes to you . . ."

That lyric became a commentary on sports and its role in society and in our fantasy lives. I read where Paul Simon, a lifelong Yankee fan, tried to explain what it meant. "It has something to do with heros," he said. "People who are all good with no bad in them. That's the way I always saw Joe DiMaggio."

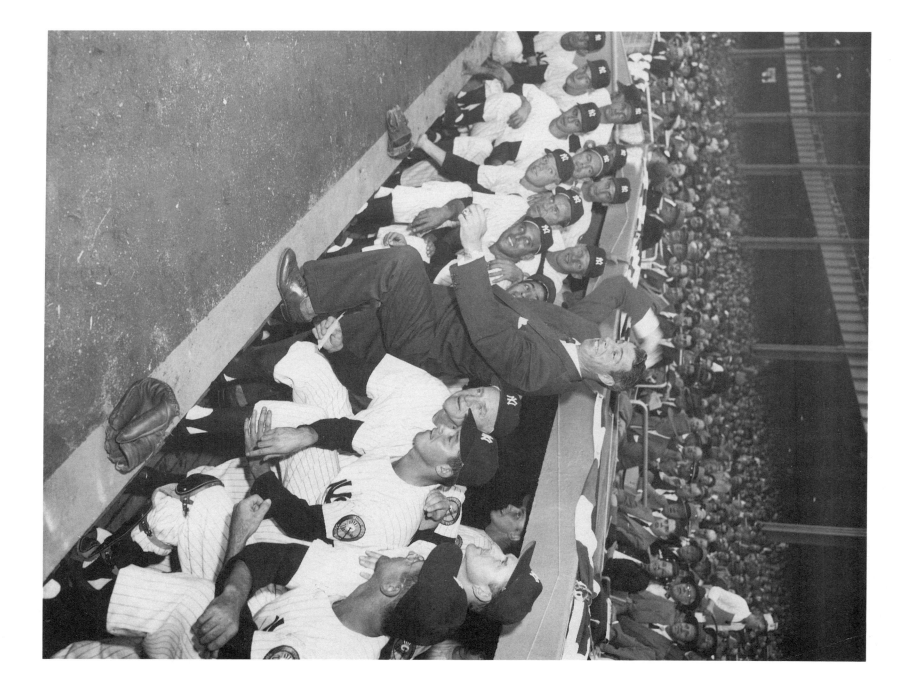

Image and Icon:
The Hero at Large

Whenever Joe DiMaggio retired as an active player, most observers considered him the equal of any man who had yet played the game, the equivalent of Babe Ruth and Ty Cobb. Yet unlike Ruth or Cobb, DiMaggio set few records.

Apart from the hitting streak, DiMaggio did not set any career or season records in any major offensive category. His only significant records were set in World Series play: tying Ruth at 10 for playing in the most Series, holding the record at 51 for games played, 199 for most at bats, and most times, 9, on a winning club.

His career statistics, while impressive, were less than that of many other players. DiMaggio retired with a career batting average of .325, with 361 home runs, 2,214 hits, and 1,537 RBI in 1,736 games. Perhaps most impressive is his number of strikeouts, 369. Until his final season, he had been more likely to hit a home run than strike out.

When he retired, his batting average ranked thirty-second all-time. Only Ted Williams, Stan Musial, and Rod Carew have since retired with an average higher than DiMaggio's. Perhaps more telling, he ranked fifteenth in career RBI, and his 361 home runs placed him tenth. If not for the war, he likely would have finished in the top five in each category. His career slugging percentage of .579 is still sixth best all-time, behind Ruth, Williams, Gehrig, Foxx, and Greenberg.

Since his retirement, subsequent performances by other players

Yankee Stadium Opening Day festivities in 1952 were marked by the return of Joe DiMaggio to throw out the first ball in his first season since his retirement. (Photograph courtesy of the Boston Herald)

have outstripped DiMaggio's career record. In the last forty-five years, it has become common for some observers to discount DiMaggio as a product of the New York media, one whose genius came about primarily through the success of his team.

That assertion obscures several facts. Many New York writers became blasé about his talent and set expectations that even he could not reach. When DiMaggio was at his peak, and the remarkable commonplace, some of his best performances were overlooked in favor of lesser contributions by other players. And while DiMaggio benefitted from the accomplishments of his team, DiMaggio's Yankees were not always the unstoppable force and immovable object their World Series record implied.

Before the war, DiMaggio's Yankees may well have been that team. The fact that they did not win a World Championship in each of those six seasons is almost more surprising than the fact that they won five; they were that good. But after the war, the Yankees were not nearly as talented, and the competition, the Indians of Feller and the Red Sox of Williams, was much better. DiMaggio, too, was not the player he was before the war. But that's when his contributions to the Yankees became more critical, and his successes and failures stood out as never before.

That is when he lived up to his stellar reputation; his play after the war cemented his status as a hero. Every time DiMaggio dragged himself off the disabled list and led the Yankees on a come-from-behind charge to the pennant, his standing rose. Before embarking on this project, I too, thought DiMaggio's reputation was, at least in part, a product of public relations. On a few rare occasions, his achievements may have been overstated. But over the course of his career, particularly after the war, DiMaggio led and his teammates followed.

Just as DiMaggio got better as the pressure increased during the fifty-six-game hitting streak, he also got better during a pennant race, when each game, each inning, and each at bat was increasingly critical. To come through under such conditions once in a while is not unique. Most players do and some have developed sterling reputations based on only one or two clutch performances. DiMaggio came through over and over again. His unmatched record of success at crucial times, using his glove and baserunning just as effectively as his bat, is as spectacular and prodigious as hitting in fifty-six consecutive games, perhaps even more so. Fifty-six games was just part of one season. DiMaggio faced the pressure of the pennant race countless times over fourteen seasons.

His unequaled ability to produce under pressure, often while physi-

Joe DiMaggio became a baseball announcer in New York following his retirement from baseball. He is shown interviewing old friend Billy Martin at Yankee Stadium in April 1952. (Photograph courtesy of the Boston Herald)

cally disabled, is precisely what made him such a hero to so many. The life of a fan lacks the drama inherent in baseball, yet the day-to-day pressure to succeed, particularly at work, is not so dissimilar. Most of us are satisfied if our efforts simply break even; our reward is a semblance of security. If we don't screw up, we get another chance the next day.

DiMaggio did more than that. Not only did he not screw up, he flourished day after day. His efforts lifted those around him. He was proof it was possible not just to survive, but to thrive. In his journey from North Beach to the Hall of Fame, he lived everyone's fantasy of moving from obscurity to immortality.

Other players, like Ruth and Cobb, or later, Williams, Musial, Mays, and Aaron, racked up better numbers. But no player, ever, not even Ruth, played better when playing well meant the difference between his team winning and his team losing. If Reggie Jackson deserves to be called Mr. October, then DiMaggio deserves to be called Mr. August, Mr. September, Mr. One-Game-Behind, and Mr. When-Everything-Looks-Most-Hopeless.

Ask a Red Sox fan of the late 1940s and early 1950s about DiMag-

The great Yankee outfield of Charlie Keller (l), Joe DiMaggio, and Tommy Henrich meet for Old-Timers' Day at Yankee Stadium on July 29, 1961. (Photograph by Bob Olen)

gio. Boston was a better team nearly every day of every season until late in the year, when they had to beat the Yankees. Over and over, DiMaggio stood in their way. Each spring from 1947 through 1951, *The Sporting News* picked the Red Sox to win the American League pennant. They never did. DiMaggio's Yankees won four times, and when they did not, 1948, DiMaggio helped to beat the Red Sox when he wasn't even on the field.

To be sure, there were and are better hitters than DiMaggio, better fielders, better base runners, outfielders with better throwing arms, hitters with more power. Even in his own era, he was rarely the very best at anything, winning just two home-run titles and two batting championships. But when asked to pick the best player, or select someone who had all the qualities of such a characterization, DiMaggio was the answer. When he retired, he was more than just a player. He was a hero, not only to fans, but to teammates and opponents.

Like most professional athletes, upon retirement DiMaggio faced a crisis. What was he going to do?

Since the age of sixteen, Joe DiMaggio had but one role. He was a ballplayer. There had not been a moment in his adult life, not even when a husband and father, when he was not a ballplayer first.

Many professional athletes falter in retirement. A few have success in other fields, like Dominic DiMaggio, who became a wealthy and successful businessman. Some make a transition to another role in their sport. But most former athletes are ill-prepared for life in the real world. All too often, marriages fail, money is lost, or alcohol is found. The remainder of an athlete's life pales in comparison to his earlier

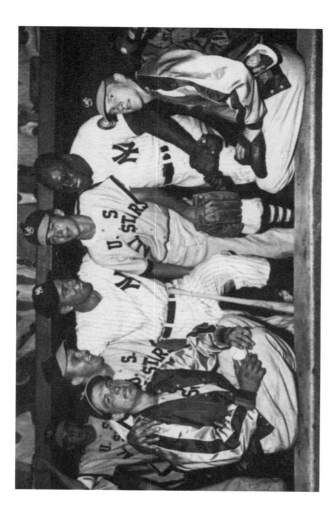

Joe DiMaggio is paired with then reigning world heavyweight boxing champion Jersey Joe Walcott as they greet young players before the start of the 7th Annual Hearst Sandlot Classic in 1952. Note the young Tony Kubek sitting on the right side of the dugout. (Photograph courtesy of the Boston Herald)

DiMaggio chats with syndicated columnist Walter Winchell at Gilmore Field in Hollywood during a cancer fund benefit game in 1953. (Photograph courtesy of the Boston Herald)

success on the field. Their lives spin off into a series of small personal tragedies, or they become caricatures of their former selves, telling the same stories of past glory over and over again, as if the past can live again with each retelling.

DiMaggio accomplished something more difficult. After retirement, DiMaggio maintained his earlier status. His profession became being himself; his job, to be Joe DiMaggio, living hero.

Just as DiMaggio felt he could not let down his teammates on the field or friends at Shor's, he has aspired to a similar standard in retirement. DiMaggio could have done *anything* after baseball. On a few occasions, he tried to do something else, but was never comfortable in another role. Eventually, he chose to remain Joe DiMaggio, and accept the public benefits and private deprivations that come with that identity. In a sense, Joe had little choice in the matter. Since the age of sixteen, he had never been anyone else.

The day he quit baseball, the Yankees retired DiMaggio's number 5 and sent his uniform and glove to Cooperstown to await the inevitable election to the Hall of Fame. One day later, the Yankees signed DiMaggio to a contract worth $100,000 to serve as a television announcer, replacing Dizzy Dean as the host of the pregame and postgame interviews on Yankee broadcasts. The job enabled DiMaggio to remain in New York much of the year, stay close to baseball, and live according to his accustomed patterns.

He maintained his home in San Francisco, living upstairs on a floor by himself in the house he bought for his parents, while his widowed

Joe DiMaggio and wife, Marilyn Monroe, are shown dining at El Morocco in New York in September 1954. Monroe had just flown east to shoot several scenes for her classic film The Seven Year Itch. *(Photograph courtesy of the* Boston Herald*)*

sister Marie lived downstairs. In the off-season, DiMaggio played golf and occasionally went down to the wharf to DiMaggio's Grotto, where he whiled away afternoons with his brother Tom.

In New York, he stayed in a hotel and appeared at Shor's, hanging out with friend George Solotaire and others. He attended the occasional football game or boxing match, and popped up in gossip columns whenever spotted with a beautiful woman on his arm. DiMaggio was no undignified skirt-chaser. He kept his private life private, and the bedroom door closed.

Once the 1952 season started, DiMaggio interviewed players before and after Yankee games. He was uncomfortable before the camera. Joe looked stiff, and when he spoke, he tended to clip off words. He was so worried about misspeaking and damaging his reputation, he insisted his part in the interviews be scripted.

DiMaggio was a lackluster replacement for the glib and entertaining Dizzy Dean. While he improved, the work was unsatisfying, and he quit after only one season.

Marilyn Monroe and Joe DiMaggio in 1953. (Photograph from Transcendental Graphics, Mark Rucker)

DiMaggio was not hurting financially, although neither was he fabulously wealthy. A variety of endorsements brought nearly $100,000 per year, and DiMaggio had few expenses apart from the care of his son, attending military school in California, and his New York hotel. When Joe went out, others paid. That had always been the case and remained so now.

He remained in the public eye, making appearances at charity functions, award dinners, golf outings, and giving the odd, brief interview, commenting on the current Yankees, or handicapping the pennant race, all activities that maintained his public image. While Joe did not appear especially happy in retirement, neither did he appear to regret his decision. Away from the baseball wars, he looked healthier and more fit than ever.

Then he met Marilyn Monroe.

In the spring of 1952, Joe DiMaggio, even in retirement, was perhaps the best-known and most-admired man in America. Marilyn Monroe was a young movie actress and nude calendar model whose talent seemed limited to her physique. She was admired too, by many of those who also admired DiMaggio, but for her more physical assets.

In the spring of 1952, Monroe appeared in a few publicity photographs with Gus Zernial, a power-hitting outfielder for the Philadelphia Athletics. DiMaggio saw the photographs, and through Zernial learned that Dave Marsh was the press agent who'd set up the shoot. Joe had connections in Hollywood and contacted Marsh. Sensing the publicity potential of the pairing, Marsh arranged for a date between DiMaggio and Monroe.

Monroe knew who DiMaggio was; she knew he was a ballplayer, but she was not particularly impressed. She was introduced to famous men all the time. Marilyn met Joe for dinner, arrived late, and was reportedly cool until Mickey Rooney, whom she had worked with before, spotted the couple and sat down.

Rooney was polite to Monroe but fawned over DiMaggio, a reaction she found intriguing. When they left, Marilyn drove Joe home, which he found intriguing.

DiMaggio called Monroe every day, asking for a date, and she turned him down every day for a week before finally caving in. They were soon in close company.

DiMaggio had always been attracted to blondes, particularly show-biz blondes, and Monroe was the blondest, albeit bleached, show-biz blonde there ever was. In turn, Marilyn herself had always been at-

As the Justice of the Peace looks on, Joe DiMaggio kisses his bride, Marilyn Monroe, on their wedding day in 1953. It was the second marriage for both. (Photograph from Transcendental Graphics, Mark Rucker)

The 1955 Induction Class at the Baseball Hall of Fame: (l–r) Joe DiMaggio, Gabby Hartnett, Frank "Home Run" Baker, Ted Lyons, Ray Schalk, and Dazzy Vance. (Wide World photograph)

tracted to older, successful men. In that, each was suited to the other. But while each fulfilled the other's notion of Mr. and Ms. Right, they were not perfectly paired. DiMaggio enjoyed San Francisco; Monroe was Miss Hollywood. DiMaggio was private, and insecure in public; Monroe needed publicity to boost her self-esteem. Joe thought Hollywood was full of phonies, and hated it. Marilyn knew Hollywood was full of phonies, and thrived in it. He expected her to adapt to who he was. She expected him to appreciate who she was.

The couple dated throughout 1952 and 1953. The press had a field day reporting the romance, even as DiMaggio resisted their attempts to sensationalize it. DiMaggio gave Monroe's career a boost and a veneer of respectability, while Marilyn kept Joe in the public eye, ensuring that no one got the impression he was not enjoying life after baseball. In retirement, DiMaggio's star was rising, and after the publication of Ernest Hemingway's *The Old Man and the Sea* in 1952, it rose further. Hemingway provided a concrete expression of how many felt about DiMaggio, using him symbolically as the ultimate example of someone who demonstrated grace under pressure.

As the relationship alternately warmed and cooled, Joe became eligible for election to the Baseball Hall of Fame in 1953. The mandatory waiting period was one year. The current five-year waiting period was not put into effect until 1954.

Joe DiMaggio and his wife, Marilyn Monroe, walk the streets near their San Francisco home prior to embarking on a trip that would take the couple to Hawaii and Japan. Monroe would also entertain American troops in Korea during the trip. (Photograph courtesy of the Boston Herald*)*

DiMaggio was disappointed when he received only 117 votes in 1953, far short of the 198 needed for election, and he finished behind seven other players in the balloting. The New York press speculated that DiMaggio was a victim of the anti-Yankee bias of those BBWA members who voted in the election.

That may have been true, but except for Lou Gehrig, who received special dispensation, and those who were inducted in the Hall's first year, 1936, no player had yet been elected in his first year of eligibility. BBWA voters were still catching up with nearly one hundred years of baseball history. The record for quickest entry to the Hall was held by Mel Ott, who was elected in his third year of eligibility in 1951.

Some baseball historians subsequently have used DiMaggio's eventual three-year wait to support arguments that diminish his achievements. But, unlike today, first-ballot election was unknown in 1953.

DiMaggio was more successful in his personal life than in his bid for the Hall of Fame. He and Marilyn Monroe followed their hearts even when better instincts may have told them not to. They fell in love, and on January 14, 1954, were married in a small civil ceremony in San Francisco.

Problems started almost immediately. They traveled to Japan, where Joe conducted a series of baseball clinics with Lefty O'Doul. When the couple returned to the United States, they lived briefly in San Francisco, then moved back to Los Angeles at Monroe's insistence.

Apart from physical attraction and genuine concern for one another,

Joe DiMaggio and wife, Marilyn Monroe, are shown upon their arrival from Japan on February 25, 1954. Monroe, who was seriously ill with bronchial pneumonia at the time, had just returned from a tour of Korean military bases. In the meantime, her husband conducted baseball clinics in Japan. (Photograph courtesy of the Boston Herald*)*

they had little in common. DiMaggio wanted a stay-at-home wife. Monroe desired a husband who wanted to do more than play golf and watch television. She complained that Joe never asked anyone over and never wanted to go out. In midsummer, they went back to the Far East, but DiMaggio remained in Tokyo while Monroe entertained troops in Korea. Upon her return, she uttered the now famous remark, "Joe, you've never heard such cheering," to which DiMaggio quickly and accurately responded, "Yes. I have." Her aspiration for public acclaim was to a level he had long since attained.

The marriage deteriorated. DiMaggio disliked her Hollywood friends and hated hanging out on movie sets. He was jealous and did not trust his wife. He wanted her to quit the movies. Marilyn wanted Joe to socialize more and talk to her. He refused to change, and she couldn't. They argued and fought. Finally, on October 27, 1954, they divorced.

Had the relationship ended with the divorce, it would not have remained the object of interest it is today. But DiMaggio and Monroe were not finished with each other. Neither could quite let the other go.

The depth of DiMaggio's attachment is illustrated by an incident that seems out of character. Today, it would be the subject of tabloid television, and would be considered, at best, harassment.

Shortly after the divorce DiMaggio was told Monroe was having an affair with another man. DiMaggio and several male friends, including Frank Sinatra, who was close to both Joe and Marilyn, went to an apartment where they were told they could find the ex-Mrs. DiMaggio and friend.

Accounts differ as to what happened next. DiMaggio either went to the wrong apartment by mistake or was led there by one of his com-

Rome's Ciampino Airport is the venue for Joe DiMaggio's first pitch to photographers covering the former Yankee's trek to visit relatives in Sicily in August 1955. (Photograph courtesy of the Boston Herald)

panions who feared a scene. He allegedly kicked the door in. Monroe was nowhere to be found. She was in an apartment upstairs.

The incident is telling. During DiMaggio's career in baseball, he allowed his emotions to take over in public only twice: approaching Whit Wyatt in the World Series, and kicking the ground after Gionfriddo's catch. But Monroe was under DiMaggio's skin. The incident was hushed up and did not become public knowledge until a year later. The female occupant of the wrong apartment eventually sued DiMaggio for $200,000, but settled out of court for much less. Joe narrowly averted a scandal of the highest order.

DiMaggio regained control of his feelings and learned to live with the breakup. Over much of the next decade, he and Monroe continued to see each other sporadically, most often when Monroe was on the rebound from another relationship or foundering under the pressures of stardom. To his credit, he never repeated his repugnant behavior and became a loyal and compassionate ally to Marilyn Monroe.

Just as DiMaggio tried to resume his relationship with Dorothy Arnold after their divorce, over much of the next decade he tried to do so with Monroe. But the relationship just wouldn't work. After a few weeks or months together, the same old problems would reappear.

DiMaggio fared better in Hall of Fame balloting. In 1954, he barely missed election, collecting 175 votes, just short of the 189 required. Finally, in 1955, DiMaggio led all eligible players with 223 votes, thirty-five more than needed, tying DiMaggio with Ott and Sisler for quickest entry into the Hall to that date.

Joe was inducted on July 25, 1955, along with Frank "Home Run" Baker, Ray Schalk, Dazzy Vance, Ted Lyons, and Gabby Hartnett. DiMaggio's presence drew the most fans to the ceremony since the Hall first opened in 1936.

He flew to Cooperstown with Yankee owner Dan Topping in Topping's amphibious plane. DiMaggio was the last of the inductees to speak at the ceremony on the lawn outside the Hall.

"This is a great day," he said. "It's certainly a long step from that time twenty years ago when I was riding to St. Petersburg with Frank Crosetti and Tony Lazzeri. They asked me to take the wheel and I had to say, 'I don't drive.' At that point, I thought I'd never be a big leaguer.

"In the minors we used to talk about what makes a big leaguer. I learned the answer when I reported to the Yankees. I was sitting on the bench in the dressing room when someone clapped me on the back and said, 'Welcome to the Yankees.'

"I turned around, and it was Lou Gehrig. I always watched every move Lou Gehrig made—on and off the ball field—and tried to pattern

Joe DiMaggio waves to a sold-out Yankee Stadium on Old-Timers' Day on July 28, 1962. (Photograph by Bob Olen)

myself after him. I'm proud, indeed, to be put alongside Lou, Bill Dickey, my other old teammate, and those great players of my time and before.

"I also want to pay special tribute to Joe McCarthy, for all the help he gave me at the beginning of my career. Now the last chapter has been written, and I can close the book."

DiMaggio's plaque reads simply, *Joseph Paul DiMaggio / New York A.L. 1936 to 1951 / Hit safely in 56 consecutive games for major league record, 1941. Hit two home-runs in one inning, 1936. Hit 3 home-runs in one game (3 times). Holds numerous batting records. Played in 10 World Series (51 games) and 11 All-Star games. Most Valuable Player A.L. 1939, 1941, 1947.*

DiMaggio's postelection retirement continued in much the same fashion, although he continued to guard his privacy and became ever more protective of his public image. He became a vice president of a pasta company in charge of public relations on the West Coast, turned down a lukewarm overture from the Yankees to become a coach, trav-

Joe DiMaggio enters the offices of the Westwood Village Mortuary to make the funeral arrangements for his former wife Marilyn Monroe. (Photograph courtesy of the *Boston Herald*)

Joe DiMaggio is escorted by his son, Joe Jr., at the funeral service for his ex-wife Marilyn Monroe. (Photograph courtesy of the *Boston Herald*)

eled to Italy, served as chairman for the National Paraplegic Foundation—a veterans group—and eventually took another job with V. H. Monette Company, a supplier of commissaries on American military bases. He played a lot of golf and lived quietly. On those occasions when he saw Monroe, there was no publicity. He would not allow it.

In 1961, DiMaggio returned to spring training with the Yankees as special assistant to Ralph Houk, although his duties consisted of little more than working with a few hitters and talking to the press. DiMaggio obviously enjoyed himself and it looked as if he might return to baseball, but Joe never asked and the Yankees apparently never offered a permanent role.

On August 4, 1962, for reasons still not entirely clear, Monroe overdosed on barbiturates, an apparent suicide. DiMaggio was in the public eye again. In obvious pain, he took charge of her funeral arrangements, banned most of her Hollywood friends, and oversaw a quiet, dignified service. Immediately afterward, he had roses placed on her grave twice a week, a touching gesture that continued through 1982 when Joe stopped after the custom became too public.

In the years since her death, Monroe's life has taken on a mythic quality, like the lives of James Dean or Elvis Presley. Her relationship with DiMaggio is part of this. For many Americans under the age of forty who are not sports fans, DiMaggio is best known not as a ballplayer, but for his marriage to Monroe. As her legend grew, so has the dimension of their relationship. The public has chosen to ignore the more prosaic and tawdry elements in favor of a highly romantic interpretation. DiMaggio has been cast as an inherently sympathetic figure, a man who lived with loss and publicly mourned.

Seen in this light, DiMaggio's stature as a hero has increased. To quote Campbell on the hero again, "Every one of us shares the supreme ordeal . . . not in the bright moments of his tribe's great victories, but in the silence of his personal despair." The public perceived him as a more complete person, a man who not only accomplished great things on the field but acted honorably at a time of great stress; a man who apparently lived his life by the standard he demonstrated as a player. Whether that perception is wholly accurate does not seem to matter; it is what people want to believe and allows them to believe in Joe DiMaggio. DiMaggio's relationship with Monroe remains the defining element of his post-baseball life.

DiMaggio next came into public view in the fall of 1967. The hit film *The Graduate* featured a song written by Paul Simon and performed by Simon and Garfunkel titled "Mrs. Robinson." Just as Hemingway

invoked DiMaggio as a symbol in *The Old Man and the Sea*, Simon did so too, asking, "Where have you gone, Joe DiMaggio? A nation turns its lonely eyes to you."

DiMaggio didn't understand the song. He complained to friends he had not "gone" anywhere. That was not the point. While DiMaggio had not gone anywhere, Simon noted that what he once stood for appeared to be fading from American life.

In October of 1967, DiMaggio surprised everyone by agreeing to serve as an executive vice president for Charlie Finley and the Oakland A's. He might have preferred a similar position with the Yankees, but no one asked. When Finley asked, DiMaggio accepted.

While DiMaggio's title was vice president, he never had a desk in the Oakland front office. His primary duty was to act as batting coach under Oakland manager Bob Kennedy. DiMaggio served two years in Oakland and worked with some of the best young talent in baseball, including Sal Bando, Joe Rudi, Rick Monday, and Reggie Jackson. All were players of great promise who lacked only experience. His old fans, however, were shocked to see the dignified DiMaggio in the garish Oakland uniform, wearing white spikes. He looked out of place in any uniform but the Yankee pinstripes.

The Athletics' young hitters did improve under DiMaggio's tutelage, although it is impossible to gauge his influence. He was popular with the players. They needled him by playing "Mrs. Robinson" in the clubhouse, but DiMaggio was unperturbed and took their antics in

(l–r) Baseball Commissioner Bowie Kuhn, Mrs. Babe (Claire) Ruth, and Joe DiMaggio at the Major League Baseball Centennial Dinner in 1969. (Photograph courtesy of the Boston Herald)

stride. The A's moved up from a last-place finish in 1967 to finish sixth in 1968 at 82–80, and a year later, they finished second to Minnesota in the American League's new divisional setup as Reggie Jackson cracked 47 home runs and Sal Bando knocked in over 100 runs.

But Finley, as usual, changed managers before the 1969 season. He replaced Kennedy with Hank Bauer, DiMaggio's old teammate, then fired Bauer with two weeks left in the season and replaced him with John McNamara. With each change, Joe's role diminished, and he grew tired of the travel. He served as coach though spring training of 1969, then resigned. A few years later, those same A's became the first team since the Yankees to win three straight world championships.

Soon after DiMaggio left the A's, Baseball Commissioner Bowie Kuhn made overtures to DiMaggio about working for the Commissioner's office but didn't follow through. DiMaggio disliked being teased, and grew more cautious when approached by others seeking his involvement in anything.

As baseball celebrated its centennial in 1969, DiMaggio received increased acclaim. On July 21, he was selected as baseball's "Greatest Living Player," and a member of the "Greatest Living Team." A month before, on June 8, the Yankees honored both DiMaggio and the recently retired Mickey Mantle with their own plaques in the Yankee outfield, joining monuments to Miller Huggins, Jacob Ruppert, Ed Barrow, Ruth, and Gehrig.

In the early 1970s, DiMaggio was approached by a group that tried to buy the Yankees, but nothing happened and DiMaggio eventually

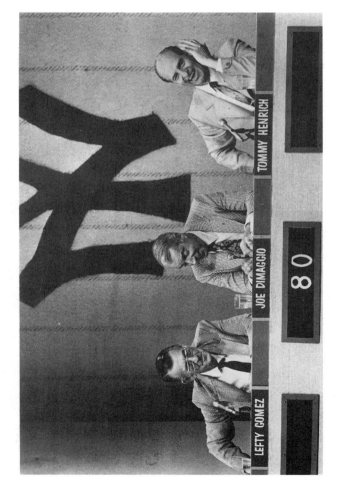

In 1972, DiMaggio appeared on the syndicated sports quiz show "Sports Challenge" with former teammates Lefty Gomez and Tommy Henrich. The stars are breaking up after viewing a tape showing the young DiMaggio legging a single into a double. (Photograph courtesy of the Boston Herald)

felt used. Still, his stint with the A's and the publicity he received during baseball's centennial served him well.

In 1972, Joe began serving as television spokesperson for a New York bank, Bowery Savings. The public trusted DiMaggio, and deposits at the bank soared. Soon after, he filled a similar role as national spokesperson for Mr. Coffee, and the coffee maker became one of the best-known products in America. His original three-year deal with Mr. Coffee netted one million dollars, more than his total salary as a professional ballplayer.

DiMaggio had come a long way as a public speaker. He no longer looked stiff, and spoke in a relaxed, offhand manner. Moreover, advertisers discovered DiMaggio was much admired by American men over age thirty-five, the demographic group with the most disposable income. The endorsements made DiMaggio rich, kept him in the public eye, yet made few demands on his time. He was amused when children referred to him as "Mr. Coffee." Other advertisers approached DiMaggio, but he turned most of them down, not wanting to damage his image.

As DiMaggio aged, he began to feel more at ease in public. He spoke easily at dinners, and seemed to enjoy the attention of fans. Usually, his public appearances were confined to banquets or old-timers' games, but he clearly enjoyed being remembered, and adapted

DiMaggio watches his putt fall for a birdie at the first hole of a Pro-Am Charity Tournament held in September 1979 at Pleasant Valley Country Club. (Photograph by Peter Southwick, courtesy of the Boston Herald*)*

nicely to his role as one of baseball's elder statesmen. He looked forward to talking with old teammates and opponents, many of whom now found him far more affable than he had been as a player.

He seemed happy, traveling the country as Joe DiMaggio, American Icon, keeping his hand in the game as a member of the board of directors for the Baltimore Orioles. In the mid-1980s, as baseball's memorabilia market took off, no player took better advantage than Joe DiMaggio.

As the boys who were Joe DiMaggio fans in the 1930s and 1940s reached middle age, they became ever more solicitous of their own memories, and desired tangible proof of the past. DiMaggio was their hero. They turned their attention, and their dollars, toward baseball memorabilia.

While the memorabilia market enabled many old ballplayers to make a healthy living selling autographs and other such items, the hysteria of the fad also cost them some privacy. In only a few years it became virtually impossible for DiMaggio or many other former players to make a public appearance without being hounded by autograph seekers waving bats, balls, photographs, and baseball cards. As a huge market developed for such memorabilia, players like DiMaggio signed on with card show promoters and card companies to manage their activities.

For many former players, the memorabilia market became a double-edged sword. While it provided income many times more what

On June 9, 1991, President George Bush presented the Presidential Medal of Freedom to Ted Williams and Joe DiMaggio. It had been fifty years since both men had captured headlines with their batting heroics. (Photograph by Rich Lipski, courtesy of the Washington Post*)*

Joe DiMaggio and Ted Williams enjoy each other's company at the 1991 Hall of Fame induction ceremony at Cooperstown. The induction marked the fiftieth anniversary of the duo's much-celebrated summer of '41. (Photograph by Bill Brett, courtesy of the Boston Globe)

they earned as players, the men were reduced to a kind of commodity, an autograph-making machine whose value is based almost entirely on their flourishing script, not on appreciation of their actual accomplishments.

Today, a ball signed by Joe DiMaggio is worth about $400—more than that of any living player. His signature, and his right to sign certain kinds of memorabilia, is under exclusive contract with the companies that market those items.

Yet somehow DiMaggio has retained his unique sense of privacy and dignity. In a telling moment, the baseball writer Peter Gammons and Oakland A's pitcher Bob Welch spotted DiMaggio calmly waiting in line to receive an occupancy permit to return to his home in the Marina District in San Francisco a few days following the 1989 earthquake. No one bothered DiMaggio, and he asked for no special favors. When Gammons asked him about it a few years later, Joe responded, "That's why I love it at home, in San Francisco. I am allowed to live my life."

DiMaggio received a burst of publicity in 1991, when baseball celebrated the fiftieth anniversary of both his 56-game hitting streak and Ted Williams's .401 batting average. DiMaggio and Williams appeared together at many celebrations, and each received a Medal of Freedom

Joe and Vince DiMaggio hold court at Old-Timers' Day at Fenway Park in May 1986. (Photograph by Bill Greene, courtesy of the Boston Globe)

from U.S. President George Bush. DiMaggio is now regarded as a national treasure. And he is.

In recent years, Joe DiMaggio has been slowed somewhat by health problems, but he remains more active than most men his age. He recently moved from his beloved San Francisco to Florida, but still makes regular trips to the city of his birth. He helps support a hospital, the Joe DiMaggio Children's Hospital in Florida, but characteristically prefers to keep the depth of his involvement private. Inquiries to him by writers or anyone else must be made in writing and go through his attorneys. On the rare occasions when DiMaggio agrees to an interview, the interviewer is told in advance that Joe will not respond to questions about either Marilyn Monroe or Joe Jr. Several times each season, DiMaggio slips into a private box at Joe Robbie Stadium in Miami or the Oakland Coliseum to take in a baseball game.

Recently, DiMaggio provided a brief glimpse into his private life. Joe is the great-grandfather of two girls. On Halloween in 1994, Joe DiMaggio, the dignified, proud ballplayer, hero to millions, appeared

Carl Yastrzemski shares a laugh with Joe DiMaggio at the 1986 Red Sox Old-Timers' Day game at Fenway Park. (Photograph by Barry Chin, courtesy of the Boston Herald)

as grand marshal of the annual "Great Pumpkin Parade" in Half Moon Bay, California. When a reporter asked him why Joe DiMaggio, the great ballplayer, deigned to appear in so undignified a setting, DiMaggio quietly replied that it was because the girls asked him. They wanted to ride in the parade.

As DiMaggio enters his eighth decade, he remains an enduring symbol of another age and another time. A time when baseball was not fettered with the distractions of strikes and lockouts, when the most important battles took place on the field, in a pennant race, and a player's reputation was earned not by what he said or how he behaved, but by the way he played the game.

Joe DiMaggio played baseball the way the game was meant to be played. When talking to old ballplayers, or reading what they told others about DiMaggio, one phrase is used repeatedly: "the best player I ever saw." In 1933, in the first few weeks of DiMaggio's professional career, Billy Raimondi said precisely that. So did San Francisco sportswriter Abe Kemp in 1935. Ted Williams says it today, over forty years since DiMaggio last played the game.

Most players would agree with Jerry Coleman, who in a 1989 interview with Dom Forker in his book *The Men of Autumn* said "Joe was the greatest all-around player I ever saw. The way he handled himself, the team, the game, was impeccable. He understood his role thoroughly. He had incredible mystique. No one else ever did it better.

Every player is insecure. The pressure to succeed is great. But he wasn't a normal player. He had to be perfect every day. Joe wasn't happy when he wasn't perfect. He had to be DiMaggio every day."

Casey Stengel, the one man in baseball DiMaggio feuded with, may have said better than anyone what Joe DiMaggio meant to those around him. When Stengel was serving as manager of the New York Mets, DiMaggio appeared at an old-timers' game at Shea Stadium. After the game, an interviewer asked him about DiMaggio.

In his own inimitable, stream-of-consciousness fashion, Stengel spoke for many when he said, "We had Mr. DiMaggio who walked out there today and I want to tell you that DiMaggio, with the cheers he received, every one of them should have been given by myself and I should have yelled all winter during my off-season because of the success the club had with him at the bat and the wonderful catches he made in the outfield."

Joe DiMaggio himself has rarely offered an assessment of his own life. Compared with modern-day sports heroes, his reticence about his own accomplishments is unique. In a rare moment of insight, he told one interviewer, "I'm just a ballplayer with only one ambition, to give all I've got to help my club win. I've never played any other way." If that ambition exacted a personal price, in DiMaggio's own terms, the end justified the means. It made him a hero, and forever bound him to that definition. He lived the way he did in order to accomplish what he set out to do: win ball games.

He did that. Better than anyone else ever has.

The Yankee Clipper returns to Fenway Park on May 17, 1986. Fenway Park was the scene of many of his greatest games. It was here be received his loudest ovations outside of Yankee Stadium. (Photograph by Peter Travers, courtesy of the Boston Red Sox)

The Clipper: Safe Haven at Last

Thomas Boswell

Washington, July 1983—In a parking lot beside RFK Stadium this week, two dozen middle-aged men, most of them dressed like Connecticut Avenue lawyers, chased one senior citizen as he left the Cracker Jack Old-timers' Classic. Pens and autograph pads in hand, the adults pursued the silver-haired sixty-eight-year-old man, just as they probably lapped at his heels during his days of legend from 1936 until 1951 when he was the Yankee Clipper and, some claim, the greatest player in baseball history.

"Joe, Joe," cried one fellow, "we played a round of golf together five years ago in Jersey." The hero stopped to sign. Finally, he was at ease with age

and this endless foolishness called fame. At last, it was almost a pleasure to be Joe DiMaggio.

As DiMaggio opened his hotel door, he tucked in his shirt and buckled his belt. Once he might have been too formal or too leery to open his door when he was still in disarray. Now he takes things as they come and wonders why it took him so long to learn the trick. Now he'll let his hair down, to a degree, and chat for ninety minutes about almost anything.

DiMaggio knows many baseball fans were either children or unborn when he retired. They never saw him play. Since he's spent much of his life avoiding interviews, he's also left a spotty

record of his thoughts about the game he loved. Many current fans have never heard him, either.

"It's only in the last few years that I outgrew that [reticence]," said DiMaggio. "It has been a tremendous change for me. I finally conquered that part . . . I find myself a lot more comfortable with people now. It gradually disappeared with the years.

"It sounds strange, but going through those TV commercials [over the last ten years] for Mr. Coffee and the Bowery bank in New York has helped a lot. I gradually broke down the barriers."

Perhaps sadly, it took DiMaggio sixty years to learn that even the simplest communication—outside, perhaps, the close-knit settings of family or long friendship—is a form of acting, a hard and conscious and practiced task of projecting some bearable public version of yourself.

"For a long time [until he was almost sixty], I would cringe, avoid crowds. It was not for reasons of being aloof . . . I just didn't feel natural. People said, 'You're so relaxed on the ball field.' I'd say, 'But I knew what I was doing . . .'

"Before a camera, or a group of people, I didn't have a performance to give. [So] I was very, very shy. I wanted to be away from people. I thought I didn't have that much to offer, that much to say, so I used to go into my shell."

What did he find that he had to offer?

"My gentleness," he said softly. " . . . I'm one of the easiest-[going] guys, and I'm patient with people. Usually I don't mind standing and signing . . . I think I should be flattered . . . the fans have been very good to me. Why not show up? I feel I owe something, as long as they want me.

"[Sometimes] I still balk. I hate banquets with a passion. There are certain people I don't ever feel at ease with . . . I don't do talk shows, though I don't mind sport shows . . . When a lot of people see you and start yelling, 'Hey, Joe,' that's embarrassing. But I'm oblivious to a lot of that now. I try to live a normal life."

Actually, DiMaggio is so infatuated with discovering that the public world need not be a recluse's nightmare that his schedule is now one long, leisurely but persistent round of appearances, cameo bows at old-timers' games and golf outings.

"I still have to work for a living," he exaggerated. "At least, I'm not really retired in the sense of doing whatever I feel like. Sometimes I wonder if I don't spend my life on airplanes. I took fourteen trips to New York last year."

If DiMaggio flies and appears and signs and generally circulates within the baseball world, then that's because he chooses to. Unmarried since he was divorced from his second wife, Marilyn Monroe, in 1955, DiMaggio leads an itinerant bachelor life, keeping a home in San Francisco, but materializing almost anywhere. The phone rings. "I'm heading to Vancouver tomorrow," DiMaggio tells an old friend. "They've built a new stadium. I'll take a tour around, see what it has to offer." Because of his large family—he's one of nine children and has a son, forty-two, by his first marriage, and two granddaughters—DiMaggio has relatives or friends almost anywhere you could stick a pin in the map.

DiMaggio is in no danger of being mistaken for the Electric Horseman. Perhaps it's a question of style, more than anything else. Where another man might seem to be flirting with the limelight so it won't forget him, DiMaggio is so confident of his place that his public appearances have the air of a royal favor. Perhaps a sense of self is as much a gift as a thing earned.

For instance, DiMaggio never reaches, and deigns to accept only a fraction of what is handed to him. When Grecian Formula offered him a quarter of a million dollars to pitch their stuff, DiMaggio declined. "It was a helluva lot of money and I had that beautiful pepper hair then," he said without a trace of

On Opening Day in 1976, Joe DiMaggio greets former world heavyweight boxing champion Joe Louis, who is just about to throw out the first pitch. Both were arguably the greatest sports heroes of their generation. (Photograph by Bob Olen)

anything in his voice. "It isn't that I don't like money, it's just...."

He shrugs. He can't explain. DiMaggio doesn't tint his hair and won't imply that he does. Just this week, Polident put out a feeler to see if he'd hawk their denture powder. "Tell 'em I've still got my own teeth," said DiMaggio to the middleman with a laugh. "Give that one to Martha Raye."

If the bustle of the world rolls off DiMaggio's back more easily than it did in his tormented decades as one of the country's dominant celebrities, it is, in part, a mere question of volume. The morning he separated from Monroe, photographers were perched in trees, watching the windows of their Beverly Hills house. He couldn't even leave his wife without answering reporters' questions on the way to the car.

Now his fame is almost oldshoe, a comfortable national institution like the way his name recurs as an American touchstone, whether in *The Old Man and the Sea*, "Mrs. Robinson," or the latest remake of *Farewell, My Lovely*.

A year ago, as DiMaggio was leaving Cooperstown after a visit to the Hall of Fame, he and a friend were deep in conversation and got lost. "That's the trouble with good b.s.," said DiMaggio. "You miss your turn."

Finally they hailed a fellow on a tractor to ask directions. The farmer, apparently unaware of DiMaggio's identity, leaned on the passenger door and, speaking across DiMaggio to the driver, began saying, "You go down about three miles...." Then, casually, in mid-sentence, he patted DiMaggio familiarly on the arm and said, "I see you, Joe," then finished his instructions. DiMaggio loves to tell this story. If only America had 200 million more such people of simple dignity, his life would be perfect. Even so, it's getting easier.

DiMaggio's present is easy to take and the past is now at a safe enough distance that redigesting it is all pleasure. He's reached the reminiscing age. Today's athletes say of the honors and records, "It doesn't mean much to me now. But I'll probably enjoy it when I'm old."

* * *

DiMaggio is enjoying it.

"You look in those old pictures at the people who attended ball games years ago. They came in straw hat, jacket and tie. Talk about a change. I know those were just the ways of the days. But now, when I see those pictures, I marvel at that. We weren't even aware of it."

DiMaggio knows it's baseball doctrine that pining for the old days gets you the raspberry. But he can't help it. He thinks his game was better.

"We only had sixteen teams then. It has to be watered down now. When they keep re-signing fellows like [Gaylord] Perry and [Jim] Kaat, what does that tell you?

"When I played ball, I played because I loved it," DiMaggio says later. "It gripes me when some of these [current] players find fault with the front office because the owner wants them to give 100 percent effort and gets mad when they don't . . .

"I played for the manager and my teammates, not for the owners. Of course, we didn't get no static from upstairs then," he says, in almost the only grammatical remnant of a childhood spent near Fisherman's Wharf in San Francisco.

For DiMaggio the game, at least as he remembers it, was an all-consuming craft—an art into which any man of honor would pour himself completely, defining himself by the pure hard line of his performance. "I wasn't one of those batting cage men. I went to the outfield every day and worked. I made it a ritual of charging ground balls so I could adjust my way of straightening up to throw . . . Dom had ability, but he didn't have room to roam," he says of his brother Dom of the Boston Red Sox. "I did . . . I expressed myself . . .

"People say I was graceful. I was not aware of it. I did everything my normal way . . . I practiced hard. I was a complete player because I worked at it. I remember how good a fungo hitter Earle Combs was. He could put the ball just inches beyond your glove."

DiMaggio wonders if this generation has spent as many hours on baseball's vital details. He remembers working with a rookie named Reggie Jackson. "Reggie didn't mind working," says DiMaggio, "but his eyes must have bothered him even then. We'd come out two hours early. He'd pound that glove and the [fly] ball would land five feet away."

Finally Jackson could catch what he could reach, but his throws became a small symbol of the age to DiMaggio. "Getting rid of the ball quickly is how you throw somebody out. Reggie takes all that windup and the fans go 'Ooooh, aaah' because he had a strong arm. But he never threw anybody out. I guess it was more important to him to show off his arm." More to his taste is Steve Garvey, a player who has his full respect.

"He's like Malicious [the race-horse]. He just keeps plodding along."

When it's time for DiMaggio to judge himself, he has a shocking preference. The fifty-six-game hitting streak is not his choice of monument. "Fifty-six is a helluva good record. Everybody's made a big thing of it. But the thing that's most important to me is that we won ten pennants and nine world titles in my thirteen years."

Only one unattained record still pricks DiMaggio to, if not pique, then an annoyed perplexity. New York brought him fame, wealth and an adoring media that gave him such an overlay of the mythical that it will probably remain forever impossible to judge where DiMaggio really belongs among the game's all-time top-ten players. But New York also brought him his cross—Yankee Stadium, a park whose Death Valley seemed constructed specially to thwart DiMaggio. Call it the House (Babe) Ruth Built and DiMaggio wanted to tear down.

"I don't like to say this about myself, but I would have hit 76 home runs [instead of 46] in 1937 if I'd played in a normal park," he says. "Mel Allen counted all the balls I hit to the warning track. I'll admit it got discouraging. I'd hit the ball 430 where it used to be 457 feet and the guy wouldn't even have to make a sensational catch . . ."

Within the last year, statistician Pete Palmer tabulated every home and away game of DiMaggio's career. Palmer found that in 880 games in Yankee Stadium, DiMaggio had 148 homers, 720 RBI and a .315 average. In 856 games on the road, he had 213 homers, 817 RBI and a .333 average. So it's likely that Death Valley cost DiMaggio perhaps 75 homers, 150 RBI and 20 points in average. In '37 DiMaggio had 27 homers on the road and 19 at home; Yankee Stadium probably cost him 10 homers and an outside chance at breaking Ruth's record.

If DiMaggio's words seem those of a prideful man, it is the last impression he would want

to give, and a largely false one, too. DiMaggio has an enormous sense of himself and his deeds, but he seldom seems full of himself. He'll tell tales on himself.

"[Manager Joe] McCarthy wouldn't let me bunt. But once I tried anyway. I fouled the ball off so [wildly] that it tipped my nose. I almost decapitated myself. I said, 'That's it for bunting.'"

Before his last season, DiMaggio talked himself into coming back. "That was my first mistake," he says, leaving the exotic impression that it was his first basic mistake in baseball judgment. "I hit .263. I remember that average better than the

good ones."

The next spring, in '52, he hung 'em up, though the Yankees told him he could play in any seventy-five games of his choosing, at no cut in salary. "It didn't take long for me to get over retiring," he says. "Within the year, I'd say, I went to one game and watched the St. Louis Browns play in '52. I stood way out in left field on a hill. Nobody saw me . . . My injuries were there. They were just too much . . .

"I knew my body. I understood myself."

Statistical Appendix

Compiled and edited by Glenn Stout

Joe DiMaggio's baseball career is much more than a collection of statistical information. His personal statistics, while impressive, pale in comparison to a number of other players'. But DiMaggio is unique. As the text points out, his numbers do not begin to tell the full story of his career. In many instances, what DiMaggio did is less significant than when he did it, an element that cannot be reflected in raw statistics.

The purpose of this appendix is to provide the essential statistical data of DiMaggio's career in the context of the performance of his team. The attention lavished on DiMaggio's 56-game hitting streak has obscured some of his other accomplishments. A complete rendering of the 56-game streak is included here, and it is supplemented by a game-by-game analysis of DiMaggio's earlier 61-game Pacific Coast League streak, his career home-run record, a record of his World Series performance, and other statistical information that together creates the most complete statistical assessment of DiMaggio's career ever to appear in print.

Data concerning DiMaggio's cumulative career, World Series, and All-Star Game records were gleaned from standard sources. The compilation of data for DiMaggio's hitting streaks was created from the author's own research in newspapers and other sources. The home-run log was discovered in an incomplete form in a file at the Baseball Hall of Fame. I have added additional information and verified its accuracy.

THE YANKEE SEASON RECORD: THE DIMAGGIO YEARS

Year	W	L	PL	2nd	GA/GB	Manager
1936	102	51	1	Detroit	19.5	McCarthy
1937	102	52	1	Detroit	13	McCarthy
1938	99	53	1	Boston	9.5	McCarthy
1939	106	45	1	Boston	17	McCarthy
1940	88	66	3	Det (1) Cle (2)	2	McCarthy
1941	101	53	1	Boston	17	McCarthy
1942	103	51	1	Boston	9	McCarthy
1946	87	67	3	Bos (1) Det (2)	17	McCarthy 35, Dickey 105, Neun 14
1947	97	57	1	Detroit	12	Harris
1948	94	60	3	Cle (1) Bos (2)	2.5	Harris
1949	97	67	1	Boston	1	Stengel
1950	98	56	1	Detroit	3	Stengel
1951	98	56	1	Cleveland	5	Stengel
Total:	1272	734	.634	Average Season Record:	98–56	.636*

*Difference in percentage is due to tie games.

JOE DIMAGGIO'S REGULAR-SEASON MINOR AND MAJOR LEAGUE BATTING RECORD

Note: **Boldface** indicates tied or led league.

WITH SAN FRANCISCO SEALS, PACIFIC COAST LEAGUE

YR	G	AB	R	H	2B	3B	HR	RBI	BB	K	AV	OB	SLG
1932	3	9	2	2	1	1	0	2	NA	NA	.222	NA	NA
1933	187	762	129	295	45	13	28	**169**			.340		
1934	101	375	58	128	18	6	12	69			.341		
1935	172	679	173	270	58	18	34	**154**			.398		
TOT.	463	1825	362	659	122	38	74	394			.361		

PCL MVP 1935
Hit safely in 61 consecutive games, 1933.

1935 PACIFIC COAST LEAGUE CHAMPIONSHIP SERIES
SAN FRANCISCO VERSUS LOS ANGELES

G	AB	R	H	2B	3B	HR	RBI	Score
1	4	2	2	0	0	0	0	SF 5 LA 0
2	3	2	2	0	0	1	3	SF 7 LA 5
3	4	2	2	1	0	0	2	SF 3 LA 4
4	4	1	1	0	0	0	0	SF 7 LA 10
5	4	1	3	0	0	0	2	SF 6 LA 3
6	4	0	0	0	0	0	0	SF 8 LA 3
TOT.	23	8	10	1	0	2	7	AVG. .434

For a more detailed and narrative description of DiMaggio's performance in the championship series, see the text.

WITH NEW YORK YANKEES, AMERICAN LEAGUE

YR	G	AB	R	H	2B	3B	HR	RBI	BB	K	AV	OB	SLG
1936	138	637	132	206	44	**15**	29	125	24	39	.323	.352	.576
1937	151	621	**151**	215	35	15	**46**	167	64	37	.346	.412	**.673**
1938	145	599	129	194	32	13	32	140	59	21	.324	.386	.581
1939	120	462	108	176	32	6	30	126	52	20	**.381**	.448	.671
1940	132	508	93	179	28	9	31	133	61	30	**.352**	.425	.626
1941	139	541	122	193	43	11	30	**125**	76	13	.357	.440	.643
1942	154	610	123	186	29	13	21	114	68	36	.305	.376	.498
1946	132	503	81	146	20	8	25	95	59	24	.290	.367	.511
1947	141	534	97	168	31	10	20	97	64	32	.315	.391	.522
1948	153	594	110	190	26	11	**39**	**155**	67	30	.320	.396	.598
1949	76	272	58	94	14	6	14	67	55	18	.346	.459	.596
1950	139	525	114	158	33	10	32	122	80	33	.301	.394	.585
1951	116	415	72	109	22	4	12	71	61	36	.263	.365	.422
TOT.	1736	6821	1390	2214	389	131	361	1537	790	369	.325	.398	.579

American League Most Valuable Player, 1939, 1941, 1947

Set major league record by hitting safely in 56 consecutive games, May 15–July 16, 1941.

Set record for most hits, rookie season (206) in 1936 (since broken).

Equaled modern major league record for most triples, game (3), August 27, 1938.

Hit two home runs, fifth inning, June 24, 1936.

Hit three home runs in a game, June 13, 1937 (2), May 23, 1948, and September 10, 1950.

Hit for cycle, July 9, 1937, and May 20, 1948.

Led American League in most times hit by pitcher (8), 1948.

Led American League in total bases, 1937, 1941, 1947.

Named to Hall of Fame 1955.

REGULAR SEASON: FIELDING AND STOLEN BASES

Note: **Boldface** indicates led the league.

MINOR LEAGUE

YR	PO	A	E	FA	POS	SB	CS
1932	4	7	1	.917	SS	0	NA
1933	407	**32**	17	.963	OF	10	NA
1934	236	11	8	.969	OF	8	NA
1935	430	**32**	21	.957	OF	24	NA
TOT.	1077	82	47	.961		42	

MAJOR LEAGUE

YR	PO	A	E	FA	POS	SB	CS
1936	339	**22**	8	.978	OF	4	0
1937	**413**	21	**17**	.962	OF	3	0
1938	366	20	15	.963	OF	6	1
1939	328	13	5	.986	OF	3	0
1940	359	5	8	.978	OF	1	2
1941	385	16	9	.978	OF	4	2
1942	409	10	8	.981	OF	4	2
1946	314	15	6	.982	OF	1	0
1947	316	2	1	**.997**	OF	3	0
1948	441	8	13	.972	OF	1	1
1949	195	1	3	.985	OF	0	1
1950	376	9	9	.977	OF/1	0	0
1951	288	11	3	.990	OF	0	0
TOT.	4529	153	105	.978		30	9

JOE DIMAGGIO IN THE ALL-STAR GAME

YR	AB	R	H	2B	3B	HR	RBI	SB	Score
1936	5	0	0	0	0	0	0	0	NL 4, AL 3
1937	4	1	1	0	0	0	0	0	AL 8, NL 3
1938	4	1	1	0	0	0	0	0	NL 4, AL 1
1939	4	1	0	0	0	0	1	1	AL 3, NL 1
1940	4	0	1	0	0	0	1	0	NL 4, AL 0
1941	4	3	1	0	0	0	1	0	AL 7, NL 5
1942	4	0	2	1	0	0	1	0	AL 3, NL 1
1947	3	0	1	0	0	0	1	0	AL 2, NL 1
1948	1	0	0	0	0	0	0	0	AL 5, NL 2
1949	1	0	2	0	0	0	3	0	AL 11, NL 7
1950	3	0	0	0	0	0	0	0	NL 4, AL 3
TOTAL	40	7	9	2	0	1	6	1	.225 BA

Fielding Totals: 150 putouts, 0 assists, 1 error, .993 FA.

JOE DIMAGGIO IN THE WORLD SERIES

YR	G	AB	R	H	2B	3B	HR	RBI	Result
1936	6	26	3	9	3	0	0	3	Yanks 4–2 over Giants
1937	5	22	2	6	0	0	1	4	Yanks 4–1 over Giants
1938	4	15	4	4	0	0	1	2	Yanks sweep Cubs
1939	4	16	3	5	0	0	1	3	Yanks sweep Reds
1941	5	19	1	5	0	0	0	3	Yanks 4–1 over Dodgers
1942	5	21	3	7	0	0	0	3	Cards 4–1 over Yanks
1947	7	26	4	6	0	0	2	5	Yanks 4–3 over Dodgers
1949	5	18	2	2	0	0	1	2	Yanks 4–1 over Dodgers
1950	4	13	2	4	1	0	0	2	Yanks sweep Phillies
1951	6	23	3	6	2	0	1	5	Yanks 4–2 over Giants
TOT:	51	199	27	54	6	0	8	30	.271 BA Yankee record: 36–14.

JOE DIMAGGIO'S 61-GAME HITTING STREAK MAY 28–JULY 25, 1933

SAN FRANCISCO SEALS, PCL RECORD

Before the streak began, DiMaggio appeared in 52 games, going 50 for 201, a batting average of .249, with 6 home runs and 24 runs scored. The Seals' record was 16–36 (.308). The Seals' record during the streak was 26–34–1 (.433).

At the beginning of the streak, DiMaggio was playing center field and batting fifth in the order. Following game 10 of the streak, DiMaggio was moved to right field. Following game 21 of the streak, DiMaggio hit third in the order. Following game 33 of the streak, DiMaggio hit fourth in the order. In the game that ended the streak, DiMaggio led off.

Game	Date	Opponent	A/H	Score	H/AB	2B	3B	HR	RBI	R
1	5/28	Portland	A	3–1	1–4	0	0	0	0	0
2	5/30	Seattle	A	10–8	3–6	1	0	0	1	0
3	5/30		A	6–7	3–4	0	1	0	3	1
4	5/31			12–13	2–4	0	1	0	1	1
5	6/1			8–7	1–5	0	0	0	0	0
6	6/2			7–5	2–5	0	1	0	1	1
7	6/3			4–13	2–4	0	0	1	1	2
8	6/4			12–5	2–4	2	0	0	2	1
9	6/4			1–10	1–3	0	0	0	1	0
10	6/6	Oakland	A	3–1	1–4	1	0	0	2	1
11	6/7			2–3	1–3	0	0	0	0	1
12	6/8			3–0	1–4	0	0	0	0	0
13	6/9			3–4	1–4	0	1	0	2	1
14	6/10			11–16	2–5	0	0	1	2	2
15	6/11			9–9	3–5	1	0	1	2	2
16	6/11			10–0	1–4	0	0	0	2	2

#	Date	Opponent	H/A	Score	Batting					
17	6/13	Seattle	H	6–1	2–4	0	0	0	1	1
18	6/14			5–7	1–3	0	0	0	0	0
19	6/15			5–8	2–4	1	1	1	3	2
20	6/16			5–12	2–5	0	0	0	1	2
21	6/17			9–6	3–4	1	0	0	2	2
22	6/18			6–1	1–3	1	1	0	1	1
23	6/18			2–5	2–2	0	0	0	0	0
24	6/20	San Francisco Missions	H	1–0	1–2	0	1	1	1	0
25	6/21			6–5	2–3	0	0	0	1	0
26	6/22			4–3	2–4	0	0	0	0	0
27	6/23			5–4	1–4	0	0	1	0	1
28	6/24			2–6	2–4	0	0	0	1	0
29	6/25			9–7	2–4	0	0	0	1	3
30	6/25			5–6	1–4	0	0	0	0	1
31	6/27	Los Angeles	A	6–7	2–3	0	1	3	3	1
32	6/28			5–6	3–5	0	0	1	1	1
33	6/29			7–11	1–5	0	0	0	0	0
34	6/30			4–6	1–4	0	0	0	0	0
35	7/1			5–10	1–4	1	0	0	0	1
36	7/2			1–5	1–4	0	0	1	1	0
37	7/2			6–3	2–4	0	0	2	2	0
38	7/4	Hollywood	H	4–8	1–5	0	0	0	0	0
39	7/4			8–2	2–5	0	0	2	2	1
40	7/5			3–4	1–4	1	0	0	0	0
41	7/6			13–5	2–5	1	0	1	1	1
42	7/7			5–7	1–5	0	0	1	1	1
43	7/8			4–12	2–4	0	0	0	0	2
44	7/8			1–2	1–3	0	0	1	1	0
45	7/9			9–12	3–6	1	1	1	1	1
46	7/9			5–4	1–3	0	0	0	2	0
47	7/11	Los Angeles	H	2–8	2–4	0	0	2	1	1
48	7/12			4–1	1–4	1	0	1	1	1
49	7/13			2–8	3–4	0	0	1	1	1
50	7/14			6–7	2–5	0	0	3	3	0
51	7/15			5–8	4–5	3	0	2	2	1
52	7/16			8–2	1–4	0	0	1	1	0
53	7/16			5–3	1–3	1	0	1	1	1
54	7/18	Sacramento	A	13–5	3–3	1	1	0	0	0
55	7/19			8–12	3–5	0	0	0	0	0
56	7/20			3–2	1–5	0	0	0	0	0
57	7/21			6–7	1–5	0	0	0	0	1
58	7/22			6–7	1–4	0	0	0	0	0
59	7/23			7–4	1–5	0	0	0	0	1
60	7/23			2–7	1–4	0	0	0	0	0
61	7/25	Oakland	H	14–5	1–5	0	0	2	2	1
TOTALS:				26–34–1	102–252 (.405)	18	4	11	54	48

JOE DIMAGGIO'S 56-GAME HITTING STREAK
MAY 15–JULY 16, 1941
MAJOR LEAGUE RECORD

Note: Night games are designated with an asterisk. If DiMaggio collected hits off more than one pitcher in a game, all pitchers are listed and the number of hits made by DiMaggio off each appears in parentheses.

Game	Date	Opp.	A/H	Score	Pitcher(s)	H/AB	2B	3B	HR	RBI	R
1	5/15	Chi	Home	1–13	E. Smith	1–4	0	0	0	0	0
2	5/16			6–5	Lee	2–4	0	0	1	1	2
3	5/17			2–3	Rigney	1–3	1	0	0	1	1
4	5/18	St.L		12–2	B. Harris (2)	3–3	1	0	0	1	3
5	5/19			1–5	Niggeling (1), Galehouse	1–3	0	0	0	0	0
6	5/20			10–9	Auker	1–5	0	0	0	0	0
7	5/21	Det		5–4	Rowe (1), Benton (1)	2–5	0	0	0	1	1
8	5/22			6–5	McKain	1–4	0	0	0	0	0
9	5/23	Bos		9–9	Newsom	1–5	0	0	0	0	0
10	5/24			7–6	E. Johnson	1–4	0	0	0	0	0
11	5/25			3–10	Grove	1–4	0	0	1	2	2
12	5/27	Wash	Away	10–8	Chase (1), Anderson (2), Carrasquel (1)	4–5	0	0	0	3	3
13*	5/28			11–7	Hudson	1–4	0	0	0	0	2
14	5/29			4–5	Sundra	1–3	0	0	0	0	0
15	5/30	Bos		7–6	E. Johnson	1–2	0	0	0	1	1
16	5/30			0–13	M. Harris	1–3	0	0	0	0	0
17	6/1	Cle		2–0	Milnar	1–4	0	1	0	1	1
18	6/1			5–3	Harder	1–4	0	0	0	0	0
19	6/2			5–7	Feller	2–4	0	0	1	2	2
20	6/3	Det		2–4	Trout	1–4	0	0	0	0	0
21	6/5			7–2	Newhouser	1–5	1	0	0	0	0
22	6/7	St.L		4–5	Muncrief (1)	3–5	0	1	0	1	2
23	6/8			9–3	Auker	2–4	0	0	2	4	3
24	6/8			8–3	Caster (1), Kramer (1)	2–4	0	1	0	0	1
25	6/10	Chi	Home	8–3	Rigney	1–5	0	0	0	0	0
26*	6/12			3–2	Lee	2–4	0	0	1	1	1
27	6/14	Cle		4–1	Feller	1–2	0	0	0	0	0
28	6/15			3–2	Bagby	1–3	0	0	0	0	0
29	6/16			6–4	Milnar	1–5	0	0	0	1	0
30	6/17	Chi		7–8	Rigney	1–4	0	0	0	0	0
31	6/18			2–3	Lee	1–4	0	0	1	2	2
32	6/19			7–2	E. Smith (1), Ross (2)	3–3	1	0	0	1	2
33	6/20	Det		14–4	Newsom (2), McKain (2)	4–5	0	0	1	3	3
34	6/21			2–7	Trout	1–4	0	0	0	0	0
35	6/22			5–4	Newhouser (1), Newsom (1)	2–5	1	0	0	0	1
36	6/24	St.L		9–1	Muncrief	1–4	0	0	0	0	0
37	6/25			7–5	Galehouse	1–4	0	0	0	0	0
38	6/26			4–1	Auker	1–4	0	1	0	1	1
39	6/27	Phi	Away	6–7	Dean	2–3	1	0	0	1	0
40	6/28			7–4	Babich (1), L. Harris (1)	2–5	0	0	1	2	2
41	6/29	Wash		9–4	Leonard	1–4	0	0	0	0	0
42	6/29			7–5	Anderson	1–5	1	0	0	0	1
43	7/1	Bos	Home	7–2	M. Harris (1), Ryba (1)	2–4	0	0	0	1	0
44	7/1			9–2	Wilson	1–3	0	0	0	0	0
45	7/2			8–4	Newsom	1–5	0	0	1	3	1
46	7/5	Phi		10–5	Marchildon	1–4	0	0	1	2	2
47	7/6			8–4	Babich (1), Hadley (3)	4–5	0	1	0	2	2
48	7/6			3–1	Knott	2–4	0	0	0	0	0
49*	7/10	St.L	Away	1–0	Niggeling	1–2	0	0	0	2	1
50	7/11			6–2	B. Harris (3)	4–5	0	0	1	2	1

G	Date	Opp	Pitcher	Score	H–AB	2B	3B	HR	RBI	R
51	7/12		Kramer (1)	7–5	2–5	1	0	0	1	1
52	7/13	Chi	Auker (1) Muncrief (1) Lyons (2) Hallett (1)	8–1	3–4	0	0	0	0	2
53	7/13		Lee	1–0	1–4	0	0	0	0	0
54	7/14		Rigney	1–7	1–3	0	0	0	0	0
55	7/15		E. Smith	5–4	2–4	1	0	1	2	1
56	7/16	Cle	Milnar (2) Krakauskas (1)	10–3	3–4	1	0	0	0	3
TOTALS:				41–13–2	91–223 (.408)	16	4	15	55	56

STREAK BREAKDOWNS: DIMAGGIO UNDER PRESSURE

Day by day, game by game, the pressure on DiMaggio to continue the streak increased. Yet, as the streak grew longer, DiMaggio hit better and the Yankees played better baseball.

G	AB	R	H	2B	3B	HR	RBI	AVG.	NY Record
May 15 thru June 5 (Game 1–Game 21, before Gehrig's funeral)									
21	82	20	29	4	3	3	15	.353	11–8–2
June 7 thru July 16 (Game 22–Game 56)									
35	141	36	62	12	1	12	40	.439	30–5
May 15 thru June 17 (Game 1–Game 30. DiMaggio breaks Yankee record)									
30	118	30	43	7	3	8	26	.364	19–9–2
June 18 thru July 16 (Game 31–Game 56)									
26	105	26	48	9	1	7	29	.457	22–4
May 15 thru July 1 (Game 1–Game 44. DiMaggio ties Keeler's record)									
44	174	43	66	12	3	12	41	.374	30–12–2
July 2 thru July 16 (Game 45–Game 56)									
12	49	13	25	4	1	3	14	.510	11–1

OTHER STREAK FACTS

At the beginning of the streak, DiMaggio was hitting .306. At the end of the streak, he was hitting .375.

Thornton Lee and Edgar Smith of the Chicago White Sox gave up the most hits to DiMaggio during the streak: six.

DiMaggio hit .524 vs. the Philadelphia Athletics, his best performance against another team, and only .300 against the Boston Red Sox, his worst performance. Ted Williams hit .520 against the Yankees in those games, and .412 during DiMaggio's streak. Yet the Yankees defeated Boston five of six games during the streak, with one game tied.

DiMaggio hit for the best average against St. Louis Browns right-hander Bob Smith, collecting five hits in six at bats (.833).

DiMaggio struck out only five times in 223 official at bats during the streak.

On seven occasions, DiMaggio went four at bats without a hit. On two occasions, he went five at bats without a hit.

In thirty-four games, DiMaggio collected only one hit. He went 1 for 2 three times, 1 for 5 seven times, 1 for 3 eight times, and 1 for 4 sixteen times.

At the beginning of the streak, the Yankees were 14–14, 5½ games out of first place. After game 56, at the end of the streak, the Yankee record was 55–27, six games ahead of second-place Cleveland.

During the streak, only two other Yankees regulars hit above .300: Phil Rizzuto hit .368 and Red Rolfe hit .305.

For the season, DiMaggio got a hit in 114 of 139 games.

JOE DIMAGGIO'S MAJOR LEAGUE REGULAR-SEASON HOME RUNS (361 TOTAL)

1936

#	Date	Opponent	A/H	NY-Opp
1	May 10	Philadelphia	H	7-2
2	May 20	Detroit	A	3-4
3	May 24	Philadelphia	A	25-2
4	May 27	Boston	A	9-8
5	June 8	St. Louis	H	12-3
6	June 21	Detroit	H	7-8
7	June 24	Chicago	A	18-11
8	June 24	Chicago	A	18-11
		both hit in same inning		
9	June 27	St. Louis	A	10-6
10	June 28 (1)	St. Louis	A	3-6
11	July 4	Washington	A	4-3
12	July 10	Cleveland	A	18-0
13	July 22	St. Louis	H	5-6
14	July 23	St. Louis	H	15-3
15	July 23	Chicago	A	12-3
16	July 26 (1)	Chicago	A	7-2
17	August 5	Boston	A	7-6
18	August 9 (1)	Philadelphia	H	10-2
19	August 16 (1)	Philadelphia	A	5-7
20	August 17	Washington	H	7-4
21	August 19	Washington	A	5-3
22	August 23 (1)	Boston	A	4-5
23	August 25	St. Louis	H	13-1
24	August 28 (2)	Detroit	H	19-4
25	August 31	Chicago	A	5-1
26	Sept. (2)	Cleveland	A	11-3
27	Sept. 13 (1)	Cleveland	H	10-7
28	Sept. 13 (1)	St. Louis	A	
29	Sept. 13 (2)	St. Louis	A	13-1

TOTAL: 29   Yankee record: 21-5   .807

1937

#	Date	Opponent	A/H	Score
30	May 10	Chicago	A	7-0
31	May 10	Chicago	H	
32	May 23	Chicago	H	
33	May 25	Cleveland	H	4-3
34	May 29 (1)	Detroit	H	9-4
35	June 5	Philadelphia	A	6-5
36	June 6	Detroit	A	4-5
37	June 7	Detroit	A	3-4
38	June 8	Chicago	A	4-5
39	June 11	St. Louis	A	10-0
40	June 11	St. Louis	A	
41	June 13	St. Louis	A	8-8
42	June 13 (2)	St. Louis	A	
43	June 13 (2)	St. Louis	A	
44	June 20 (1)	Chicago	H	8-4
45	July 1	Chicago	H	
46	July 2	Philadelphia	A	12-7
47	July 3	Washington	A	3-8
48	July 4	Washington	A	5-4
49	July 5 (2)	Boston	H	7-0
50	July 9	Washington	H	8-4
51	July 9	Washington	H	16-2
52	July 14	Detroit	A	10-2
53	July 18	Cleveland	A	5-1
54	July 20 (1)	St. Louis	A	5-4
55	July 23	Chicago	A	6-9
56	July 25 (1)	Chicago	A	12-11
57	July 27	Detroit	H	6-5
58	July 31	St. Louis	H	6-5
59	July 31	St. Louis	H	6-9

#	Date	Opponent	A/H	Score
60	August 1	St. Louis	H	14–5
61	August 3 (1)	Chicago	H	7–2
62	August 11 (1)	Boston	A	8–5
63	August 12 (2)	Boston	A	5–3
64	August 18	Washington	H	7–6
65	August 22	Philadelphia	H	4–1
66	August 26	St. Louis	A	5–1
67	August 28	St. Louis	A	5–9
68	Sept. 2	Cleveland	A	2–4
69	Sept. 6 (1)	Philadelphia	A	6–3
70	Sept. 11	Washington	H	6–4
71	Sept. 12 (2)	Washington	H	2–1
72	Sept. 18 (2)	Chicago	H	4–0
73	Sept. 20	Detroit	A	5–0
74	Sept. 28 (1)	Washington	A	9–0
75	October 3	Boston	H	6–1

TOTAL: 46   Yankee record   31–7–1   .816

1938

#	Date	Opponent	A/H	Score
76	May 1	Washington	A	3–4
77	May 2	Washington	A	3–2
78	May 5	St. Louis	H	12–10
79	May 8	Chicago	H	7–3
80	May 18	St. Louis	A	11–7
81	May 18	St. Louis	A	
82	June 3	Detroit	H	5–1
83	June 6	St. Louis	H	6–5
84	June 24	Detroit	A	8–12
85	June 25	Detroit	A	9–3
86	June 30	Philadelphia	H	13–1
87	July 2	Washington	H	12–2
88	July 4 (2)	Washington	H	4–4
89	July 12 (2)	St. Louis	H	10–5
90	July 13	St. Louis	H	15–12
91	July 13	St. Louis	H	
92	July 26 (1)	St. Louis	A	10–5
93	July 28	St. Louis	A	3–4
94	July 30	Chicago	A	9–6
95	August 4	Detroit	A	8–4
96	August 11	Washington	A	9–6
97	August 12 (1)	Philadelphia	H	4–5
98	August 16	Washington	A	16–1
99	August 21	Philadelphia	A	8–4
100	August 25 (2)	Cleveland	H	15–3
101	August 26 (1)	Cleveland	H	15–9
102	Sept. 2	Boston	H	6–4
103	Sept. 4	Washington	H	7–4
104	Sept. 7	Boston	A	4–11
105	Sept. 10	Washington	A	6–5
106	Sept. 17	Detroit	A	3–7
107	October 2	Boston	A	6–1

TOTAL: 32   Yankee Record: 23–6–1   .793

1939

#	Date	Opponent	A/H	Score
108	April 21	Washington	A	6–3
109	June 8	Chicago	A	7–2
110	June 18	Detroit	H	5–6
111	June 28 (1)	Philadelphia	A	23–2
112	June 28 (1)	Philadelphia	A	
113	June 28 (2)	Boston	A	10–0
114	July 2 (2)	Washington	A	3–7
115	July 5	St. Louis	H	6–4
116	July 25	Detroit	H	5–1
117	August 3	Detroit	H	12–3
118	August 5	Cleveland	H	6–1
119	August 6 (1)	Cleveland	H	4–5

#	Date	Opponent	A/H	Score
121	August 9	Washington	A	13–8
122	August 13 (2)	Philadelphia	A	21–0
123	August 13 (2)	Philadelphia	A	4–0
124	August 16	Washington	A	9–8
125	August 17	Washington	H	14–5
126	August 22	Chicago	H	16–4
127	August 23 (2)	Chicago	A	18–2
128	August 28	Detroit	A	6–7
129	August 28	Detroit	A	7–12
130	August 29	Detroit	A	5–5
131	Sept. 2	Detroit	A	2–1
132	Sept. 3 (2)	Boston	H	5–2
133	Sept. 6	Boston	H	8–5
134	Sept. 7	Boston	A	7–1
135	Sept. 16	Detroit	H	3–2
136	Sept. 23	Washington	A	
137	Sept. 24	Washington	A	

TOTAL: 30 Yankee Record: 20–5–1 .800

1940

#	Date	Opponent	A/H	Score
138	May 17	Chicago	A	6–1
139	May 23	Detroit	A	2–3
140	May 27	Washington	H	5–0
141	May 30 (2)	Boston	H	4–11
142	June 2 (1)	St. Louis	H	13–4
143	June 4	Chicago	H	3–7
144	June 9	Cleveland	H	4–3
145	June 16 (1)	St. Louis	A	6–12
146	June 16 (1)	Chicago	A	5–6
147	June 16 (2)	St. Louis	A	3–5
148	June 18	Chicago	H	12–9
149	June 29	Philadelphia	A	8–4
150	July 1	Washington	H	3–6
151	July 5	Philadelphia	H	10–4
152	July 13 (1)	St. Louis	H	
153	July 13 (1)	St. Louis	H	12–6
154	July 13 (2)	Cleveland	A	4–3
155	July 17	St. Louis	H	12–14
156	July 24	Cleveland	H	10–9
157	July 28 (1)	Chicago	A	3–8
158	July 28 (1)	Chicago	A	7–10
159	August 6	Boston	A	13–0
160	August 7 (1)	Philadelphia	H	19–8
161	August 10	Boston	H	15–2
162	August 13 (2)	Boston	H	5–3
163	August 13 (2)	Cleveland	H	6–5
164	August 22	Cleveland	H	4–3
165	August 23	St. Louis	H	1–2
166	August 29 (2)	Boston	A	4–16
167	Sept. 7	St. Louis	A	
168	Sept. 15 (2)	St. Louis	A	

TOTAL: 31 Yankee Record: 16–12 .571

1941

#	Date	Opponent	A/H	Score
169	April 16	Philadelphia	H	7–10
170	April 19	Washington	H	5–2
171	April 20	Philadelphia	A	19–5
172	April 21	Philadelphia	A	14–4
173	April 27	Washington	H	3–6
174	May 16	Chicago	H	6–5
175	May 27	Washington	H	10–8
176	June 3	Detroit	H	2–4
177	June 8 (1)	St. Louis	A	9–3
178	June 8 (1)	St. Louis	A	8–3
179	June 8 (2)	St. Louis	A	3–2
180	June 12	Chicago	A	3–2
181	June 15	Cleveland	H	

#	Date	Opponent	A/H	Score
182	June 19	Chicago	H	7–2
183	June 22	Detroit	H	5–4
184	June 25	St. Louis	H	7–5
185	June 27	Philadelphia	A	6–7
186	July 2	Boston	H	8–4
187	July 5	Philadelphia	H	10–5
188	July 11	St. Louis	A	6–2
189	July 20	Detroit	A	12–6
190	July 23	Cleveland	H	3–2
191	July 27 (2)	Chicago	H	3–7
192	July 29	Detroit	H	3–6
193	July 31 (2)	Detroit	H	5–0
194	August 6 (1)	Boston	A	3–6
195	August 9	Philadelphia	A	8–3
196	Sept. 23	Philadelphia	H	8–9
197	Sept. 25	Philadelphia	H	7–2
198	Sept. 25	Philadelphia	H	

Yankee Record: 20–8 .714

TOTAL: 30

1942

#	Date	Opponent	A/H	Score
199	April 15	Washington	A	9–3
200	April 22	Philadelphia	H	11–5
201	May 5	Chicago	H	5–4
202	May 5	Chicago	H	
203	May 10 (1)	Washington	H	4–3
204	May 13	Cleveland	A	2–7
205	May 13	Cleveland	A	
206	May 16 (2)	Detroit	A	2–1
207	May 29	Washington	H	16–1
208	June 3	Chicago	H	4–1
209	July 1	Philadelphia	H	4–5
210	July 4 (2)	Boston	A	4–6
211	July 18	Chicago	H	7–6
212	July 19 (1)	Chicago	H	9–2
213	July 28	Chicago	A	8–3
214	July 29 (1)	Chicago	A	5–6
215	August 16	Philadelphia	A	11–2
216	August 17	Philadelphia	A	15–0
217	Sept. 14	Cleveland	A	8–3
218	Sept. 17	Detroit	A	7–4
219	Sept. 27	Boston	A	6–7

Yankee Record: 14–5 .737

TOTAL: 21

1946

#	Date	Opponent	A/H	Score
220	April 16	Philadelphia	A	5–9
221	April 21	Washington	H	6–1
222	April 26	Washington	A	11–7
223	April 26	Washington	A	
224	May 4	Detroit	H	4–3
225	May 10	Boston	H	4–5
226	May 14	St. Louis	A	6–2
227	May 19 (2)	Cleveland	A	7–1
228	May 23	Detroit	A	12–6
229	May 26 (2)	Boston	A	4–1
230	May 30 (1)	Philadelphia	H	6–1
231	June 16 (1)	St. Louis	A	9–2
232	June 21	Detroit	A	2–6
233	June 23	Detroit	A	10–8
234	June 23	Detroit	A	
235	June 25	Cleveland	A	3–8
236	July 6	Philadelphia	H	8–5
237	August 11 (2)	Boston	A	9–1
238	August 16	Boston	A	1–4
239	August 20	Chicago	H	2–9
240	August 21	Chicago	H	10–1
241	August 21	Chicago	H	5–4
242	Sept. 4	Philadelphia	A	3–4

#	Date	Opponent	A/H	Score
243	Sept. 13	Detroit	A	5-4
244	Sept. 14	Detroit	A	4-7

TOTAL: 25   Yankee Record: 15-8 .652

1947

#	Date	Opponent	A/H	Score
245	April 20	Philadelphia	A	6-2
246	May 13	St. Louis	H	9-1
247	May 17 (1)	Chicago	A	4-3
248	May 26	Boston	H	9-3
249	June 1	Cleveland	A	11-9
250	June 1	Cleveland	A	3-4
251	June 6	Chicago	H	3-1
252	June 6	Chicago	H	2-4
253	June 7	Chicago	H	8-1
254	June 26	Cleveland	A	8-2
255	July 2	Philadelphia	H	12-2
256	July 6 (1)	Washington	A	9-4
257	July 12 (1)	St. Louis	A	4-5
258	July 15 (1)	Cleveland	A	16-6
259	July 27 (2)	St. Louis	A	10-2
260	August 24 (2)	Chicago	H	6-5
261	August 30	Boston	A	1-4
262	Sept. 1 (2)	Washington	H	6-5
263	Sept. 11 (2)	Detroit	H	11-5
264	Sept. 23 (2)	Washington	A	3-1

TOTAL: 20   Yankee Record: 14-5 .737

1948

#	Date	Opponent	A/H	Score
265	April 21	Washington	A	3-6
266	April 25	Boston	A	5-4
267	May 1	Boston	H	6-8
268	May 10	Chicago	A	9-3
269	May 20	Chicago	A	13-2
270	May 20	Chicago	A	10-2
271	May 22	Chicago	A	6-5
272	May 23 (1)	Cleveland	A	13-2
273	May 23 (1)	Cleveland	A	2-5
274	May 23 (1)	Cleveland	A	4-0
275	June 11	Cleveland	H	8-10
276	June 20 (1)	Cleveland	A	4-2
277	June 20 (2)	St. Louis	A	6-5
278	June 20 (2)	St. Louis	A	7-3
279	June 21	Cleveland	H	9-0
280	June 22	Cleveland	H	2-4
281	June 24	Cleveland	H	4-0
282	June 25	Detroit	H	2-4
283	July 9	Washington	A	8-2
284	July 21 (1)	Cleveland	H	7-3
285	July 22	Cleveland	H	6-5
286	July 25 (2)	Cleveland	H	7-3
287	July 25 (2)	Chicago	H	10-2
288	August 1	Chicago	A	8-2
289	August 14	Chicago	H	14-3
290	August 15	Philadelphia	H	3-5
291	August 21	Philadelphia	H	6-0
292	August 23	Philadelphia	H	11-1
293	August 27 (2)	Chicago	H	7-2
294	Sept. 4 (1)	Cleveland	H	6-2
295	Sept. 4 (1)	Washington	H	5-2
296	Sept. 4 (2)	Washington	H	5-3
297	Sept. 5	Washington	H	5-3
298	Sept. 10	Washington	H	11-6
299	Sept. 11	Boston	H	6-3
300	Sept. 16 (1)	Detroit	A	1-2
301	Sept. 19 (2)	St. Louis	A	9-6
302	Sept. 19 (2)	St. Louis	A	1-2
303	Sept. 20	St. Louis	A	8-7

TOTAL: 39   Yankee Record: 25-7 .781

1949

#	Date	Opponent	A/H	Score
304	June 28	Boston	A	5–4
305	June 29	Boston	A	9–7
306	June 29	Boston	A	
307	June 30	Boston	A	6–3
308	July 4 (2)	Boston	H	6–4
309	July 17 (2)	Chicago	A	3–7
310	July 20	Cleveland	H	7–3
311	August 5 (1)	St. Louis	H	10–2
312	August 7	St. Louis	H	20–2
313	August 7	St. Louis	H	
314	August 11	Boston	A	6–7
315	August 28 (1)	Chicago	A	8–7
316	Sept. 5 (1)	Philadelphia	A	13–4
317	Sept. 10	Washington	H	3–4

TOTAL: 14

Yankee Record: 9–3 .750

1950

#	Date	Opponent	A/H	Score
318	April 21	Washington	H	14–7
319	April 28	Washington	A	4–5
320	May 17	St. Louis	A	11–9
321	May 21 (1)	Cleveland	A	14–5
322	May 21 (1)	Cleveland		
323	June 2	Chicago	H	6–5
324	June 3 (2)	Chicago	H	6–3
325	June 5	Cleveland	H	2–3
326	June 6	Cleveland	H	2–16
327	June 7	Detroit	H	5–4
328	June 18 (1)	St. Louis	A	15–5
329	June 18 (2)	St. Louis	A	9–0
330	June 22	Cleveland	A	2–6
331	June 23	Detroit	A	9–10
332	June 25 (1)	Detroit	A	8–2
333	June 30 (2)	Boston	A	2–10
334	July 2	Boston	H	15–9
335	July 23	Detroit	A	5–6
336	July 26	St. Louis	A	6–3
337	July 30 (1)	Chicago	A	15–7
338	July 30 (2)	Chicago	A	4–3
339	August 18	Philadelphia	A	3–2
340	August 20 (1)	Philadelphia	A	6–4
341	Sept. 2	Washington	H	9–2
342	Sept. 10	Washington	A	8–1
343	Sept. 10	Washington		
344	Sept. 10	Washington		
345	Sept. 12	Cleveland	A	7–8
346	Sept. 14	Detroit	A	7–5
347	Sept. 16	Detroit	A	8–1
348	Sept. 19	Chicago	A	3–4
349	Sept. 23	Boston	H	8–0

TOTAL: 32

Yankee Record: 19–10 .655

1951

#	Date	Opponent	A/H	Score
350	April 27	Boston	A	3–4
351	April 28	Washington	H	6–4
352	May 20	St. Louis	H	7–3
353	May 24	Detroit	H	11–1
354	May 30 (2)	Boston	A	4–9
355	June 7	St. Louis	A	7–5
356	July 27	Chicago	H	3–1
357	July 29 (1)	Chicago	H	8–3
358	July 29 (1)	Chicago	H	
359	August 9	Washington	H	6–4
360	August 25	Chicago	A	2–3
361	Sept. 28	Boston	H	11–3

Yankee Record: 8–3 .727

TOTAL: 12
CAREER: 361

Number of games with one home run: 288
Number of games with two home runs: 32
Number of games with three home runs: 3
Number of home runs hit in doubleheaders: 3
Yankee record in all games in which DiMaggio hit one or more home runs: 235–85–3   .734   (323 games)
Number of Yankee wins in which DiMaggio hit home run(s) equal to the margin of victory: 45
Note: Discrepancy between total number of games (323) and total number of home runs (361) is due to multiple-home-run games.

HOME RUNS AGAINST OPPONENT

St. Louis: 67
Washington: 58
Chicago: 58
Detroit: 47
Boston: 46 (29 hit at Fenway Park)
Philadelphia: 45
Cleveland: 40

TOTAL AT HOME: 148
TOTAL AWAY: 213

JOE DIMAGGIO'S MAJOR LEAGUE GRAND SLAMS

#1 July 5, 1937 versus Boston at Yankee Stadium. 6th inning, Rube Walberg, pitcher. Final score: NY 8, Bos 4.

#2 July 18, 1937 versus Cleveland at Cleveland. 9th inning, Bob Feller, pitcher. Final score: NY 5, Cleve 1.

#3 October 3, 1937 versus Boston at Yankee Stadium. 7th inning, Joe Gonzales, pitcher. Final score: NY 6, Bos 1.

#4 August 28, 1939 versus Detroit at Detroit. 3rd inning, Tommy Bridges, pitcher. Final score: NY 18, Det 2.

#5 August 13, 1940 versus Boston at Yankee Stadium (game 2). 4th inning, Herb Hash, pitcher. Final score: NY 9, Bos 1.

#6 August 22, 1940 versus Cleveland at Yankee Stadium (game 2). 2nd inning, Al Milnar, pitcher. Final score: NY 15, Cle 2.

#7 April 20, 1941 versus Philadelphia at Philadelphia. 9th inning, Herman Besse, pitcher. Final score: NY 19, Phi 5.

#8 May 10, 1946 versus Boston at Yankee Stadium. 5th inning, Joe Dobson, pitcher. Final score: NY 4, Bos 5.

#9 June 1, 1947 versus Cleveland in Cleveland. 8th inning, Roger Wolff, pitcher. Final score: NY 11, Cle 9.

#10 July 22, 1948 versus Cleveland at Yankee Stadium. 5th inning, Bob Feller, pitcher. Final score: NY 6, Cle 5.

#11 September 10, 1948 versus Boston in Boston. 10th inning, Earl Caldwell, pitcher. Final score: NY 11, Bos 6.

#12 September 5, 1949 versus Philadelphia in Philadelphia (game 1). 3rd inning, Lou Brissie, pitcher. Final score: NY 13, Phil 4.

#13 May 21, 1950 versus Cleveland in Cleveland. 2nd inning, Early Wynn, pitcher. Final score: NY 14, Cle 5.

Yankee Record: 12–1

JOE DIMAGGIO AT HOME AND ON THE ROAD

As the statistics below bear out, DiMaggio was hampered by hitting in Yankee Stadium.

HOME

G	AB	R	H	2B	3B	HR	RBI	AVG.	SLG.
880	3360	648	1060	186	73	148	720	.315	.546

ROAD

G	AB	R	H	2B	3B	HR	RBI	AVG.	SLG.
856	3461	742	1154	203	58	213	817	.333	.610

JOE DIMAGGIO'S FIRST GAME
SAN FRANCISCO,
OCTOBER 1, 1932
PACIFIC COAST LEAGUE

Missions	AB	H	O	A	E
Sherlock, 2b	4	3	2	3	1
Wright, ss	3	1	3	5	0
Eckhardt, rf	4	2	2	0	0
Almada, cf	3	0	2	0	0
Gyselman, 3b	4	0	2	2	0
Dahlgren, 1b	4	0	11	0	0
Kelman, lf	3	2	0	0	0
Ricci, c	4	1	3	2	0
T. Pillette, p	3	0	0	1	0
Totals	32	9	25	13	1

San Francisco	AB	H	O	A	E
Donovan, 1b	5	2	12	2	0
J. DIMAGGIO, ss	3	1	2	2	0
Garibaldi, 2b	4	3	3	6	1
Sulik, lf	4	0	4	0	0
Hunt, rf	4	1	2	1	0
V. DiMaggio, cf	4	2	1	0	0
Wera, 3b	4	0	1	2	0
Brenzel, c	4	1	0	3	0
Davis, p	4	1	2	2	0
Totals	36	11	27	18	1

A — One out when winning run was scored.

```
Missions       101 000 010 — 3
San Francisco  002 000 101 — 4
```

Two base hits—Wright, V. DiMaggio, Sherlock. Three base hits—J. DiMaggio, Sherlock. Home run—Donovan. Stolen bases—Garibaldi 2, Sulik. Umpires—Dunn, Fanning.

PITCHING RECORD

Missions		IP	H	R	BB	HP	SO
T. Pillette	LOST	9	11	4	1	0	3

San Francisco		IP	H	R	BB	HP	SO
Davis	WON	9	9	3	1	0	1

Selected Bibliography

The sources listed below represent those books and periodical articles that were most useful in the preparation of this volume, although I caution the reader that inclusion here does not indicate the accuracy of any individual source. As previously indicated, newspapers were the primary resource used in the creation of this book. Additional books and articles pertinent to Joe DiMaggio can be found in the bibliography contained in Jack B. Moore's *Joe DiMaggio: A Bio-Bibliography* and Myron Smith's *Baseball Bibliography.*

BOOKS

Allen, Lee, et al., eds. The Baseball Encyclopedia. New York: Macmillan, 1969.

Allen, Maury. Where Have You Gone, Joe DiMaggio?: The Story of America's Last Hero. New York: E. P. Dutton, 1975.

Anderson, Dave, et al. The Yankees: The Four Fabulous Eras of Baseball's Most Famous Team. New York: Random House, 1980.

Barrow, Edward. My Fifty Years in Baseball. New York: Coward-McCann, 1951.

Berkow, Ira. "Joe DiMaggio's Return," in Beyond the Dream: Occasional Heroes of Sports. New York: Atheneum, 1975.

Cannon, Jimmy. "Joe The Center Fielder," in Esquire's Great Men and Moments in Sports.

Cinel, Dino. From Italy to San Francisco. Palo Alto: Stanford University Press, 1984.

Creamer, Robert W. Babe: The Legend Comes to Life. New York: Simon & Schuster, 1974.

Creamer, Robert W. Stengel: His Life and Times. New York: Simon & Schuster, 1984.

DeGregorio, George. Joe DiMaggio—An Informal Biography. New York: Stein and Day, 1981.

DiMaggio, Joe, and Richard Whittingham. The DiMaggio Albums. New York: G. P. Putnam's Sons, 1989.

DiMaggio, Joe. Lucky to Be a Yankee. New York: Rudolph Field, 1946.

Dobbins, Dick, and Jon Twichell. Nuggets on the Diamond: Professional Baseball in the Bay Area from the Gold Rush to the Present. San Francisco: Woodford Press, 1994.

Gallagher, Mark. *Day by Day in New York Yankee History.* New York: Leisure Press, 1983.

Forker, Dom. *The Men of Autumn.* Dallas: Taylor Publishing, 1989.

Gilbert, Bill. *They Also Served: Baseball and the Home Front, 1941–1945.* New York: Crown Publishers, 1992.

Goldstein, Richard. *Spartan Seasons: How Baseball Survived the Second World War.* New York: Macmillan, 1980.

Golenbock, Peter. *Dynasty: The New York Yankees, 1949–1964.* Englewood Cliffs, N.J.: Prentice-Hall, 1975.

Graham, Frank. *The New York Yankees, 1900–1946.* New York: G. P. Putnam's Sons, 1946.

Halberstam, David. *The Summer of '49.* New York: William Morrow, 1989.

Hemingway, Ernest. *The Old Man and the Sea.* New York: Charles Scribner's Sons, 1952.

Holtzman, Jerome. *No Cheering in the Press Box.* New York: Holt, Rinehart and Winston, 1973.

Johnson, Dick, and Glenn Stout. *Ted Williams: A Portrait in Words and Pictures.* New York: Walker and Company, 1991.

Kahn, Roger. *Joe and Marilyn: A Memory of Love.* New York: William Morrow, 1986.

LeConte, Walter. *The Ultimate New York Yankees Record Book.* New York: Leisure Press, 1984.

Meany, Tom. *Joseph Paul DiMaggio: The Yankee Clipper.* New York: A. S. Barnes, 1951.

Meany, Tom. *The Yankee Story.* New York: E. P. Dutton, 1960.

Moore, Jack B. *Joe DiMaggio: A Bio-Bibliography.* Westport, Connecticut: Greenwood Press, 1986.

Neft, David, and Richard Cohen. *The Sports Encyclopedia: Baseball,* 6th ed. New York: St. Martin's/Marek, 1985.

Salant, Nathan. *This Date in New York Yankees History.* Briarcliff Manor, N.Y.: Stein and Day, 1983.

Schoor, Gene. *Joe DiMaggio, A Biography.* New York: Doubleday, 1980.

Seidel, Michael. *Streak: Joe DiMaggio and the Summer of 1941.* New York: McGraw-Hill, 1988.

Sheed, Wilfred. "King DiMaggio," in *Baseball and Lesser Sports.* New York: HarperCollins.

Silverman, Al. *Joe DiMaggio: The Golden Year, 1941.* Englewood Cliffs, N.J.: Prentice Hall, 1969.

Smelser, Marshall. *The Life That Ruth Built.* New York: New York Times Books, 1975.

Smith, Myron. *Baseball: A Comprehensive Bibliography.* Jefferson, N.C.: MacFarland & Company, 1986.

Sullivan, George, and John Powers. *The Yankees: An Illustrated History.* Englewood Cliffs, N.J.: Prentice-Hall, 1982.

Thorn, John, and Pete Palmer, eds. *Total Baseball.* New York: Warner Books, 1989.

ARTICLES

Note: Includes only those articles that the author found most useful. Newspaper articles that are described in the text are generally not included unless the specific article is a feature of some kind. A note on newspaper sources appears in the Introduction.

Allen, Mel. "Who is the World's Greatest Ballplayer?" *Sport,* Sept. 1948, p. 20.

Anderson, Dave. "The Longest Hitting Streak." *Sports Illustrated* July 17, 1961, pp. 36–41.

Blahous, Charles. "The DiMaggio Streak: How Statistically Likely?" *The Baseball Research Journal,* pp. 41–43.

Boswell, Thomas. "At Last, DiMaggio Feels Comfortable in Public." *The Washington Post,* September 1, 1983.

Burr, Harold. "The Brothers DiMaggio." *Baseball Magazine,* July 1941, pp. 367–369.

Case, Gene. "DiMaggio's Streak Stricken?" *The Nation*, August 26/September 2, 1991, pp. 225–228.

Daniel, Dan. "Inside Joe DiMaggio." *Baseball Magazine*, February 1952, pp. 8–10.

Daniel, Dan. "Joe DiMaggio: My Friend the Yankee Clipper," in *The Sporting News Baseball Register 1950*, pp. 2–41.

DiMaggio, Joe, as told to John Ross. "The Joe DiMaggio Story," *True*.

Gildea, William. "Meeting DiMaggio: A Journey in Time." *Washington Post*, August 7, 1984.

Gould, Stephen Jay. "The Streak of Streaks." *The New York Review of Books*, 1988.

Lupica, Mike. "Where Joe DiMaggio Has Gone." *Esquire*, May 1994, pp. 51–52.

Meany, Tom. "Joe DiMaggio as I Knew Him." *Collier's*, April 19, 1952, pp. 66–70.

Merin, Samuel. "An Italian Baseball Guide," *Baseball Magazine*.

Milstein, Gilbert. "Why They Cheer Joe DiMaggio." *New York Times Magazine*, July 9, 1950, pp. 14, 41–43.

Robinson, Ray. "Joe DiMaggio in the Year of the Streak." *New York Yankees 1991 Official Yearbook*, pp. 49–53.

Sher, Jack. "DiMag, The Man behind the Poker Face." *Sport*, September 1949, pp. 16–17, 71–80.

Stout, Glenn. "The Case of the 1947 MVP Ballot." *The Sporting News*, December 20, 1993.

Stout, Glenn. "Pitching Puzzle." *Boston Magazine*, October 1989.

Stump, Al. "Why Young Players Love Joe DiMaggio." *Sport*, August 1968, pp. 16–17.

Talese, Gay. "The Silent Season of a Hero." *Esquire*, July 1966, pp. 40–45, 112.

OTHER SOURCES

Joe DiMaggio Clipping Files, Baseball Hall of Fame Library, Cooperstown, New York. This file contains literally thousands of clippings and articles, primarily from the New York *World-Telegram*.

Harold Kaese Archives, Boston Tradition in Sports Collection, Boston Public Library.

Interviews with Dick Dobbins, Dick Beverage, Bill Weiss, Billy Raimondi, Charley Walgren, and anonymous sources.

Index

Note: In this index, JDM is used for Joe DiMaggio. Individuals mentioned incidentally are not indexed.